The Peacekeeping Failure in South Sudan

The Peacekeeping Failure in South Sudan

The UN, Bias and the Peacekeeper's Mind

Mark Millar

ZED

LONDON • NEW YORK • OXFORD • NEW DELHI • SYDNEY

Zed Books
Bloomsbury Publishing Plc
50 Bedford Square, London, WC1B 3DP, UK
1385 Broadway, New York, NY 10018, USA
29 Earlsfort Terrace, Dublin 2, Ireland

BLOOMSBURY and Zed Books are trademarks of Bloomsbury Publishing Plc

First published in Great Britain 2022
This paperback edition published in 2024

Cover image: Displaced people walk past a UN armoured vehicle inside the United Nations Mission in
South Sudan, 2014. (© Andreea Campeanu/REUTERS/Alamy Stock Photo)

A catalogue record for this book is available from the British Library.

Library of Congress Cataloging-in-Publication Data

Names: Millar, Mark, 1979- author.
Title: The peacekeeping failure in South Sudan: the UN, bias and the Peacekeeper's mind / Mark Millar.
Description: New York: Zed Books, an imprint of Bloomsbury Publishing, 2022. |
Includes bibliographical references and index.
Identifiers: LCCN 2022003830 (print) | LCCN 2022003831 (ebook) | ISBN 9781350273849 (hardback) |
ISBN 9781350273856 (epub) | ISBN 9781350273863 (pdf) | ISBN 9781350273870
Subjects: LCSH: United Nations Mission in South Sudan. | United Nations–Peacekeeping forces–
South Sudan. | Peacekeeping forces–South
Sudan. | Conflict management–South Sudan. | South Sudan–History.
Classification: LCC JZ4971 .M55 2022 (print) | LCC JZ4971 (ebook) |
DDC 341.58409629–dc23/eng/20220126
LC record available at https://lccn.loc.gov/2022003830
LC ebook record available at https://lccn.loc.gov/2022003831

ISBN: HB: 978-1-3502-7384-9
PB: 978-1-3502-7388-7
ePDF: 978-1-3502-7386-3
eBook: 978-1-3502-7385-6

Typeset by Deanta Global Publishing Services, Chennai, India

To find out more about our authors and books visit www.bloomsbury.com and
sign up for our newsletters.

Contents

Illustrations

Figure

Map

Preface

This book began life, at least in my head, almost as soon as I started my career working in the world of international peace and security organizations. I began as an intern at NATO Headquarters in Brussels in 2006. I had preconceptions as to what working for the world's largest military alliance might be like. I am embarrassed to say that most of those were based on movies in which such serious organizations were housed in shiny new buildings, decked out with hundreds of screens on every wall, soaking up information to inform critical decisions of global importance. I also assumed the people inside were the kind of smart political operators and analysts that I had watched working on *The West Wing*. However, as I nervously walked through the NATO entrance the first time, that illusion quickly disappeared. There was a perceptible boundary between the impressive and bright-looking reception, which was open to the public, and where many photocalls took place, and then the dark hallways that led to the functional bureaucracy. At that time, the headquarters were still housed in the *temporary* accommodation it had moved into in the 1960s, fashioned out of a converted hospital. Because of various bureaucratic obstacles, a five-year transition to a permanent site had stretched to more than fifty years.[1] In that time, remodelling was infrequent. The interior hallways retained the dour, outdated aesthetic of the building's original purpose. Since the end of the Cold War, and the expansion of its membership, the organization had also been running out of space. The offices of new members were squeezed into gaps on the site in ramshackle prefabricated containers, giving the place an even more temporary feel. There was no wall of screens. Instead, the computers we had access to were out of date and felt like a step down from the modest public university where I had just been studying.

At the time, NATO had become embroiled in what increasingly looked like a quagmire in Afghanistan. Every day a new list of its casualties would arrive in my inbox. One of my first taskings was to compile the figures and flag observable trends to my boss. By then, the successful use of improvised explosive devices (IEDs) and their absorption into complex attacks was providing the Taliban with critical successes that should have been much more alarming to NATO than they appeared to be. My boss would express a note of concern each morning as I did my briefing, but my reports were just one of many. For every tactical misstep, there were apparent successes. Billions of dollars were successfully being funnelled into projects in the country through various NATO members, which were also the primary aid donors, as well as through the military's own quick impact projects (QIPs), which were aimed at winning the support of the populace to the aims of the NATO mission. Billions more were also being spent on security sector reform (SSR) of the Afghan army and police. Rising numbers of new hospitals, schools, bridges, roads, soldiers and policemen provided evidence of quantifiable success. There were also more anecdotal stories of a collaborative spirit with Afghan colleagues and an appreciative local population. The challenges that included vast corruption, inefficient and poorly directed aid, badly coordinated and conceptually confused state-building and SSR efforts were clear and often stated within NATO. However, more pointed criticism from external commentators that often contradicted our own data and pointed to more fundamental issues with the mission and the level of local support it enjoyed were often dismissed. The mixture of positive and negative information created a sufficiently murky and complex picture that the need to create urgency around a shift in strategy was absent.

Within the offices of NATO, it was clear that there was little appetite for dwelling on the potentially negative outcomes of the mission. This was not simply because it was uncomfortable, but it did not seem relevant to the bureaucrats that I met. Not only did Afghanistan feel physically remote, but, for the international staff that I worked with, their tasks were heavily siloed and focused on attaining short-term outputs around the exhausting task of coordinating supposed allies that, nonetheless, often found it difficult to work together. NATO civilians managed the drudgery of meetings, processes and paperwork that gave an appearance of a cohesion around decisions that were the compromise of disparate political and military world views. Where drama was more evident was in the pettier aspects of office life and the melodramas that they entailed. For example, the three most senior officials in my section could barely bring themselves to exchange a pleasantry, as some yearlong argument had allowed a deeply personal animosity to fester. Nobody confided in me the root causes of their mutual dislike, but I gathered that at least part of it was related to different working styles, personalities and partisan ways of looking at the world that reflected their national and personal backgrounds. My boss, the head of the section, accused his two deputies of withholding information and banished them from meetings as punishment. The deputies responded by telling whoever would listen that they believed the head to be incompetent, while also confirming his suspicions by pettily ordering other interns not to share information with me. It is likely that at some point amid this unseemly feud the tide in Afghanistan irrevocably turned.

Time and again over the next decade in my work for the UK government, the United Nations (UN), humanitarian agencies and non-governmental organizations (NGOs) I was surrounded by personalities, organizational cultures and structures that seemed at odds with the grave nature of the work to which they were supposed to be dedicated. During this time, the popular British television sitcom *The Office* was enjoying success, being remade into multiple versions around the world. In explaining its international appeal, one of its originators Ricky Gervais commented on the universality of its themes. Whether it was India, Chile or Germany (all of which remade versions of the show), the idiosyncrasies and pettiness of office life were recognizable between all cultures. In an interview, Gervais suggested that somewhere in a NASA building some of the smartest people on earth were probably arguing over who had the bigger chair. These human elements, rather than the high purposes for which people had gathered, defined the experience of an organization.

Over my career, I have watched various bureaucracies that were staffed by people who were intelligent, empathetic and capable of strong rational thinking consistently work to support policies and strategies that were antithetic to sensible decision-making. There was something about the way their work had been structured that did not put a premium on optimal decision-making. In 2018, I had the chance to take a career break, and I delved into resolving this problem that had irritated me for more than a decade. I followed my partner back to the UK and did research on peacekeeping decision-making in South Sudan, a country that I had spent time working as a conflict analyst and where the United Nations Mission in South Sudan (UNMISS) had struggled to perform effectively. That research is the basis for this book. Following the completion of the masters, for which that research was designed, I conducted additional interviews and spent another year working in South Sudan, which provided additional material that was used in the compilation of this book.

Acknowledgements

I would like to thank my partner Clo, without whose love and support this book would not have been possible. I would also like to thank the Norwegian Refugee Council, which generously allowed me time away from my work to finish the final drafts. While conducting research at the University of Kent, Ingvild Bode was my academic supervisor and provided excellent guidance and insight. If this book is coherent to its reader, she deserves much of the credit. I would also like to thank Nadine Ansorg, who also provided much needed and superb supervision as well as the wider team of the School of Politics and International Relations at the University of Kent. Thanks to John Karlsrud and Harmonie Toros, who acted as examiners to my initial thesis and whose comments for improvements I have developed for the purposes of this book. I am exceptionally grateful for the many individuals who let me interview them. The candid insights that they allowed me into their work is the basis of this book. Thanks to Amelia Kyazze, who helped me collect my thoughts as I transitioned my research for publishing. I would also like to thank the many friends and family who patiently had to listen to me as I squeezed the random thoughts that litter this book out over several years. Finally, I would like to thank the people of South Sudan, who deserved better.

Abbreviations

APC	Armoured Personnel Carrier
ARCSS	Agreement for the Resolution of Conflict in South Sudan
ASG	Assistant Secretary General
AU	African Union
CMT	Crisis Management Team
CPA	Comprehensive Peace Agreement
CTSAMVM	Ceasefire and Transitional Security Arrangement Monitoring and Verification Mechanism
D/SRSG (Political)	Deputy Special Representative of the Secretary General (Political)
D/SRSG (RC/HC)	Deputy Special Representative of the Secretary General (Resident Coordinator/Humanitarian Coordinator)
FPU	Formed Police Unit
HCT	Humanitarian Country Team
HIPPO	High-Level Panel on Peace Operations
HRW	Human Rights Watch
ICRC	International Committee of the Red Cross
IGAD	Inter-Governmental Authority on Development
IOM	International Organization for Migration
JMAC	Joint Mission Analysis Centre
JMEC	Joint Monitoring and Evaluation Commission

MINUSMA	Mission Multidimensionnelle Intégrée des Nations Unies pour la stabilisation au Mali (*United Nations Multidimensional Integrated Stabilization Mission in Mali*)
MONUSCO	Mission de l'Organisation des Nations Unies pour la stabilisation en République démocratique du Congo (*United Nations Stabilization Mission in the Democratic Republic of the Congo*)
MSF	Médecins sans frontières
NGO	Non-Governmental Organization
OLS	Operation Lifeline Sudan
POC AA	Protection of Civilians Area Adjacent
POC	Protection of Civilians
R-ARCSS	Revitalized Agreement for the Resolution of Conflict in South Sudan
SAF	Sudanese Armed Forces
SOFA	Status of Forces Agreement
SPLA	Sudan People's Liberation Army
SPLA/iO	Sudan People's Liberation Army/in Opposition
SRSG	Special Representative of the Secretary General
SSDA/CF	South Sudan Defense Army/Cobra Faction
SSLA	South Sudan Liberation Army
SSNPS	South Sudan National Police Service
TCC	Troop-Contributing Country
TGoNU	Transitional Government of National Unity
UAV	Unmanned Aerial Vehicle
UNAMA	United Nations Assistance Mission in Afghanistan

UNCT	United Nations Country Team
UNDSS	United Nations Department of Safety and Security
UNHCR	United Nations High Commissioner for Refugees
UNISFA	United Nations Interim Security Force in Abyei
UNMIL	United Nations Mission in Liberia
UNMIS	United Nations Mission in Sudan
UNMISS	United Nations Mission in South Sudan
UNOCI	United Nations Operation in Côte d'Ivoire
UNOIOS	UN Office of Internal Oversight Services
UNPOL	United Nations Police
UNSC	United Nations Security Council
UPDF	Ugandan People's Defense Force
USG	Under-Secretary General

Map of South Sudan

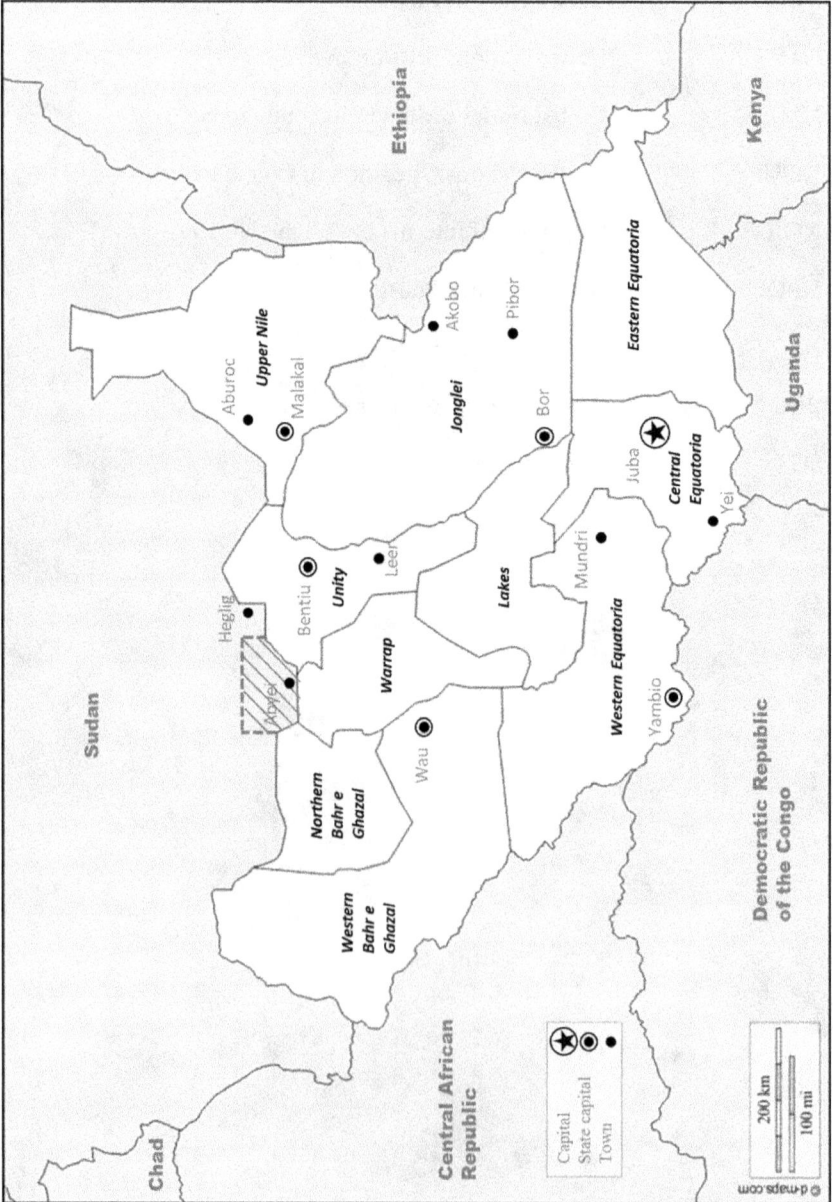

Map 1 Base map reproduced with kind permission of d-maps.com. https://d-maps.com/carte.php?num_car=21114 &lang=en Place names and locations added by author.

Surrounded

To explain how I have come to understand the failures of the UN peacekeeping mission in South Sudan, it is necessary to describe a few of the years in which I worked in the country and later as part of the UN Headquarters in New York. In this chapter, I will provide a snapshot of the country at a pivotal moment in its civil war and offer a personal reflection on the values that I brought into that context and the unexpected ways that I reacted. At the same time, I will describe my experiences of working within a UN system that is shaped by specific organizational pressures. The chapter will help situate for the reader my place in the country and the UN and create some understanding of the experiences that I have drawn on to create an interpretation of how UN peacekeeping failed in South Sudan. The insight that underpins this book is that situation, personal values and psychology met in a cognition that, together with the organizational setting, shaped the way that I felt and acted that was part of an ordinary means to understand the world around me. My assumption is that others within South Sudan at that time and operating in a similar setting, including peacekeeping decision-makers, constructed the world through similar mechanisms that are unlikely to be the most optimal means to achieve stated objectives.

A trip south

In the first week of July 2016, I was part of a small UN humanitarian team of five people that travelled by road from Juba, the capital city of South Sudan, to Yei about 150 kilometres southwest in Central Equatoria state. I was a conflict analyst working for the UN-affiliated International Organization for Migration (IOM). I had chosen to make the trip based on recent security incidents in the area. At that moment, the civil war that had ravaged South Sudan for the previous two and a half years was in abeyance following the signing of a peace agreement the previous year. But that agreement had been entered into with minimal good faith by either side. Numerous breaches of the ceasefire had taken place. The government had used the interruption to clamp down on perceived dissent in the west and south of the country, where communities that had hitherto stayed out of the war, lived. Yei was a focal point for this strategy in the south.

The roots of the national conflict that began in 2013 are complex and will be explored more fully later in the book. However, the rivalry of elite politicians belonging to the two most prominent communities in the country, the Dinka and the Nuer, played a significant role. That dynamic had also helped define the first years of the conflict in which violence was focused on the north-east quadrant of the country where the borders of territory, in which those communities were dominant, met. By 2016, that dynamic had started to change.

The Kakwa, Pajulu and Kuku communities that occupy the area around Yei are just a few of the many Equatorian communities that inhabit the three Equatoria states (Western, Central and Eastern) that loosely correspond to the Equatoria province of the Anglo-Egyptian Condominium that helped define administrative units in the postcolonial period.[1] Equatorians are a diverse mixture of communities that include agriculturalists and pastoralists from different ethnocultural backgrounds but together comprise the third-largest group in the country behind the Dinka and Nuer. They also live in some of the most fertile and minerally rich sections of the country. In the colonial period, Equatorians had some privileges in the British administration in the south, including their participation in the Equatorial Corps, part of the Sudan Defense Force, which largely excluded Dinka and Nuer. That allowed the community greater leadership of a proto-nationalist southern Sudanese cause when rebellion loomed in the same year as Sudan's independence in 1955. This followed an unsatisfactory postcolonial arrangement in which southerners were in danger of being overshadowed by more powerful northern elites with which they had significant religious and cultural differences.[2] However, the political concessions of Khartoum at the conclusion of the First Sudanese Civil War in 1972, and the emerging political aspirations of members of the more numerous Dinka and Nuer within a single administrative unit of Southern Sudan, diminished Equatorian influence and participation in future political struggles.[3] During the Second Sudanese Civil War (1983 to 2005), the Equatorian region hosted pivotal actions including Operation Thunderbolt in which the main rebel group, the Sudan People's Liberation Army (SPLA), seized control of Yei from the Sudan Armed Forces (SAF). Notwithstanding the contribution of Equatorian soldiers to that liberation effort, a myth became pervasive within the Dinka-dominated

SPLA that Equatorian communities had played a peripheral role in the fighting, further undermining their political stature.

Following South Sudan's independence in 2011, the desire of disparate Equatorian communities to separate themselves from attempts at political hegemony by more populous South Sudan groups became increasingly important. This included defending their community against perceived encroachment by members of a triumphant Dinka community on land and mineral rights in the south.[4] However, Equatorian pleas for a more devolved system of governance, in which it felt better able to protect its distinct interests, could be viewed with suspicion by the Sudan People's Liberation Movement (SPLM), the political organization of the SPLA, whose war experience was shaped by an authoritarian outlook that was weary of divisive splits that undermined its attempts to advocate for a unified South Sudan identity. Nonetheless, at the start of the national conflict in 2013, the Equatorian community remained largely loyal to the government led by the Dinka president, Salva Kiir, while also pushing for reform to a centralized control of power which had favoured Dinka and Nuer elites.

When that political effort failed, including after the sacking of the Central Equatorian governor and arrest of the governor of Western Equatoria in 2015, some Equatorian groups became increasingly restless and aggressive responses to perceived provocations became more frequent. This included violent resistance to Dinka pastoralists entering the south in 2015, as well as increased numbers of Equatorians joining the armed government opposition. The government countered harshly in a way that only fuelled further dissent. At the end of 2015 and the start of 2016, the SPLA, which now existed as the official army of the South Sudan state, led coordinated security operations in an area associated with the opposition, north of Yei.[5] However, the SPLA involved in the operation were largely Dinka, operating in a territory that was less familiar to them than it was to the militia they were hunting. As is common in this kind of asymmetric conflict, the frustration of fighting an invisible foe meant that soft and available targets, in the form of the perceived civilian support base, became the subject of those operations. Reports of villages being destroyed as well as murder, rape and civilian displacement followed.[6] Additional security forces were moved to Yei. The detention of young men in the town and surrounding areas by the feared National Security Services (NSS) became more common. I received reports of individuals being arrested during the night, tortured and occasionally killed. Such stories were easy to believe. The South Sudan security services' history of arbitrary arrests and use of torture were familiar. The previous year my own colleague, an Equatorian, had been abducted, detained and savagely beaten. Their only crime appears to have been their association with humanitarians and suspicions that they supported the collation of information that the government perceived to be critical of it. Having beaten them to the point that they were bloodied and bruised all over, the officers drilled a hole in their feet.

The relationship between the local community and government in Yei had become further exacerbated by the deployment of a government paramilitary group to the area that had its roots in a Dinka militia known as the Mathiang Anyoor. That group had been responsible for many of the massacres that had taken place at the outset of the conflict in Juba in 2013. By 2016, they had been notionally incorporated into the regular SPLA but operated through a separate command structure associated with hardliners within the government.[7] Interviews that I carried out in Yei revealed widely felt outrage from frequent incidents of violence and harassment by those forces. That outrage became even more furious in May 2016, when individuals associated with that force shot and killed a nun who had been travelling through the town in an ambulance.[8]

When we arrived in Yei at the start of July, none of these tensions were immediately apparent. In fact, having become used to seeing towns that had been decimated by violence in other parts of the country, there was a sense of relief to arrive in a place that appeared calm and, by the standards of the day, thriving. Shops and restaurants were open, and the market was busy and well stocked. While we knew that there was an enhanced military presence in the area, it was not immediately evident, at least compared to other parts of the country. Even in Juba, the constant movement of well-armed soldiers round the city contributed to a perpetual sense of unease. Yei in contrast appeared outwardly peaceful, and it was tempting to make comparisons with the decades old reputation it had as a cosmopolitan trading hub. Before the second civil war of independence broke out, Yei had used its position on a crossroads to nearby Uganda and the Democratic Republic of Congo (DRC), as well as its rich surrounding agricultural areas, to become known as a significant market town that earned it the local moniker 'Small London'.[9] The civil war of independence had disrupted that spirit, but signs of its more cosmopolitan past were returning. In addition to visible economic activity, investors and farmers had begun plans for long-term growth. One project associated with George Clooney and funded by Nespresso had planted more than 20,000 coffee trees, betting on a brighter and more prosperous future.[10]

Hope, however, was more difficult to come by after the sun went down. Young men were disappearing at night. Sometimes they were being arrested by the newly arrived security forces but increasingly we were told they were leaving the town. The question of where they were going, however, was met with furtive glances and non-committal shrugs. A few quietly confided that they had gone to be with anti-government militias that were clandestinely gathering in bush areas around the town.

In the preceding weeks, the number of security incidents in Juba between the SPLA and the opposition forces, which were allowed to be there as part of the peace agreement, had been increasing. The political arrangement on which security relied looked fragile with the question increasingly being of when, not if, it would fail. With increasing violence across the west and south, a return to violence meant that the next phase of the war would be a truly national one with all the dangers that such a geographical escalation implied. My research in Yei was supposed to create data to provide another salvo of warnings about the imminent and dire trajectory of the conflict. Whether it would have had any effect seemed doubtful. In my career, I had found the responsiveness of policymakers to expert interpretation of available information to be sluggish at best. However, events superseded the objectives of the research. On 8 July 2016, four days into my trip to Yei, a fight broke out between soldiers of opposing forces outside of the president's palace in Juba, triggering a series of events that definitively ended the peace. As news arrived in Yei that the war had started again, thousands of civilians begin to stream out of the town, taking what little belongings they could and moving towards refugee camps in nearby Uganda.

On 10 July, following a respite in the violence in Juba, my team made the decision to try and make the journey back to the capital by road. For the first time since arriving in the country, other than in an exercise, I donned my bullet proof vest and UN helmet. The town that we left was different from the one we had arrived in. The military had set up roadblocks around it, ostensibly to protect it from external threats but also trapping civilians inside. Those people who had not fled stayed inside their homes. The shops and businesses were closed. The streets, aside from anxious looking soldiers, were deserted. As we left, my driver muttered to me that the journey was a mistake. His usual cheery confidence had disappeared. Instead, he gripped the wheel tightly, intensely scanning the road and the thick bush that lined it. I cannot remember how responsive I was to these fears, or whether I was even sympathetic to his concerns. To my shame, it is possible, if not likely, that I was dismissive. Approximately twenty minutes outside of the town, we were stopped by a call on the radio from Juba. Fighting had begun again in the capital, and under no circumstances should we try and enter the city. Much to my driver's relief, we turned around and sought a more secure location to base ourselves than the private hotel that we had been staying. We drove back through the military checkpoints and arrived at the gates of the only UN compound in town, belonging to UN High Commissioner for Refugees (UNHCR). With some negotiation over how our accommodation bills would be paid, we were welcomed inside. Over the forthcoming days, the colleague I was travelling with set up to support her team in Juba by satellite phone as they were frantically trying to negotiate access for vital humanitarian aid to the huge, displaced populations that were emerging in the city. I set to work compiling my notes and eking out whatever information I could from the contacts that we had made in the town and its implications for the latest round of violence.

By 12 July, it had become clear that against the odds the leader of the opposition, Riek Machar, had survived a huge government onslaught against his compound and had fled Juba. The likelihood was that he would try to flee the country moving through territory where friendly forces could facilitate his escape. That meant he would be moving in our direction as the most direct route to the border. I wrote up the possible scenarios. The Equatorian militia close to Yei, which we knew existed and supported the opposition, could support Machar by harassing government forces and providing protection to the escaping party. A less likely, but possible action, was that that same militia could attack Yei in a way that might provide a safe waypoint on Machar's way to Uganda or the DRC, or else a diversion to pull pursuing forces from the hunt. These scenarios were running through my brain one night as I was sitting alone at the edge of the freight container that was my temporary home. The air was thick with heat. Insects buzzed hurriedly around me. Save their noise and a very occasional burst of distant gunfire, which was sufficiently common in South Sudan that it could be relegated to background noise, the evening was peaceful. I received a message on my phone from a colleague asking me how I was doing. To this concerned pleasantry, I began to enthusiastically relay the dramatic escalation of events. When the colleague offered the observation that my tone sounded more excited than worried, I felt a sudden flush of pride at my bravado and responded with something embarrassingly glib. The colleague made it clear that they were not offering the observation as a compliment.

On 14 July, a small plane chartered by IOM arrived in Yei to extract us. The next day, I was back to work in Juba and began to see first-hand the devastation that had been wrought over the previous week. Buildings across the city bore the scars of bullet holes, rockets and shells. Shops and compounds lay broken and open, their contents looted or smashed by the orgy of violence that had taken place. Hundreds had been killed. As many, and likely many more, were subjected to rape and sexual assault. The streets were quiet. Tens of thousands had left their homes, cramming themselves into UN bases or else humanitarian and religious compounds where they felt some degree of safety. In Yei, an attack by the opposition did not materialize. Machar's escape route bypassed the town, but he relied on militias from the area to shepherd his passage to safety in the DRC. In the months that followed, there was a devastating offensive by the government around Yei that looked punitive. The severity of the violence was such that it led to concerns that the war crimes committed were a prelude to a genocide (see Chapter 8).

Me and the context

In my office I began to collate the reports I needed to make sense of the resurgence of conflict. I began to trawl through the evidence to piece together the steps that had led to the fresh outbreak of fighting. It was not difficult. As had happened previously in the country, the immediate triggers were the result of a clear path of escalation. I noted again that the United Nations Mission in South Sudan (UNMISS), in a grim repetition of previous tragedies, had failed to proactively deploy what capabilities it had available to it to show force and potentially deescalate the situation. During the violence, they had largely stayed inside their bases.

As I fulfilled my professional duties, I also began to take stock of my own feelings. I looked for the sadness and horror that felt should have been normal, based on events that I was documenting. I found little evidence that such a sympathetic response existed. I returned to that moment in Yei and my flush of excitement that was far from the terror that I knew the people in town must have felt. The memory created a peculiar psychological sensation. I found it difficult to reconcile those feelings, cold and uncaring beyond my own personal enthusiasm, with the individual that I thought I was. Several years later, a therapist, who was helping me with a low-level depression that I came to know in the intervening years, generously suggested that the guilt I came to associate with those feelings was at least somewhat unjustified. They offered the explanation that in a moment of intensity I subconsciously disassociated. I stopped myself from consideration of potentially debilitating horrors in a way that allowed me to continue being effective in my role. I may have also given outweighed importance to a moment in which I overestimated my personal culpability in a self-flagellating expression of survivor's guilt. These analyses rang partially true and helped provide some peace of mind. However, a more complete examination offered a less comfortable but probably more complete interpretation.

I was a white, male, Westerner, working for an international organization on a UN compound. While not impervious to harm, those considerations ensured its likelihood was greatly reduced. Freed from that concern, I could view the situation in a more dispassionate way that was appropriate to my privileged and somewhat protected position. As such, the situation, as tragic as it was, also created professionally satisfying outcomes. With shame I recollect that I found professional self-worth as the unfolding reality confirmed my earlier predictions. Moreover, analysts are often judged by their fieldwork. The chance to be in proximity to a moment of action, felt professionally vindicating. Even more uncomfortable was the recognition that there was also a desirable aesthetic to the moment. The seemingly heroic tableau of sitting nonchalantly on the frontline of conflict created a desirable image through its similarities to moments from fictional representations that I had absorbed into my own mythology and was a type of saviorism. In trying to explain my feelings, I therefore found an ugly rationality which related to the subconscious values that I brought into the context and were reinforced by my organizational setting. For better or worse, those personal elements would define how I approached my work and interpreted the world around me.

In the belly of the beast

In 2017, after three and a half years in South Sudan, I left the country to take up a role at the UN Headquarters (UNHQ) in New York, attached to the Secretary General's Executive Office as part of the Executive Committee Secretariat. The Executive Committee was the weekly cabinet-style meeting that was chaired by the Secretary General and included the heads of the UN's various departments as well as regularly the leaders of the largest UN agencies, funds and programmes. My role was to coordinate research and compile the information packs that accompanied the topics discussed each week. During the meetings, I regularly sat in to take notes and write up a summary of the discussion. I also continued to write analysis on South Sudan, holding the portfolio for the country on behalf of the Research and Liaison Unit, attached to the UN Operations and Crisis Centre.

I took up the role with some trepidation. When I first arrived in South Sudan, I had worked for UNMISS as an analyst in their operations centre. During that assignment, the role of UN officials based in New York was regarded with some scorn. The UNHQ teams were perceived as out of touch but demanding. Multiple UNMISS departments generated reams of daily reporting for the UNHQ. However, information only flowed in one direction and, even then, seemed to have limited impact on policy. The UN officials who visited from headquarters showed little interest in the strategic context. Their talking points altered little between each trip, even as the context dramatically changed. UNMISS colleagues commonly described the insatiable, yet seemingly meaningless, appetite for information from UNHQ as *feeding the beast*. Those who had previously worked in New York additionally warned of an atmosphere that could be dysfunctional and even toxic. I was told to expect Machiavellianism as senior officials jostled to position themselves, and their departments, above one another. As an analyst, I was warned that interest in my work would also be limited. Much of the work on strategy was done among senior leaders without reference to the analytical components of the organization.

Entering the UNHQ building for the first time, it is difficult to not be impressed. I would recommend reaching it by the ferry that crosses the East River that allows the best vantage point to view the shimmering monolith perched at the edge of the water. Entering through the large open reception hall of the General Assembly building is like entering a cathedral, not least because of the set of stained-glass windows designed by Marc Chagall that sit to the side of its entrance. However, the large replica of the Sputnik satellite that hangs above your head suggests a more agnostic, if no less grand, spirit. The huge assembly rooms are inspiring, even before considering the extraordinary breadth of human history that they have hosted. Pieces of archaeology and works of art pepper other parts of the building giving it a feeling of a museum more than a place of work. However, as you leave the area open to the public and move to the large main building that houses the offices of the UN Secretariat, the décor becomes more recognizably corporate and mundane. At the bottom of the Secretariat tower, there is a café usually serving a long line of slightly harried looking staff. Above, there are thirty-seven floors of nondescript offices and meeting rooms about which there is little to be said other than that they look much like any office in any other part of the world.

On arriving, I put aside the preconceptions of my former colleagues and determined to be open and collaborative. Once I had grasped my core duties on the Executive Committee, I reached out to the South Sudan Integrated Operational Team (IOT), responsible for coordinating all issues regarding the country. I knew the IOT lacked staff with strong knowledge of the context, and it occasionally fumbled when handling information. On one occasion, while I was there it showed a map as part of a closed-door presentation to the UN Security Council (UNSC) that illustrated areas of influence of belligerents. The map was at least three years out of date and wildly incorrect. Even though none of the representatives of the UNSC noticed the mistake, the incident was embarrassing. I offered support but found that each suggestion was met with a polite counteroffer to let me know if I was needed. Privately, it was suggested to me that the IOT was a guarded unit, whose task priorities were at least equivalent to its value as a vehicle for its managers' careers. Informal collaboration with staff from other departments diluted their perceived control of the portfolio, and I was never invited to help.

I concentrated on supporting the Executive Committee for which there was a huge amount of work. Each two-hour meeting covered three or four main topics. Each topic was supported by a two-page text background briefing and an information pack with various related infographics. The development of these products could be wrought, with the content having to be mediated between departments with differing, and sometimes competing, agendas. On occasions, I was asked to remove information that I believed to be essential to understanding the given topic. The reasoning was generally explained to me as being the necessity of avoiding misinterpretations that could be perceived as indicative of the UN Secretariat stating positions that were objectionable to UN member states, regardless of their factuality. The suspicion that even a background document for a closed meeting of high-level UN staff was subject to such scrutiny was not unfounded, as the influence of member states were ever present. I heard senior staff complain when pushed to commit to a paper deemed mildly controversial that they were not willing to be the subject of a démarche from a member state. Although not having formal disciplinary implications, being mentioned in a démarche could nonetheless complicate an otherwise successful UN staff career.

Even within the Executive Committee's members, the most senior staff of the UN showed their susceptibility to external influences. When on one occasion the Secretary General opened a discussion around a topic that had as its focus a key foreign policy of a permanent member of the UNSC, the first person to speak was a head of department who was also a national of the country in question. They expressed exasperated bafflement that the topic had reached the level of the Executive Committee and characterized the policy as an unmitigated good. What followed was a nervous silence as the other senior staff stared fixedly at the papers in front of them, refusing to be the next person to speak. Without any further interventions the discussion prematurely ended, and the next topic began.

The lengths to which senior policymakers avoided controversy stifled meaningful discussion. Attendees of the Executive Committee invariably stuck to pre-prepared talking points that extolled their department's achievements while offering little in innovative policy suggestions. At the end of a meeting, those of us charged with writing the summary struggled to reimagine the dreary interactions into something that suggested a pointed discussion of the topic had taken place, and as demanded by our bosses. Picking out action points beyond inevitable calls for further meetings, consultations or conferences were even more difficult. A notable exception to these high-level interventions was the high commissioner of human rights, Zeid Raad Al Hussein. His interjections could be passionate and sharp and offered specific and direct public positions for the UN to take on human rights issues. In an unusual decision in 2018, he declined to take up a second term in his office. Resistance to his directness and confrontational style appear to have played a role in his resignation as he complained that to have carried on in his role might have also meant 'bending a knee in supplication'.[11]

A person and an organization

My experiences in New York were a world away from sitting in a UN base in Yei. There was no sensory connection to the topics on which I worked. The richness of the context became less relevant, and my professional satisfaction was less tied to outcomes of actual situations and more on the compliments of those senior to me in the organization. Their interests became my interests. Things that I had hitherto regarded as unimportant, such as the quality of a well-constructed paragraph or a clean and properly branded infographic, took on an outweighed importance in their capacity to reflect well on the department that I represented. When asked to reflect on my time in New York I have often compared it to the classic horror story, *Stepford Wives*, in which through mysterious forces individuals are cajoled to adopt a singular compliant persona. The passing multitude of UN staffers in the lobby show a highly diverse workforce in terms of nationalities, ethnicities and gender. However, the value of that diversity diminished with the acceptance of a single way of working. A narrower mindset predominated, based on a desire to please a hierarchy that operated within tight political constraints.

Conclusions

In South Sudan, I believe my perception of the world in which I worked was inevitably as much a product of the person I was, and the values that I brought with me as the context in which I worked. I also understood that those values were not always related to the individual that I understood or wanted myself to be. In New York, I saw my understanding of the world change as I sought to fit in with an organization that was buffeted between individual career interests and the interests of an international system that constrained the way that work was done.

When the time came to try and understand what had happened in South Sudan and the various failures of the UN, of which the events in 2016 were only one example, my own experiences were significant. Those insights provided a means to understand UNMISS decisions that did not look strictly rational. Intuitively, I understood what had led to the various mistakes that took place, but I lacked the language to explain it to anyone who was not part of that same system. My knowledge of international relations had not equipped me to describe what I increasingly viewed as a cognitive process that created understanding that informed decisions within the UN. In the next chapter I will describe the steps that took me from that intuitive understanding to a more academic framework that borrows from organizational, decision and cognitive theories as well as international relations studies to build a model that better accounts for peacekeeping decision-making that created suboptimal action in South Sudan.

Towards a peacekeeping mindset

Back to school

In 2018, I returned to academia to turn my practitioner's observations into a theory. In this chapter, I shall consider some of the international relations lenses that I initially explored to understand how UN action takes place. That includes looking at realist-institutionalist, sociological-institutionalist and more technical approaches. The insufficiencies of these approaches to explain what I had seen, drew me to other methods more commonly found in organizational studies and decision theory to understand psychological and cognitive bases of action. Through this framework, a UN peacekeeping mindset becomes discernible as a better means to explain action in South Sudan. That mindset also opens the possibility of a better way to understand UN peacekeeping in other contexts as well as to make predictions regarding future action.

The realist-institutionalist

One of the simplest ways to understand UN action is that the organization simply exists to deconflict and legitimize the actions of the world's great powers. As suggested in the previous chapter, these interests have a very real impact on the way that the UN conducts itself, even behind closed doors. As Abbott and Snidel succinctly put it:

> States are the principal actors in world politics, and they use IO's [international organizations] to create social orderings appropriate to their pursuit of shared goals.[1]

Those interests do not create uniform or predictable action. Rather, they reflect the anarchic organization of international relations shaped by strategic interdependence. Legalistic and non-interventionist approaches, such as those often favoured by China and Russia, can exist even as other nations seek progress in changing peacekeeping norms that create the basis for interventions.

Action as understood as a product of this rationalist-institutionalist understanding of the UN does not necessarily correspond to espoused values and stated intentions. The UN can be used as a forum within which to signal values. Ignoring, or deliberately misinterpreting, the resource implications of commitments associated with asserting those values creates instances of 'organizational hypocrisy'[2] in which states act according to their operative interests. A significant example of this are the commitment gaps that appear in peacekeeping operations where the UNSC fail to authorize adequate resources to achieve a particular mandate. Commitment gaps will be discussed in greater length in relation to the United Nations Mission in South Sudan (UNMISS) later in this book.

When state interests are the primary guiding factor for an international organization, the functionaries that carry out the work of the UN thereby become agents charged with enacting those interests. A principal/agent relationship develops. However, inherent in that relationship is a sense that agents maintain some power to determine how action takes place as well as being able to influence the principal's understanding of the world. The agent's control of *expert* information and proximity to the subject of the principal's decisions allow it to shape information that informs choice alternatives for the principal. This approach has generated useful insights on how the contents of mandates and the resourcing of peacekeeping missions are made[3] as well as the relationship between the UNSC and the UN Secretariat.[4]

A realist-institutionalist approach has therefore been useful in creating insights as to the way that states organize themselves and interact with international organizations, as well as the manner that those organizations respond to that interaction. The lens is less useful when examining lower-level decision-making of the type that is the subject of this book, other than to highlight the pervasive nature of those principal and agent interests that may still influence more junior functionaries even when exercised at a distance.

The sociological-institutionalist

Some scholars have noted that bureaucracies are capable of influencing action beyond what belongs to the interests of states or the organization. For example, individual bureaucrats can become norm entrepreneurs by shaping action, using the mechanics of the organization to create change in ways that create benefits beyond those of narrow state and organizational interests.[5]

However, when bureaucracies are seen as entities that exist independently of interests, it is also possible to see within their organization problematic behaviour that can negatively impact the way they carry out the actions for which they were designed. Martha Finnemore and Michael Barnett have portrayed the UN bureaucracy as a context within which rigid organizational rules and structures regulate knowledge and activity. The corresponding dysfunctionality at an operational level creates suboptimal peacekeeping responses such as those seen in Rwanda in 1994. As they explained in their book *Rules for the World*:

> The social stuff of which they [International Organizations] are made – specifically, their rules and the nature of their authority – yields insight into the ways that they exercise power and how their good intentions can sometimes lead to unfortunate and tragic outcomes.[6]

Others, such as Severine Autesserre, see the UN as existing in a much wider landscape of international 'interveners', comprised of a multitude of international organizations and diplomatic missions, which develop and share 'collective understandings'.[7] Autesserre creates a richer understanding of the daily lives of the mass of individuals that work in emergency contexts through the practice, habits and narratives that constitute their reality. She demonstrates how this undermines the perceived value of locally embedded understandings of the context.[8] The information that flows up towards the principals and determines appropriate action in those contexts is therefore likely to be flawed.

While Barnett, Finnemore and Autesserre offer a different focus in their approach (sociological vs anthropological) and unit of analysis (higher-level bureaucrats vs lower-level interveners), there is a common appreciation of organizations as being societal units with corresponding culturally specific practices that inform the construction of knowledge and corresponding action. That interpretation aligns with a sociological-institutionalist approach to understanding organizational action within international relations.[9] This approach also shifts focus on the primary driver of action away from interests and towards the organization itself. A broad interpretation of how action can be driven by the organization is that it creates a *logic of appropriateness* which leads decision-makers to reflect organizational rules, structures and social practices in appropriate action. Appropriateness can be contrasted with the *logic of consequences*[10] in which individuals can make more objective judgements and better incorporate rational actor preferences.

A sociological-institutionalist approach creates significant understanding as to potential sources of dysfunction at an operational level. However, sociological-institutionalist approaches can also relegate individuals to relatively powerless roles amid larger sociological forces with implications as to how we understand individual agency and accountability.

The technical approach

A final significant approach to accounting for peacekeeping action is in its descriptions of action as defined by the technical capabilities available to a peacekeeping mission. Capability limitations are significant elements of the two approaches outlined earlier. Rationalist-institutionalists highlight the role of interests in creating resource, or commitment, gaps that undermine capabilities in peacekeeping missions. Sociological institutionalists see inadequate human resource mechanisms and training gaps, as well as rigid rules and hierarchies, as creating cadres unsuited to being responsive to local contexts.

Other scholars have focused more on the technical nature of capability limitations that are more atheoretical in their approach. These approaches can be a means to retain focus on technical components in peacekeeping missions such as the absorption of new technologies[11] or assessing peacekeeper's tactical readiness to respond to different thematic challenges, including their ability to carry out protection of civilian roles.[12] Such approaches are also prevalent in the UN's own analysis of peacekeeping in the frequent reviews and panels aimed at improving peacekeeping action. This approach is useful for isolating analysis around technical problems to apply corresponding technical fixes. However, they provide the narrowest snapshot of a system, often deliberately, in a way that avoids the political implications of a broader structural lens. This makes them less useful in considering a complete understanding of peacekeeping action.

An alternative approach

As useful as existing frameworks are, they all have limitations. Firstly, their scope can be fragmented in their tendency to focus on different components. Rationalist-institutionalist approaches are most useful when applied to senior policy levels including interactions within the UNSC, as well as between the UNSC and UN Secretariat. Sociological-institutionalist approaches, on the other hand, provide insights that help explain operational-level action. A focus on technical limitations helps explain tactical level action. Even when such approaches are applied in an overlapping way,[13] they struggle to effectively convey a system-wide understanding of processes that make decisions that create action. This also obscures the fact that the UN exists as an open interconnected system where external and internal stimulus can be expected to have a system-wide impact.

Another problem with existing approaches is that I struggled to recognize my own experiences within them. Except for the work done on norm entrepreneurs, the personalities of individuals are often lost even as they are critical to the way that information is mediated, and decision alternatives defined. To form a framework for this research, I therefore sought out those disciplines within which individuals, as part of larger systems, were a greater focus. Specifically, I borrowed from studies of organizational behaviour, psychology, decision theory and cognitive science.

The organizational mind

Writing in the 1940s the organizational theorist Herbert Simon was the first to see within individual behaviour, when situated within organizational systems, a susceptibility to decision-making that was at odds with economic understandings of a rational agent.[14] In explaining this Simon suggested that, notwithstanding the many outward components of decision-making processes, decisions ultimately take place within a human mind and therefore cognitive limitations need to be accounted for when trying to understand how they are made. Unable to compute a potentially infinite number of choice alternatives, as demanded by a truly rational choice, a decision-maker is compelled to limit the factors that they consider to those that are pertinent:

> One can leave out of account those aspects of reality – and that means most aspects – that appear irrelevant at a given time. Administrators (and everyone else, for that matter) take into account just a few of the factors of the situation regarded as the most relevant.[15]

How a decision-maker might compile those relevant factors will depend on what is being demanded from the given task within the context of organizational priorities. More succinctly, he suggests a cognitive understanding of organizational decision-making as

> shaped by a scissors whose two blades are the structure of the task and the computational capabilities of the actor.[16]

Simon's understanding that individuals were not strictly rational and interpreted the world around them to fit cognitive limitations and suit organizational functions had significant implications for decision theory that reverberate today. However, his characterization of the human mind feels mechanistic in its reduction to computational functions that are dedicated to organizational tasks.

It was in the decades that followed Simon's initial work that the cognitive revolution created a more intricate understanding of individuality within social and organizational settings. The movement away from behaviourist approaches to cognitive ones created new concepts within social psychology. These included Solomon Asch's experiments, showing the need of individuals to make decisions that demonstrate group conformity[17] and Leon Festinger's discovery of individual decision-making behaviour that reduces the mental discomfort caused by contradictory beliefs, otherwise known as cognitive dissonance.[18] According to these psychological approaches, people prioritized individual needs for cognitive comfort and ease above more practical elements, including those that might better serve more optimal decision-making.

In the 1970s, Daniel Kahneman and Amos Tversky added further to the cognitive model with their work on prospect theory. In their experiments, they identified how individuals consistently subjectively frame an outcome or transaction in ways other than that expected of a rational agent with the result that they systematically violate the axioms of expected utility theory, that correspond to most people's understanding of rational choice.[19] This was done because of bias in decision-making. While ostensibly an economic theory, the discoveries provided further evidence of the importance of psychology in decision-making behaviour. They demonstrated how individuals apply bias to compensate for missing or uncertain information, rather than trying to rationally incorporate that uncertainty into their calculation of choice alternatives. The suggestion developed further by Kahneman suggested that an individual's need for certainty to create personal cognitive ease takes priority over their commitment to more complex, and potentially discomfiting, rational decision-making.[20]

An application of cognitive approaches is not unknown in the study of international relations.[21] However, such approaches have often focused on the role of individuals that exist either as elite decision-makers[22] or else as individuals generating knowledge as experts.[23] What remains less understood is how these individual cognitive processes impact systemic elements of behaviour within international organizations. Within sociological-institutionalist frameworks, cognition has been used more recently to incorporate analysis of lower-level functionaries. For example, the *logic of appropriateness*, mentioned previously, has more recently been interpreted as the following of 'cognitive scripts' that reinforce the legitimacy of institutions and shapes action within them among functionaries.[24] However, this only reiterates existing sociological-institutionalist ideas by reinforcing notions of following collective behaviour rather than individuals interacting with their organizational reality to create action that is simultaneously systemic and individual.

In business studies where the application of cognitive science is more advanced, this cognitive approach has generated insight into understanding systemic events through individual cognition. For example, the role of cognitive bias among auditors has been interpreted as a reason for catastrophic and systemic business failures that had international ramifications in the early 2000s.[25]

Bounded rationality, bias, behaviours and suboptimal decision-making

Having recognized the importance of an approach that is tied to organizational, decision and cognition theories, there is a need to define exactly how such a framework can be applied. Specifically, how can it be used to understand UN peacekeeping decision-making in South Sudan and build on the understanding of UN action that already exists? To start, I have returned to Simon who first coined the term 'bounded rationality' to describe the constructed world within which an administrator necessarily lives to create appropriate decision-making alternatives within an organizational context. Those elements that appear extraneous to that context are filtered to create a smaller range of choices manageable within the limitations of the human mind. Simon further suggests that a decision arising from a bounded rationality, in and of itself, is likely to be suboptimal because of the tendency towards *satisficing* choices. In such choices, decision-makers seek outcomes that just pass the threshold of acceptability according to perceived organizational priorities, rather than pursuing more risky *maximizing* solutions.[26]

Where information is unknown or uncertain, the known parameters of the bounded rationality, within which individual and organizational expectations are captured, will create an anchor for choice alternatives. Individuals may incorrectly value information so as to better correspond to a preferred interpretation of reality. This is a bias that will be more likely to lead to suboptimal decisions, given its relation to a flawed valuation of data.

A traditionally conceived *rational* organization, as originally described by the likes of Max Weber, has mechanisms that should mitigate against bounded rationalities that are too narrow, and their inherent tendency towards bias. Large modern organizations have access to experts that when efficiently organized allow them to gather the most relevant information required for the optimal selection of choice alternatives. The division of labour between different departments decreases the possibility that a single bias viewpoint dominates decision-making. In reality, organizations create behaviours that promote conformity and cohesion. This undermines diverse and independent viewpoints in favour of choice alternatives that support the coherence of an organizational bounded rationality. *Bounded rationality, bias* and *behaviour* therefore combine to undermine optimal decision-making. In the following text, I will attempt to explore each of these concepts in greater depth to understand how they might specifically relate to the context of UN peacekeeping.

A peacekeeping bounded rationality

A bounded rationality as viewed by an individual-decision maker within the UN must necessarily fulfil the psychological needs of that person in the organization within which they are situated. Put simply, a bounded rationality will provide the answer to two basic questions. Firstly, 'What is important to my organization?' Secondly, in fulfilment of their own needs, they will ask, 'What is important to me?' I have offered four potential answers that broadly capture the most likely answers to these questions.

a) Individual values – *'I must justify my professional self-image, by carrying out my duties according to my values within the resources available to me.'*

The first is perhaps the most obvious and correlates most closely to how Simon might have originally conceived a practical minded functionary. Specifically, within UN peacekeeping, officials are responding to duties, roles and responsibilities with set tasks that have been organizationally defined. The broader objectives of those tasks are set within mission mandates. In an individual fulfilling their tasks to what they perceive is the best of their abilities creates self-worth regarded as an 'emotional sine qua non'. Failure to meet the standards of that self-conception represents a 'self-rejection' that can be the cause of debilitating emotional pain and is generally avoided by 'successful' professionals.[27]

However, the nature of what constitutes the self-image of a *good* professional is value laden. This research takes the cognitive-affective personality approach, in which behaviour and attitudes can be best predicted by understanding the interaction of an individual with a stable psychological system within a given situation.[28] Available external resources, available internal resources, external stimuli including extreme situations such as those found in peacekeeping create differing expectations of oneself. In this book, I will primarily focus on the three different heads of UNMISS to understand how their individual personalities, and the shifting world around them, created a fluid perception of what constituted a *good professional* and, in so doing, created an element of bounded rationality that changed according to different situations. For example, political, diplomatic, administrative and operational expertise were variously considered as *important* professional values, depending on the individual.

b) UNSC and UN Secretariat interests – 'I must satisfy those above me in the hierarchy.'

Even with a diversification in types of organizational structure away from a classic bureaucratic hierarchy, the prevalence of hierarchy as a societal structure still means that people have become 'so accustomed to the idea of superiority and subordination' that even in less formal organizations the need to please those 'above' is evident.'[29] That instinct is likely to be considerably more important in an organization such as the UN in which hierarchical stratification is pronounced and embedded in its rites and rituals including an elaborate grading system of seniority.[30]

Deference to hierarchy from those decision-makers working at the field level of a peacekeeping mission can constitute a deference to those interests that emanate from senior leadership within the UNSC and the UN Secretariat. As described in the previous chapter, the UNSC deploys a range of means to make its interests felt among senior staff of the UN. This includes informal arrangements and lobbying by member states over who leads UN Secretariat departments as well as agencies, funds and programmes.[31] The UNSC can also hold influence over its nationals that occupy senior positions in the Secretariat.

The UNSC can more directly intervene when senior UN staff act in a way; they perceive to be contrary to their interests. When Kai Eide opened negotiations with the Taliban while being Special Representative of the Secretary General (SRSG) at UNAMA, he did so against the backdrop of 'considerable pressure from UN headquarters and the Security Council against engagement'.[32] When Choi Young-Jin used military force to intervene in the conflict in Sierra Leone as SRSG of UNOCI, he was criticized by a member of the UNSC.[33] The UNSC can also make positive examples of individuals. Kofi Annan's significant role in the decision failures that contributed to the UN's catastrophic performance in Rwanda in 1994 did not impede his ascension to Secretary General. Notably his actions were more closely aligned to the interests of members of the UNSC, who were reluctant to extend their involvement in the troubled country.

Another means by which the UNSC communicate their interests to UN peacekeeping staff are the resources which they make available to respective missions. The so-called commitment gap (the gap between a peacekeeping mandate and the resources available to achieve that mandate) has been a common feature of peacekeeping since their inception and been raised by the Secretariat as a considerable impediment to its ability to carry out mission mandates.[34] The level to which the UNSC authorizes resources communicates the level of its commitment to an individual context.[35] A wary SRSG is likely to evaluate expectations according to the political and material support evident in mission resourcing rather than the heady values of a mission's mandate.

Other interests that will impact the decision-making environment are those within the senior staff of the UN Secretariat. These are not always directly aligned with the UNSC. Often, they relate to a preference in New York to avoid involvement that might overextend the organization in volatile and uncertain contexts. Senior staff have an interest in avoiding personal association with visible professional failures that are more likely with large peacekeeping operations in dangerous and unpredictable environments, particularly where they know that UNSC commitment is low. In the creation of UNMISS, for example, the UN Secretariat initially tried to avoid a Chapter VII mandate that necessitated a deeper operational commitment to South Sudan, including the possibility that it could be obliged to use force to intervene in attacks on civilians. The Secretariat instead argued that a Chapter VI mandate, without such expectations, was more appropriate to the context.[36] As the principal, the UNSC ultimately overruled the Secretariat, but the latter continued to act in a way that showed a clear preference to avoid Chapter VII commitments.

c) Organizational myth – *'I must protect the positive shared image of the organization and myself within the organization.'*

A bureaucracy creates a social system within which mechanisms are reconstructed as symbols, rites and rituals. These constitute a type of culture that takes on an inflated importance in the mind of the employee.[37] Some individual's values may lead them to rebel against these rites and rituals. However, the individual need for conformity suggests a greater likelihood that they will adhere to the organizational culture. Current orthodoxy in organizational management suggests that strong 'organizational-fit' should correspond to career advancement and hiring and promotion practices should be used to incentivize organizational conformity.[38] In the UN, the use of core competencies and core values in recruitment creates a means to define individual conformity to an organizational identity at the outset.

A UN cultural identity will also likely be even more prominent than a normal organizational culture, given the quasi-religious nature of its organizational myth. Within its founding document, the opening line, 'We the peoples of the United Nations', delineates the grandiose authority that underpins the organization's legitimacy. One of the founding figures of the early organization of the UN in general, and peacekeeping in particular, Dag Hammarskjöld, looms large in the myth. His use of language leant a quasi-religious purpose to the organization reflected in his personal writings, as well as his public conceptualization of the UN's role.

> The principles of the Charter are, by far, greater than the Organization in which they are embodied, and the aims which they are to safeguard are holier than the policies of any single nation or people.[39]

Today, it is not unusual to see ambitious bureaucrats in New York with a copy of Markings, a collection of Hammarskjöld's spiritual musings on professional life, posed subtly in their office. However, focus on an organizational myth can create world views that are simultaneously expansive (lifting decisions outside the scope of narrow interests) while also inward-looking (satisfaction with a fixed self-image that precludes reform). Abraham Zaleznik sees within organizational myth the tendency for corporations to embrace their mythology in a way that creates inefficiency, as staff focus on its unchanging 'inner life'. Far from motivating an organization to show itself worthy of its myth, it breeds insularity and lessens responsiveness to a changing environment.[40] The core message of its myth fades into irrelevance as energies are directed towards the maintenance of symbols, rites and rituals, and focus is on maintaining a generic positive representation of the organization. Of particular relevance in this research is the tendency for a focus on organizational myth to overemphasize the risks of actions that have the potential to undermine the organization's reputation. This lessens a decision-maker's appetite for uncertainty in a way that disincentivizes the contemplation of a broader range of decision alternatives.

An example of the significance of myth may be seen in the response of the UN to the Haitian cholera crisis of the 2010s that killed approximately 10,000 people. Notwithstanding the evidence against it, it took six years of repeated denials and delayed action[41] before the UN publicly accepted its responsibility for introducing the disease to the local population.[42] The accusations, while true, directly challenged the myth of the UN through its implication of incompetence and apparent indifference to the suffering of the local population. The organizational myth encouraged officials to be circumspect of information that might have prompted more timely remedial action.

d) System appropriateness –
'*I must act correctly according to the system.*'

The way in which the UN places a high priority in the observance of rules and structural expectations also skews decision-making by creating irrational value around rule following that detracts from focus on more practical elements of a task. It was notable in this research that the UN generally did not punish instances of poor decision-making and even rewarded bad decision-makers. The common factor is that these decision-makers did not break any implicit or explicit rules. Such a narrow definition of job performance inevitably skews decision-making by creating appropriateness around process rather than task objectives. This idea corresponds closely to Barnett and Finnemore's ideas as to how pathologies of dysfunction are created in bureaucratic rule following.

In 2017, UN Resident Coordinator for Myanmar Renata Lok-Dessallien was moved from her position following media accusations that she suppressed information about human rights abuses to maintain focus on cooperation with the government on development issues.[43] The subsequent investigation by the UN confirmed 'instances of deliberately de-dramatizing events in reports prepared by the Resident Coordinator', which played a role in the UN's failures in the country during the genocide against the Rohingya community. However, the report is also at pains to suggest that the resident coordinator acted according to the rules suggesting that she 'framed her coordination of the country team in terms of the guidance received from New York'.[44] Within the UN system, such adherence to the rules cannot be faulted even in the face of catastrophic failure. Lok-Dessallien subsequently secured a promotion to the resident coordinator role in India in 2019.

Bias fills uncertainty

The parameters of a bounded rationality create a preferred framework for UN decision-makers to define choice alternatives. It reflects the mechanism by which organizational decision-makers distil the chaotic nature of reality and its infinite choice alternatives to those manageable elements that are pertinent to the structure of the task. However, an individual's understanding of values, interests, organizational myth and system appropriateness take on an outweighed importance within that rationality particularly when other elements of a task decision are unknown or uncertain. This increases the likelihood of bias.

Bias allows information about the world to be interpreted through subconscious processes that minimize cognitive contradictions and promote cognitive ease in a way that is important to the psychological well-being of individual decision-makers.[45] Faced with contradictory or uncertain information, a decision-maker will show a subconscious preference for an interpretation of the world that confirms existing beliefs within an organizational bounded rationality. The focus will be on matching to that interpretation a satisficing solution. This is likely even if a more rational choice is to incorporate more uncertain elements or pursue riskier maximizing strategies. Uncertain or maximizing alternatives that contradict the bounded rationality and create risk will likely be a source of psychological discomfort that will cause an individual to subconsciously turn away from them. The tendency for individuals to resort to bias to resolve complex and uncertain problems is central to the experiments of Tversky and Kahneman and has been widely observed in organizational decision-making.[46]

In ordinary circumstances, where a broadly stable *reality* exists through the acceptance of shared knowledge between the UN and other entities capable of creating understandings of reality (governmental, civil society, media etc.), suboptimality within decision-making may be limited by the need to demonstrate responsiveness to commonly accepted *truths* that more closely correspond to an objective reality. Organizational myth will compel the UN to act in situations where the necessity of its intervention cannot be generally denied. For example, in relation to the UN's involvement in Haiti, they changed their reaction to the cholera outbreak when their responsibility for the public health crisis was established through shared understandings with which an organizational interpretation could not compete.

However, shared stable understandings of reality are contingent upon the availability of information delivered in a sufficiently slow and predictable way that a network of disparate organizations can negotiate and agree upon shared meanings. In a dynamic situation, such as a warzone, the stability of that reality degrades as entities struggle to find information and agree on meanings in a fast-changing environment. A conflict will undermine the availability and certainty of information as well as the capacity of diffuse networks to support a single, stable understanding. In that environment, an organization such as the UN must be self-reliant in the absorption of information and creation of understandings. In that more isolated environment, a bounded rationality becomes more significant to the appraisal of information and construction of reality. The bounded rationality provides an arbitrary anchor that biases the decision-maker to certain choice alternatives and incentivizes the avoidance of alternative contradictory external understandings.

Bias pushes decision-makers to favour existing beliefs and experiences that are connected to values, myths, interests and appropriateness as they interpret the world to develop choice alternatives. In the following text, I have suggested three types of bias that I will refer to in the chapters of this book as they were the most prevalent based on observations of UNMISS.

a) Confirmation bias refers to, 'the seeking or interpreting of evidence in ways that are partial to existing beliefs'.[47] A significant amount of empirical evidence exists to suggest that individuals are susceptible to seeking out,[48] interpreting[49] and remembering[50] information in such a way so as to better conform to an existing and deeply held hypothesis. Within my framework such hypotheses (or beliefs) are those that have been developed as *correct* according to at least one component of the bounded rationality. That can lead to overweighting the importance of information that corresponds to an individual or organizational perspective that is either a broad world view or a narrower piece of policy established to give coherence to the bounded rationality.

b) Availability bias refers to the tendency of individuals to make judgements, 'by the ease with which relevant instances come to mind'.[51] The availability of such instances in a person's mind will affect the ability of an individual to predict the likelihood of an event.[52] The vividness of instances, where they have had negative or positive connotations to the person experiencing them, also create associations that shape the way an individual perceives social reality and the values that they attach to it.[53] In this book, availability bias most commonly relates to those experiences that are important to the way an individual interprets and composes their sense of a professional *self*. For example, memories associated with previous individual professional successes are likely to be more available to a decision-maker, given their positive association. That may prompt an individual to place importance on perceived understanding from that moment, even when its relevance to a current situation is limited. Organizations are also likely to only assimilate information that reinforces the bounded rationality. Information that contradicts the bounded rationality is marginalized or forgotten and is no longer available even when it has the potential to inform more optimal decisions in the future. For example, information about critical incidents can become unavailable because reviews of the incident were either never done or never given prominence in the organization.

c) **Substitution bias,** otherwise referred to as *attribute substitution,* refers to the application of a stereotype[54] or reference to a prototypical case that can be applied to replace missing or uncertain information.[55] The bias can also account for positive and negative associations attached to individuals and organizations by decision-makers, even when those associations are not correlated.[56] For example, a UN official may view a government official more positively simply because they are part of the same culture or system of international governance to which they assign positive connotations.

Behaviours enable bias

The central hypothesis of this book is that the failures of peacekeeping in South Sudan were the product of a failure to properly account for unknown or uncertain factors in a rational way. Instead, decision-makers persistently showed preference for, or improperly valued, known information to align their choice alternatives more closely to a bounded rationality that promoted cognitive coherence that created certainty. Contradictory information was improperly undervalued or left out of the development of choice alternatives.

As suggested earlier, well-developed bureaucracies have inherent capacities to mitigate bias. These include the availability of diverse experts within specialized departments, the range of which should make the assimilation of information and its proper valuation more likely. The division of departments should inhibit the development of fixed organizational *beliefs* or the need to rely on individual experiences. A bureaucratic organization also creates an emotional detachment from a decision that should inhibit bias responses. An organization should have a coherent and consistent risk profile that allows it to accurately assess risk, accounting for, rather than removing, known uncertainties in decision-making. To understand why bounded rationality and bias created suboptimal decision-making in South Sudan, it is therefore necessary to understand why those mechanisms to deter bias in decision-making failed.

Within UNMISS, it was possible to identify certain behaviours that undermined a diversity of viewpoints and skewed the way in which a decision-maker frames a problem or anchors their decision. *Frames* relate to the different ways that the same information can be presented in the mind of a decision-maker to elicit differing responses. *Anchors* refer to those base values which can be chosen by a decision-maker as a basis on which decisions are made. Framing and anchoring mistakes can include wrongly classifying groups when considering threats or else arbitrarily making a risk threshold needlessly high. These behaviours are simultaneously articulations of existing bias while also shaping information selection and interpretation in a way that reinforces the logic of that bias. The repetition of certain frames and anchors legitimizes their reuse, often without accounting for whether their use has been previously accurate or successful. The following represents four ways in which behaviours within organizations allow incorrect frames and anchors to be adopted and then embedded within the UN in a way that nullifies the inherent capacity of the organization to mitigate bias.

a) **Inside views** are the consequence of decision-makers arbitrarily restricting the boundaries of a decision process by limiting inputs from those outside of a small group, often comprised of those who follow the same bounded rationality. The tendency is for those within the inside view to overstate the uniqueness of their task in a way that undermines the potential value of external viewpoints. It legitimizes the application of solutions that reflect the shared understandings from the small group according to the limited frame and arbitrary anchors that they agree upon.[57]

b) **Groupthink** occurs when the desire for conformity and perceived harmony means that those within a group overweight the importance of consensus in decision-making over critical evaluation. The group is more likely to undervalue the opinions of those views that appear disruptive in their divergence. The group artificially promotes optimism and certainty around harmonious decision-making.[58]

Groupthink is likely to lead to an emulation of the inside views of senior officials by more junior staff. This may be in expectation of professional reward in the form of senior appreciation for confirming their assertions.[59] Vying for such acknowledgement is likely to be pronounced in what William Ouchi defined as 'type A' organizations, where the importance of senior individualism undermines the value of internal consultations and horizontal information sharing.[60] In a hierarchal and process-oriented culture such as the UN, more junior staff are left out of senior decision-making. Their involvement in the organization is limited to arbitrary and irrelevant aspects of the organization's life. As Deal and Kennedy observe in process-oriented cultures:

> They [the employees] start developing artificial ties to elements of the world in the organization; small events take on major importance – a certain telephone call, that snippet of paper, or the section head's latest memo.[61]

In an environment that does not value individual junior perspectives, emulation of senior mindsets becomes one of the few ways to demonstrate value within the organization. Competition will exist between departments to create interpretations of information that satisfy senior perspectives.

Barnett and Finnemore suggest that the way in which the UN system functioned in the lead up to Rwanda and Srebrenica meant that it struggled to assign appropriate significance to events outside of the official interpretation. Processes 'generated indifference', and it became 'tolerable, even desirable, to disregard mass violations of human rights'.[62] In their place, they suggested that UNAMIR exhibited a type of groupthink favouring 'assimilated information' based on systemic understandings, even as new information contradicted the decisions that stemmed from it.[63]

c) Risk aversion refers to the tendency to reference incorrect risk frameworks in decision-making. This behaviour becomes increasingly irrational as decision-makers are willing to accept significant losses to avoid even small chances of encountering risk.[64] The pursuit of risk-averse strategies can thus inadvertently become risk-seeking. For example, a peacekeeping mission may refuse to deploy military assets to avoid circumstances where harm (to UN soldiers) is more likely or else avoid postures perceived as confrontational. However, when the risks of confrontation are only moderate while the lack of deployment makes the likelihood of encouraging future belligerent aggression high, then that decision becomes irrational.

d) The **sunk-cost fallacy** refers to the irrational tendency to incorporate past investments into present decisions even when those investments are irrelevant.[65] The tendency undermines a decision-maker's ability to critically examine their past mistakes as they seek to justify past behaviour in future decisions.[66] In situations of uncertainty, such justification can escalate to maintain the correctness of decisions even in the face of information that suggest those decisions are suboptimal.[67] A decision-maker that has a personal attachment to that investment can exacerbate this tendency as they seek to justify their role in the original decision.[68]

Methodology

In the following figure, I have summarized the key components of my hypothesis as to how decision-making processes took place with the context of UNMISS (Figure 1). It is likely that many similarities will be found with other peacekeeping missions and UN entities in general, creating predictability in UN action.

To test these assertions in relation to UNMISS, I have chosen to focus on the role of the South Sudan Office of the Special Representative of the Secretary General (SRSG) and the decisions that were made within the offices of the three individuals that occupied the role of SRSG between 2011 and 2021. I will focus on how they, and the staff around them, behaved in relation to six critical decision events. All those decisions relate to the *protection of civilians* component of the UNMISS mandate. From its inception in 2011, UNMISS had a strong protection of civilians component. In the years prior to 2014, this was outlined in sections: 3 (b) (iv), 3 (b) (v), and 3 (b) (vi) of its initial mandate and thereafter in section 4 (a). When nationwide conflict started in 2013, the UNMISS protection of civilians role became its primary task. Those efforts became centred around activities at Protection of Civilians sites (POC sites) in UNMISS bases where people had fled to escape violence. Between 2014 and 2016, UNMISS opened five major POC sites. Although POC sites were not unprecedented in peacekeeping missions, the size and extended duration of these sites provided novel challenges to a traditional peacekeeping posture.[69] Before examining those decision events more closely I will provide some additional background to the context, including some of the root causes of the conflict, as well as the organization of UNMISS. This should be useful to anyone who is new to the subject.

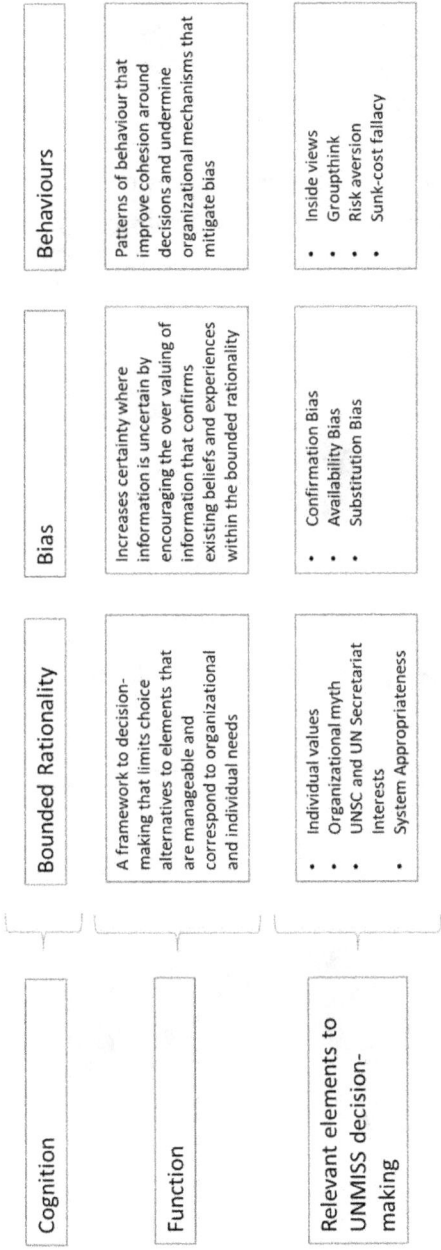

Cognition	Bounded Rationality	Bias	Behaviours
Function	A framework to decision-making that limits choice alternatives to elements that are manageable and correspond to organizational and individual needs	Increases certainty where information is uncertain by encouraging the over valuing of information that confirms existing beliefs and experiences within the bounded rationality	Patterns of behaviour that improve cohesion around decisions and undermine organizational mechanisms that mitigate bias
Relevant elements to UNMISS decision-making	• Individual values • Organizational myth • UNSC and UN Secretariat Interests • System Appropriateness	• Confirmation Bias • Availability Bias • Substitution Bias	• Inside views • Groupthink • Risk aversion • Sunk-cost fallacy

Figure 1 Summary of terms used in theoretical framework.

As part of the research for this book, I conducted fifty-two interviews in 2020 and 2021 with serving and former members of UNMISS, officials from humanitarian organizations, including UN and NGO staff, as well as independent analysts who work primarily on South Sudan. Those interviews were conducted anonymously given the potential for professional repercussions on those involved. I have also included observations that I made during my time working on the country between 2014 and 2021. These contributions are often subjective, and I have tried to be clear in the text as to the personal nature of those observations. Hopefully they contribute to setting the environment in a way that will be useful to those unfamiliar with the country or the day-to-day life or working in an emergency setting.

Hope for a better future

South Sudan up to 2011

In early 2021, I accepted a new job in South Sudan. It was the first time I had been back in almost four years, and with the ten-year anniversary of its independence it was a landmark year. On arriving at the airport, it was a relief to see that the long-delayed renovation of the new terminal had been completed. I did not have to struggle through the battered and frequently flooded tents that had been serving as the country's international airport the last time I left. Nonetheless, the chaotic arrival hall was familiar. Outside, the streets were similarly bustling. At the crowded tea shops that dotted the road leading away from the airport, people were engrossed in discussions. The tea shop serves as a traditional mainstay of social life in Juba and offers a chance for all ages and walks of life to meet and converse. The animated nature of the conversations and visible smiles of the discussants were testament to both the passions and pleasure with which debate is enjoyed in the country. At those shops, you might encounter Dinka, Nuer, the local Bari community or any member of the sixty-four tribes of South Sudan. You may hear local languages, but you'd be equally likely to hear people from different communities sharing perspectives in the lingua franca of Juba Arabic, or, increasingly, English. This common scene belies the unfair image of a country irrevocably riven by tribal differences where political disagreements are only settled through violence.

Juba also showed pockets of prosperity that offer a wider selection of more contemporary public spaces and are testament to a remarkable resilience that ensures the country continues to grow despite an unpromising environment for entrepreneurship. Small boutiques have emerged alongside swanky hotels, modern cafes and large nightclubs. In these spaces, you can find expatriate diplomats and humanitarian workers but also many young middle-class South Sudanese. Many of those young people have spent time overseas, their families pushed to Uganda or Kenya as well as farther afield during decades of conflict.

Many have returned from the United States, the UK and Australia, their diaspora status marked by accents from other parts of the world that they may also call home. Despite their differences, a common refrain from these young, educated individuals is disdain for the tribal politics of their homeland. On social media, they largely embrace a unifying Junubeen identity, the Arabic slang for all southerners.

Even among this open-minded group, there are tensions. Gender politics continue to create disagreements on topics such as polygamy or dowry obligations that are still commonly practised in South Sudan and create arguments between modernists and traditionalists. A more deep-seated tension is around those offspring of government officials and politicians who have most obviously benefitted from patronage in a kleptocratic state that has mobilized individuals along communal lines to assist in their plundering of resources.[1] The most unapologetic of these flaunt their wealth online and in the bars of Juba, Nairobi and Kampala even as an embryonic youth-led civil society, which decries the ruinous corruption of the state, struggles to be heard. In recent times, the latter have increasingly challenged a generation that they see as having been profligate in its stewardship of what was in 2021, still the world's youngest county. In Juba that challenging spirit can be seen in art (most visibly through movements such as the Anataban art collective), academia (such as the Sudd Institute) and increasingly the organization of civil action.

Those that are trying to disrupt the established political order face significant difficulties. Shortly after I arrived, a new civil society group hoped to capitalize on widespread disaffection by calling for 'mass-protests' that emulated the civil action that had brought about recent political change in Sudan.[2] The government arrested the alleged ringleaders, and some officials threatened to shoot protesters.[3] On the scheduled day of protests on 30 August, the streets were quiet. Unlike Sudan, a country that has a strong history of professional trade unions and an established middle class capable of the high level of civic organization that such protests require, political movement in South Sudan has out of necessity been organized along different lines. Since the First Sudan Civil War, protest has more often been expressed through violent resistance, often guided through highly centralized and authoritarian military structures in which individuals were often mobilized along communal lines. Those entrenched instincts continue to underpin a system of governance in which freedom of expression outside of the legitimatized platform of the SPLM is limited. Taking an unauthorized photograph in public in Juba is still likely to lead to an arrest, or at least being forced to pay a bribe to escape arrest. Despite the country ostensibly being at peace, a 9.00 pm curfew was aggressively enforced on foreigners. The country retained the label 'not free' in Freedom House's global freedom assessments in 2021.

The failure of the protests, however, masks the profound disappointment that many South Sudanese continue to feel about the lost opportunity of the first decade of independence. In my four-year absence, progress in service delivery had been lacklustre. The roads in Juba remained a mixture of pitted tarmac and murram that were battered and damaged with each rainy season. Traffic lights that had been built throughout the city only a few years earlier were almost entirely broken. Some had been vandalized, while others entirely uprooted. Across the country, the situation was considerably worse. In 2021, less than a third of people had access to electricity. About the same had access to safe water. Only one doctor was available for every 65,000 people, and about half of the child population were out of school in 2020. A food crisis existed throughout the country, with some areas experiencing famine-type conditions.[4]

On the route between the airport and my guesthouse, we were stopped by the traffic police. To drivers in Juba, this had become a daily expectation, and many junctions were crowded with the white uniformed officers speculatively stopping vehicles looking for any infraction that they might be able to benefit financially from. It was the second time that day that I had been stopped by an official seeking money, having been asked for $20 by a policeman at the airport who had accompanied me, unrequested, through the arrival hall. A never-ending budgetary crisis created months (and sometimes years) of long delays in the payment of civil servants' salaries. Those salaries were already paltry. Despite them being doubled in 2021, an ordinary soldier would still expect no more than the equivalent of about $7 per month. The most senior general in the security sector would only expect about $34 from their official pay.[5] Any interaction with official bureaucracy, especially with security services that were armed and capable of exerting an additional menace, carried an inherent risk of encountering extortion.

General poverty in the city remained visibly high. An informal camp for displaced people that had been built on a cemetery in the centre of town at the start of the conflict was still there, with fragile-looking shelters sown together with sheets emblazoned with the logos of various UN agencies. They represented a tiny handful of the approximately four million people, more than a third of the total population, which remained displaced either inside the country or as refugees, mostly in neighbouring Uganda.[6] This displacement was a product of the civil war that began at the end of 2013. Despite the signing of a peace agreement in 2018 and the establishment of a unity government, confidence has remained sufficiently low that the vast proportion of displaced had yet to venture back to their homes. The families in the cemetery lived next to a hotel complex popular with expatriates, many of whom worked for those same agencies that had branded the temporary shelters. At the hotel's restaurant, a single course would easily exceed a civil servant's monthly salary. When I visited the same hotel later that evening, I brought with me a large roll of paper money. There had been a 14,000 per cent increase in the exchange rate of the South Sudanese Pound to the US dollar since I first went to the country in early 2014. Though larger new notes had been produced, bills for groups still required a small pile of cash. What was an inconvenience to expatriates had dire consequences for many South Sudanese, who had watched the value of their salaries and savings all but disappear over the previous years.

Employment was difficult to come by. As suggested earlier, jobs with the government could be unreliable and poorly paid. Notwithstanding an abundance of enthusiasm, the private sector was underdeveloped and had struggled to expand through years of conflict. Work within humanitarian organizations, whether UN or NGO, provided a prized source of income and stability. However, by the time I arrived, falling global aid and lowering international interest in the country had seen many of the budgets, on which these jobs rely, starting to disappear. Competition for employment was becoming fierce with increasing stories of humanitarian organizations being harassed in communities where young men in particular felt unfairly marginalized from opportunities.[7] Food insecurity was also dire. While some parts of the country faced famine-like conditions, others struggled to afford staples that had been rising in price. Imports, on which the country still relied, continued to be disrupted by intermittent violence on key trade routes in addition to the impact of COVID-19. Falling aid budgets were also affecting the ability of humanitarians to respond. In 2021, the World Food Programme (WFP) had been forced to cut its rations in critical areas affecting hundreds of thousands of people in need.[8]

Notwithstanding, the proven resilience of its people, the situation had created a pervasive mood of pessimism. My colleagues privately berated the country's leaders that had thrown away the future of the country. Their faith in the transitional peace government, which was led by the same leaders that had started the conflict in 2013, was low.

In the pervasive pessimism of that moment, it was hard to imagine that before the violence of 2013 many had reason to believe that the darkest period of South Sudan's history was behind it. For most of the 1980s, the southern states of Sudan were engulfed in a vicious civil war, the brutality of which created a humanitarian disaster. The intercession of NGO and UN humanitarian agencies organized under a consortium known as Operation Lifeline Sudan (OLS) helped avert a worse catastrophe.[9] UN involvement under the OLS continued until the war finally came to a halt twenty-two years after it had begun, in 2005. The Comprehensive Peace Agreement (CPA) that concluded the conflict also heralded a new stage of involvement by the UN with the establishment of the United Nations Mission in Sudan (UNMIS). UNMIS supported the implementation of the CPA until a referendum, in which 98.3 per cent of the population of Sudan's southern states voted in favour of independence. The new state of South Sudan was declared on 9 July 2011.

On 8 July 2011, UNMIS was rebadged and given a new mandate to support the establishment of the country. To many of the staff of the newly established United Nations Mission in South Sudan (UNMISS), particularly those that had been involved since the days of the OLS, there was a sense of euphoria and optimism as tens of thousands of people gathered in Juba to celebrate the first day of the new country.[10] Not only had the country successfully emerged from one of Africa's longest and most destructive conflicts, but it appeared united in a common goal. The links that many humanitarians and analysts had forged with local South Sudanese officials during the civil wars of independence created a sense of collaboration on which it was believed an accelerated process of development could take place.

The challenges were daunting. Independence meant an inexperienced government tackling some of the world's worst human development indicators on behalf of its ten million people. This task was more complex given the decades of underinvestment in which history played a role. A British colonial strategy known as the *southern policy* had exacerbated the isolation of southern communities and undermined modernization.[11] During discussions around independence, the administration in Khartoum continued to prioritize a more urbanized and Arabic Islamic north that was a root cause of the first civil war in 1955. Following rapprochement that helped end that conflict, economic turmoil in the 1970s again diluted northern elites' commitment to continued coexistence on an equal basis. In 1983, another war broke out, effectively ending official development in the south. By the time the conflict ended in 2005, physical infrastructure in the south was largely non-existent. Only 14 kilometres of paved road existed in a country the size of France on the signing of the CPA.[12] The need for basic infrastructure was even more apparent in a country with a landscape that presents huge logistical challenges. At the heart of the country stands *The*

Sudd, a vast swamp whose Arabic name derives from the word for *barrier* or *obstruction* and is fed by a colossal rainy season that lasts up to six months each year, turning many of the country's roads into impassable rivers. Up to 60 per cent of the country can be inaccessible to road vehicles for up to half of the year.[13] In recent years, areas around the Sudd have faced catastrophic floods that regularly affect more than a million people, destroying crops and displacing tens of thousands. Climate change is escalating the severity of this already annual natural disaster.

In addition to development and transportation challenges, the political geography of South Sudan was fraught. It is made up of a patchwork of different communities divided into tribes and subdivided into sections, age sets and clans, associated with seventy different languages.[14] Flexible communal identities and competing patronage and familial claims on loyalty adds to the complexity. The two largest and most powerful groups in South Sudan are the Dinka and Nuer, accounting for 36 and 16 per cent of the population, respectively.[15] In an environment that lacks proper mechanisms to mediate legitimate claims to political and economic resources, these identity groups can be mobilized to compete and can express their rivalries through large violent confrontations. This includes cattle raiding, which can spark battles that claim hundreds of lives in a single incident.[16] During the civil war, this communal competition was fanned by Khartoum through their sponsorship of groups willing to show any level of allegiance to its authority. In an era in which Kalashnikov rifles became ubiquitous, replacing less lethal forms of weaponry, this sponsorship forged confrontations of such intensity that the geographical and temporal scope of cyclical violence associated with communal competition increased markedly. The lack of investment in local governance ensured that mechanisms, which might have otherwise created some local cohesion and resilience to modern types of conflict, largely did not exist.

In the fight for independence, communal competition had devastating consequences. In 1991, a split in the main South Sudanese rebel group, the Sudan People's Liberation Army (SPLA), saw the creation of a splinter faction. The breakaway faction believed that the goals of the SPLA had been undermined by the authoritarian and partial style of the SPLA's leader John Garang that favoured his Dinka community. The subsequent violence led to an internecine conflict in which both sides perpetrated heinous acts against civilians on a communal basis. The most notorious of these was the massacre of at least 2,000 Dinka civilians at Bor in November 1991 by forces loyal to the Nuer commander, and a leader of the breakaway SPLA-Nasir Faction, Riek Machar.[17]

Notwithstanding these divisions, when an opportunity for a negotiated peace emerged, Garang advocated for a reconciliation among all groups in the south. He brought long-standing enemies together under a *big tent policy* based on their rejoining the SPLA. When Garang was appointed president of the Autonomous Region of Southern Sudan,[18] his erstwhile enemy, Riek Machar, became the vice president. When Garang was killed in a helicopter crash only weeks after assuming the position, the task of maintaining the complex and fragile alliances that he had built fell to one of his generals, Salva Kiir, who also came from the Dinka community.

International rescue

With the 2005 peace also came an outpouring of international support. The United States took the strongest interest in the new country. During the war of the southern states, a campaign of popular support for US action against the Khartoum government had galvanized a peculiar mix of A-list Hollywood celebrities and evangelical Christians.[19] For the US administration, support for *oppressed Christian freedom fighters* against *an oppressive Islamist government* was a welcome, seemingly unambiguous, distraction from the otherwise dismal story of US foreign affairs, which was at the time defined by its unpopular misadventures in Afghanistan and Iraq. It also served as a guise for the United States to intensify international attempts to isolate Khartoum's leader Omar al-Bashir, whose regime the United States had opposed since his military coup in 1989 and support of Iraq and Osama bin Laden in the 1990s.[20] While the US administration under George W. Bush avoided calls for a military intervention, they used the moment to tighten sanctions on Khartoum, hobbling the government and forcing it to negotiate with Garang.[21] The US administration repackaged its geopolitical objectives as an act of benevolence, as its officials started to use the term *midwife* to describe its support birthing the new country.[22] The United States also paid for that title by being the largest donor in the lead-up to independence. By some reckoning during the CPA period, it was spending approximately $2 billion a year on assistance to Sudan largely targeting the south.[23] The importance of the United States to South Sudan's independence project was perhaps most visibly apparent in Kiir's ever-present black Stetson hat. The original was reputed to have been a present from Bush in 2006.[24]

Norway also played an important role in the formation of the new country. The NGO, Norwegian People's Aid, formed such a close relationship with the

SPLA during the conflict years that some military officials partially attributed their support to successes in the war.[25] The Norwegian government also provided mediators during subsequent peace processes and played an important role in convening and negotiating the CPA. Norway was also one of the largest contributors of financial assistance in the lead-up to independence, along with the United States and the UK, which was still connected to the country through its colonial history. Those three countries formed the *Troika*, an informal-yet-powerful diplomatic group with a shared interest in the success of the country.

South Sudan was not entirely dependent on aid. It also had access to considerable resources. With the peace agreement it inherited a share of Sudan's oil wealth, with much of its reserves falling within the borders that would make up the new South Sudan. Private investors, particularly from China and Malaysia, poured money into the country to exploit existing oil reserves as well as to explore new and promising areas. This included licences for the huge Block B concession into which the likes of the US Exxon Mobil, French Total and Kuwait's Kufpec also invested.[26] In 2011, GDP per capita was estimated to be more than $1,500, almost double its neighbours in Kenya and Uganda. The government's budget was a respectable $2.3 billion.[27]

Caution ahead

There was therefore good reason for exuberance in the years that followed the signing of the CPA. However, if there was a cautious tone, it was more often to be heard from the humanitarian and peacekeeping organizations that faced the realities of translating the hopes of the international community and the new government in Juba into reality. Just before the 2011 referendum, the NGO Oxfam was one of many voices trying to temper the celebrations, reminding the international community that

> The chronic poverty, lack of development and the threat of violence that blight people's daily lives will not disappear after the referendum. Whatever the outcome of the vote, these long-term issues need to be addressed.[28]

The UN had struggled in its role across the Sudan region during the CPA period. Khartoum particularly could be obstructive to its operations and expelled UNMIS's first Special Representative of the Secretary General (SRSG). Among the SPLA, which existed as the de facto authority in the south, there was equal suspicion of the international community that the UN embodied. While the

OLS may have been a lifeline, the ability of the Sudan government to control aspects of the humanitarian operation created accusations of collusion with Khartoum.[29] Equally, having been largely viewed as the oppressed party during the civil war, increased focus on the SPLA as a perpetrator of human rights abuses after 2005 created suspicion around the expectations that might be attached to continued support from the international community.[30]

UNMIS succeeded in those parts of its mandate that had strong support from its hosts in the south of the country. This included its support to basic services and, despite obstruction in Khartoum, it delivered on its promise to hold a referendum in 2011 that credibly articulated the desire of the southern states to secede from Sudan. However, it failed to resolve many of the border disputes that existed between the south and north and struggled to create institutions that were necessary for the success of a new South Sudan administration. Even more worrisome was that violence associated with sustained competition between communities continued and even rose during this period. Members of the SPLM accused Khartoum of inciting violence.[31] However, competition between communities over traditionally contested resources, such as cattle, as well as new resources that emerged with the political settlement, such as state appointments and corresponding access to oil revenues, meant that much of the conflict was driven internally. The SPLA were also involved in instigating incidents of local violence, often with the collusion of SPLM officials.[32] Notwithstanding its mandate, 'to protect civilians under imminent threat of physical violence,'[33] UNMIS showed little capacity to manage these tensions. Despite having a troop ceiling of up to 10,000 soldiers, one senior SPLM official warned that that UNMIS looked like, 'a leopard with no teeth. Once the sheep know this they will play around'.[34]

After 2007, UNMIS ceded its responsibilities in the Darfur region to the United Nations-African Union Hybrid Mission in Darfur (UNAMID). That mission placed peacekeepers between Khartoum backed militias and the SAF on one side and militias with links to the SPLA on the other. The violence that the UN faced in Darfur was traumatizing. In the years between the establishment of UNAMID and the end of UNMIS in 2011, more than half of all global peacekeeping fatalities arising out of malicious incidents were in Sudan.[35] And as the referendum and subsequent independence of the south loomed, tensions ratcheted up in the border areas, with the north taking over the disputed border region of Abyei in May 2011. A collapse of the CPA was only avoided with the deployment of yet another peacekeeping mission to Sudan in the form of the United Nations Interim Security Force for Abyei (UNISFA).

When the referendum finally was held, and South Sudan was able to declare its independence, the UN had only a short time to consider what the appropriate successor to UNMIS would look like. It was influenced by the difficult experiences of UNMIS, UNAMID and UNISFA that created a desire to limit further exposure of the organization to a context in which it already felt overextended and ill-equipped to respond. UN planners were cautious. They initially proposed a new mission operating under a Chapter VI mandate with the South Sudan government leading on all state-building and protection of civilian roles. UNMISS would be available to support protection of civilians activities in a 'worst case scenario'.[36] However, the sentiment from South Sudan's international supporters, that the country needed access to the best possible start meant that the United States especially pushed for a more robust and proactive role than UN planners had deemed realistic. This included placing the mission completely under a Chapter VII mandate that gave it a proactive role in the protection of civilians including an obligation to intervene with force, if necessary. UNMISS would still also be expected to support an extensive list of state-building activities.

In its 2011 mandate, UNMISS was authorized to perform three primary tasks, including (a) support for peace consolidation; (b) support for the government in exercising conflict prevention, mitigation and resolution and protection of civilians and (c) support for capacity building within the government to establish rule of law and strengthen its security and justice sectors. Within these broad goals, the UNSC called on UNMISS to deliver against a range of specific activities which included support to the formulation of governance policies, promotion of participation in politics, setting up of conflict prevention including an early warning mechanism, monitoring of human rights, protecting civilians under imminent threat, creating the conditions for safe humanitarian delivery, supporting security sector reform, national disarmament demobilization and reintegration, building police capacity, developing a military justice system, facilitating a protective environment for children and demining activities.

To the dismay of the UN Secretariat, having been pushed into an expansive role to achieve a laundry list of diverse activities in a combustible environment, the UNSC only authorized the minimal size of force required to achieve it. UNMISS was allocated 7,000 military personnel and 900 police. In comparison, when the UN Mission in Liberia (UNMIL) was established in 2003, it was allocated more than double the personnel for a country that was one-fifth in size and only a third of the population of South Sudan's.[37]

Scepticism on the future of UNMISS and the likelihood of success of the new state was shared by many on the ground within UNMIS, particularly among those who worked outside of the Juba headquarters and saw first-hand the many challenges the new country faced. However, within the capital itself there remained an influential group that offered a more positive outlook based on optimism around how the goodwill of a grateful South Sudanese would provide the basis of a successful mission. As one UN official recounted of the months before the transition:

> I think there was a huge amount of ignorance that was in the capital itself. I think that infected media reports, NGO reports, UN reports. I think there was a euphoric utopian engagement around that. I think that built into who they appointed as [UNMISS] SRSG.[38]

The UNMISS organization

As its predecessor, UNMISS was organized as a *multi-dimensional* mission to achieve its broad remit with the Norwegian politician, Hilde Johnson, appointed as its SRSG. The concept of multidimensional peacekeeping theoretically allowed it to achieve broad stabilization, peacebuilding and state-building objectives that were more complex than those assigned to conventional military missions. As suggested, the mission would be led by a civilian SRSG, who held the rank equivalent to Under-Secretary-General (USG), making them answerable directly to the Secretary General. The SRSG played a significant role in developing reports and shaping the Secretary General's understanding of the context. The SRSG directs how the mission manages knowledge to develop organizational understandings that inform UN action and policy developed in New York. While the Secretary General is the official link between the mission and the UNSC, where policy decisions regarding UNMISS would be made, the SRSG would also regularly report directly and in person to the Council. While individual members of the UNSC have their own national means to collect information and create knowledge about South Sudan, the SRSG plays an important role in influencing their understandings through their regular reporting. An SRSG acts as a political intermediary in issues of relevance to the UNSC and are empowered to act without consulting the Council. This extends to tactical action using UN military and includes directing specific operations as well as setting the organizational environment to prepare the military for foreseeable threats and future responses within the scope of their mandate.

Responsibility for much of the organization of UNMISS remained with several departments primarily operating out of New York. In 2011, the Department of Peacekeeping Operations (DPKO) and the Department of Field Support (DFS) had greater control of the administration of budgets, staff and assets than their successor departments, the Department of Peace Operations (DPO) and Department of Operational Support, currently do. The heads of those departments were equal in seniority to the SRSG, and had a significant stake in the strategic and operational decisions of the mission. Their physical proximity to the Secretary General and UNSC in New York would have meant they had a powerful voice when advocating for policy approaches within the mission. DPKO would have had additional decision-making leverage through their chairmanship of the New York-based South Sudan Integrated Operational Team (IOT) that acted as a conduit for working-level interactions between the UN and the Security Council penholder. Tensions could exist when the IOT sought to lead on policy recommendations to the UNSC that UNMISS felt was their preserve.

At the field level, the SRSG had notional control over all aspects of its operations inside the country and an extensive team to fulfil the mission's mandated objectives. Beneath the SRSG sat two deputy Special Representatives of the Secretary General (D/SRSG). These exist at an assistant Secretary General (ASG) level, and are also directly appointed by the Secretary General. The D/SRSG (Political) led offices that comprised approximately 500 civilians serving as political and civil affairs officers, human rights officers as well as the staff supporting rule of law and security institutions. The D/SRSG (Political) was well integrated within the mission and reported directly to the SRSG.

The D/SRSG, Humanitarian Coordinator and Resident Coordinator (D/SRSG (HC/RC)) is referred to as *triple-hatted* because of their combined roles. The S/SRSG (HC/RC) initially led departments within UNMISS of approximately 260 people including disarmament, demobilization and reintegration teams as well as peacebuilding, women's protection and HIV/Aids programmes. However, the more influential role of the D/SRSG (HC/RC) is as Resident Coordinator (RC), which gives them leadership of the UN Country Team (UNCT) that comprises the heads of UN agencies operating in the country. They also chaired the Humanitarian Country Team (HCT) in their capacity as Humanitarian Coordinator (HC), which is a broader decision-making forum that includes NGO representatives and humanitarian cluster leads. The D/SRSG (RC/HC) thus played a role more independent from the mission that included being able to engage in public advocacy on humanitarian issues separate from UNMISS. They could also coordinate policy responses within the humanitarian community independent of the SRSG. Their RC/HC role was separately administered through the United Nations Development Programme (UNDP),[39] and its humanitarian function was notionally protected from control by the mission through the principle of distinction.[40]

The mission's force commander also directly reports to the SRSG but is more junior to the D/SRSGs. They are responsible for tasking the military component of the mission, which is made up of a patchwork of troop-contributing countries (TCCs), and are employed at a D-2 level, the most senior of the professional grades of the UN. The force commander remains an active member of their parent armed forces even while directly employed by the UN.

Unlike the force commander, TCC soldiers are not directly employed by the UN. However, they are obliged to act under the authority of the UN within the broad remit of the *Policy on Authority, Command and Control.* However, TCCs retain considerable autonomy. Caveat positions on the use of TCCs are agreed between individual governments and the UN Secretariat prior to deployment. Although the military chain of command is notionally vested in the peacekeeping mission, reports of TCCs acting according to national military doctrine and according to their respective national chains of command in critical situations are common. In South Sudan, the consequence was that tactical postures and deployments in UNMISS had to be negotiated between the SRSG, force commander and respective TCCs.

UNMISS policy was ultimately directed by the UNSC. This was articulated through resolutions that relate to the regularly reviewed mandate, the authorization of forces and the mechanisms related to sanctions on the country. The UNSC also made statements that clarified its position and applied public pressure on the South Sudanese government when it was perceived to transgress international commitments.

In 2011, UNMISS was able to take advantage of a pre-existing infrastructure footprint built under UNMIS. Its civilian and military personnel were established in offices in each of the ten states in the country. Additionally, it had begun to populate thirty-five county support bases. This created operational opportunities but also considerable logistics challenges. Notwithstanding the fact that UNMISS was capable of operating and maintaining more than 3,000 UN-owned vehicles, the tough demands of the climate and terrain created shortfalls. By 2013, as many as a quarter of UN vehicles were reported to have met the 'write-off criteria'.[41] UNMISS leadership also complained about a lack of all-terrain vehicles and riverine capacities creating a constant mobility crisis within the mission.[42]

A more serious problem related to the paucity of air assets available to the mission. Despite its large number of staff operating in a huge country, in which many roads were impassable for up to six months of the year, the air assets available to the mission were limited. In 2011, it was able to operate twenty-three rotary-wing and nine fixed-wing air assets.[43] During the rainy season, these crafts provided the only realistic means to move people and equipment between its bases, conduct patrolling in vulnerable areas, as well as any reconnaissance activities. UNMISS staff interviewed for this book suggested that the overly restrictive contracts governing the use of these assets added a significant obstacle to their efficient use. In effect, those aircraft that did not come from TCCs had to follow standard commercial rules that could be difficult to comply with in an emergency context. Following the shooting down of one of its helicopters in 2012, the introduction of a flight assurance system created a layer of bureaucracy that could be punishingly inefficient as well as being deliberately manipulated by the government to obstruct UNMISS movement.

UNMISS also struggled to maintain the military hardware that was needed for a robust peacekeeping posture. An interviewee suggested that national supply chains had proven inadequate to meet the tactical readiness of TCCs including shortfalls in critical areas such as ammunition.[44] Another significant deficiency was the availability of tactical air assets. While there were provisions for seven 'military-type air assets',[45] throughout the war such air assets were not deployed. Attempts by UNMISS to deploy unmanned aerial vehicles (UAVs) and attack helicopters were persistently blocked by the South Sudan government.[46] This severely limited the scope of air cover for patrolling in risky environments and reconnaissance activities.

It is also evident that UNMISS was poorly administered in the years leading up to 2013, meaning that it is likely that what assets it had available were often deployed inadequately. The UN Office of Internal Oversight Services (OIOS) found in 2013 that in four critical administrative areas UNMISS were either categorized as unsatisfactory or only partially satisfactory. This included a particularly damning assessment of its air transportation management.[47] Part of UNMISS's administrative problems stemmed from the notoriously rigid UN human resource processes. UN staff complained to me of the difficulty hiring talented individuals in a timely fashion for critical roles. Firing inadequate or problematic staff members could be even more difficult. As one UN official commented:

Even when I've had problems with staff, and I've spoken to HR about it, they've just said to ignore them, it's more difficult to fire them than it's worth. It's just a travesty.[48]

When I joined UNMISS in 2014, I was told that even by the low standards of UN peacekeeping the administration in South Sudan was seen as problematic. In my first week, I came across a friend, who had started at the same time in a supply area of the main UN base. He worked in logistics, and with a wry smile he swept his arm across a dozen or so freight containers. Some looked as though they had not been touched for months or possibly years. 'We have no idea what is in any of these', he explained. He further complained that his colleagues, some of whom had been in their roles for years including as part of UNMIS, were not interested in finding out either.

Conclusion

Independence was met with a sense of celebration from within the country as well as many of the international governments and private companies that had a vested interest in the success of the new nation. That exuberance was informed by an expectation that leant heavily on the myth of an unproblematic independence struggle and an extremely optimistic understanding of what might be achieved through state-building activities, at which the UN found itself at the centre. Within the UN there was more ambivalence. Early planners of UNMISS were sceptical, and more generally there was an institutional reluctance to be drawn into a complex and potentially violent situation, particularly without proper resources.

By 2011, the staff of UNMIS had some reason to feel pleased with their efforts and hopeful for its successor mission. Notwithstanding, the failure to resolve many of the issues of the CPA, they had nonetheless delivered a successful referendum and created the, albeit fragile, foundations for the new country of South Sudan to exist. That had been achieved with a broadly constructive relationship between UNMIS staff in Juba and SPLM officials. While the UN's experience in Sudan had on occasions been a violent one, UNMISS would exist without being beholden to the constantly obstructive influence of Khartoum that undermined its predecessor. At the same time, the situations that appeared the most intractable in Darfur and Abyei had been removed from the responsibility of UNMISS when first UNAMID and then UNISFA were created. That justified a perspective that the UN could limit the role of the new UNMISS to one that could focus on its state-building responsibilities.

However, a positive outlook was based on a selective analysis of recent history that many within the new mission disagreed with. Violent areas of friction within the new country were evident from UNMIS' experience. A poorly trained security services looked incapable of sufficiently projecting the authority of the government while also being implicated in some attacks on civilians. Moreover, if the new staff of UNMISS may have been relieved to have distanced themselves from having to work with the difficult Khartoum, incentives for the SPLM to collaborate with the UN in projects from which they did not directly benefit diminished significantly.

With hindsight, the illusory nature of the 'euphoria' of 2011 is clear. Security in the country looked fragile, and with independence increased competition between individuals and communities over new state resources would be inevitable. The same close relationship that UN staff had had with the SPLM in the previous years could not be guaranteed. Nonetheless, the UN baulked at the idea of further commitments to protect civilians. It was hamstrung by the same practical limitations as other peacekeeping missions, which meant its ability to be flexible and pursue tactical military objectives in a dangerous environment looked poor. A lack of the right equipment and a relatively small number of soldiers for its mandate undermined its ability to pursue more protection of civilians roles, if required. UNMISS was also poorly administered, further hampering its capacity to be effective.

Based on my interviews, these misgivings were widely known at the time. However, in its first two years, the mission made only halting efforts to structure itself to make the most of its limited resources to meet emerging threats, even as they became more and more evident. That difficulty appears to have been rooted in divergent understandings of the context within the mission and the appropriate posture of UNMISS. It fell to the SRSG to adjudicate on the merits of contradictory interpretations of the situation including how UNMISS' limited resources would be prioritized. By 2013, this had critical implications.

The capital erupts

December 2013

That the optimism that some felt around independence was misplaced became apparent at the outbreak of war in December 2013. Ultimately, it would consume the entire country, displacing a third of its people and leading to the deaths of hundreds of thousands.[1] In this chapter, I will discuss the events leading up to the outbreak of violence that marked the start of the war. This includes a discussion of a situation that showed highly visible and consistent signs of stress that implied clear threats to stability and should have led to better peacekeeping responses. I will describe how divergent interpretations of the context emerged within the United Nations Mission in South Sudan (UNMISS) and how critical the role of Special Representative of the Secretary General (SRSG) was in adjudicating the shared understanding through which organizational action was tied. In the conclusion, I will suggest that decision-making became concentrated within a small number of decision-makers and was partial to one perspective that created certainty through an inside view of reality. That view relied heavily on a bounded rationality that encouraged availability and substitution bias to process information in a way that, notwithstanding the known limitations of UNMISS, undermined the mission's ability to create an optimal response to emerging threats.

A violent start

In 2011, South Sudan looked fragile. While grappling with a huge state-building operation, UNMISS was also expected to contend with multiple security threats. As described in the last chapter, disputes over border demarcations between the south and the north, particularly around the oil rich region of Abyei, existed from the outset of the Comprehensive Peace Agreement (CPA).

Not only did Khartoum lay claim to Abyei but nomadic groups aligned with, and often sponsored by, Khartoum violently resisted claims to the area by the south.[2] Between the signing of the CPA and independence, deadly clashes because of these tensions were frequent. In 2011, just three months before South Sudan achieved independence, the Sudan militarily occupied the Abyei region threatening a return to all-out war. This was only averted following a UN-brokered ceasefire and the establishment of UNISFA, which was agreed just weeks before independence. Tensions persisted along the border however, with both Juba and Khartoum trading accusations that the other was supporting insurgencies in their respective countries. The next year, South Sudan turned attacker by invading the Heglig area of Sudan. This created tensions between the government in Juba and the international community, with the former feeling the failure of the latter to support them, and even criticize their actions, showed new limits to the 'friendships' of the CPA years.[3]

It was also about this time that a militia force began to emerge out of traditional armed cattle herders along the border area. Young men in South Sudan pastoral communities have a long history of being organized into pseudo military defence structures, primarily tasked with the protection of their community's cattle. Cattle represents a hugely significant component of how communal life in parts of South Sudan, especially among the Nuer and Dinka, is organized. It is central to aspects of a community's economic life as well as well as playing an important role in social functions through cattle transfers as part of marriage negotiations and dispute resolution. The most visible symbolic importance of the cow can be seen in those ceremonies that precede reconciliation discussions between communities and begin with the slaughter of a white bull known in Dinka as *Achuiil* and in Nuer as *Ca Keth Dek*.[4] Working through progressively more responsible roles in the cattle camp and eventually becoming responsible for defence and raiding activities also represents an idealized route to manhood for some pastoralists. During the second civil war, the armed components of the cattle camps became increasingly well-armed and organized and were occasionally co-opted into the military operations of armed groups. Within the Dinka community, these armed youths are loosely referred to as *titweng* or *gelweng*. Among the Nuer, the *White Army* is commonly used to refer to a similar group of armed cattle herders that were also involved in the notorious massacre of Dinka civilians in Bor in 1991.[5] With independence, the practice of co-opting youth into violent political projects did not end but entered an ad hoc relationship with the state and powerful individuals that reflected broader power dynamics in the country. In response to the border crisis in 2011, associates of the president were alleged to have armed and trained a Dinka youth militia in the north that would later be known as the Mathiang Anyoor.[6] However, at the same time in other parts of the country, notably among the Nuer White Army in Jonglei, the state attempted to forcefully disarm and demobilize youths, stirring up resentment and provoking a violent backlash. A tendency of UNMISS to characterize the threat of these groups as a generic *youth* problem or a technical *disarmament* issue meant that it was ill-prepared to understand their role in political violence two years later.

Competition over large but finite resources, that became available with independence, also played a role in fuelling violence. In 2011, South Sudan was the third largest sub-Saharan oil producer and that wealth was largely controlled by the state, creating a concentration of power and wealth in state institutions. Frenzied competition ensued to access political positions that offered rewards above and beyond official remittances. Disappointment among candidates participating in the 2010 local elections triggered as many as seven insurgencies in the following months.[7]

Attempts by the state to address these security challenges could be clumsy. As suggested earlier, disarmament campaigns brought the government into direct conflict with the very communities that it was supposed to protect. Systematic human rights abuses by the Sudan People's Liberation Army (SPLA) were commonplace during these campaigns.[8] Even in its handling of more benign displays of anti-establishment sentiment, the security forces struggled to find an appropriately soft touch. During a peaceful protest in Wau, concerning administrative changes in the local government in 2012, eight civilians were killed.[9] The government was largely unapologetic for its actions doing little to rebuff the perception that its world view still belonged to a military elite shaped by decades of war.[10]

When heavy-handed security methods proved ineffective, the government turned to a tactic that Khartoum had deployed to accommodate erstwhile foes through material incentives. When the government reached an agreement with the South Sudan Liberation Army (SSLA) to end their insurgency in Unity State in 2013, they agreed to no less than eight of the SSLA's leaders being made generals in the SPLA and another 3,700 of its soldiers being integrated into the military.[11] This tactic became an increasingly regular need to absorb more and more soldiers. That created pressures on a bloated defence force and undermined expensive security sector reform efforts sponsored by the United States and UK governments, aimed at creating a streamlined professional army. By 2013, the SPLA had 745 generals, more than the combined forces of the entire US military. The total size of its army was more than 200,000 personnel,[12] making it technically larger than the army of neighbouring Ethiopia, which has ten times the population. South Sudan's defence budget was also larger than that of Ethiopia's and Kenya's combined.[13] The failure to reform the SPLA ensured that society remained highly militarized and that rivalry between military commanders over limited resources created discontent in the ranks. The leader of the occasional rebel group in the South Sudan Defense Army/Cobra Faction (SSDA/CF), David Yau, launched his 2011 insurgency partially as a consequence of having been disappointed by the military appointment he had been granted following his participation in a previous rebellion.[14]

The haves and the have-nots

For those that successfully found access to state resources, the rewards for the unscrupulous could be huge. Corruption proliferated on a massive scale. In 2012, Kiir accused his own staff of theft of $4 billion of public money.[15] Prosecution of corruption was insignificant and the corrupt rich, alongside those who had made legitimate fortunes from the opportunities of peace, were part of an increasingly visible elite class in Juba. Shiny modern offices and apartment blocks and an ever-growing number of expensive Land Cruisers on the poorly paved streets contrasted sharply with the dire poverty that existed in the rest of the country.

Among those left out of the immediate financial dividends of independence, anger was festering. The rapid growth in the wealth of the elites was not matched by improvements in the country's development indicators that remained among the worst in the world. According to a survey of public opinion conducted by the International Republican Institute in 2013, most of the population believed the country was moving in the wrong direction.[16] This was an opinion that was shared by many international observers. By 2013, the country was considered by the Failed States Index[17] as being in the top five most failed states in the world. The global risk consultancy company Maplecroft classified risk in the country as 'extreme'.[18]

2013 political crisis

By 2013, fundamental problems with the country's governance, security infrastructure and economic inequality were the backdrop to a growing political crisis that was playing out in Juba. In January, President Kiir fired more than 100 senior military staff amid rumours that he was concerned about a potential coup. On 23 July, he sacked his entire cabinet including his vice president, and political rival, Riek Machar. This followed persistent rumours that Machar was attempting to concentrate power for himself and intended to challenge Kiir for the presidency in 2015.[19] The move by Kiir was deeply concerning given that Machar had been appointed to his position by John Garang as an attempt to create national unity in the country. The situation prompted concerns that the political crisis could divide the country along ethnic lines between Nuer and Dinka communities, from which Machar and Kiir hailed respectively, just as it had in 1991.

On 6 December 2013, Machar, and a group of senior politicians from the ruling party held a press conference accusing Kiir of 'misguided leadership'.[20] They signalled their intent to use a meeting of senior officials of the party on 14 December to effectively end Kiir's candidacy in the 2015 elections. On 15 December, there was confusion over an alleged order by Kiir that Nuer soldiers, based in the capital, should be disarmed to prevent a potential coup.[21] On 16 December, a group of the Dinka Mathiang Anyoor youth militia, supported by Dinka members of the regular security forces, were involved in the targeting and killing of Nuer soldiers and civilians.[22] This included moving through Nuer civilian neighbourhoods seeking civilians that were hiding and then killing them indiscriminately.[23]

The violence created chaos in Juba with thousands of civilians fleeing the city or forcing their way into the two UNMISS bases in the capital, for protection.[24] On 18 December, an SPLA general based in Jonglei, Peter Gadet, led a Nuer contingent in mutiny against the government. He took the strategically important town of Bor, less than 150 kilometres from Juba. Within a week, Nuer officers across the country had rebelled under the banner of Machar, who had narrowly escaped the capital. In Jonglei, the Nuer militia, the White Army, also mobilized to support Gadet's attack on Bor, promising revenge for the attacks on Nuer in the capital. Thereafter the country divided, largely along communal lines with fierce battles being fought in Unity, Upper Nile and Jonglei states. By February 2014, tens of thousands had been reported to have been killed[25] and almost three-quarters of a million people were reported to have been displaced.[26]

A culture of non-confrontation

In the two and a half years before Juba imploded, UNMISS had struggled to come to grips with the challenges of effectively using an undermanned, under-resourced and under-motivated peacekeeping force tactically to achieve mandated goals. A failure to understand how to prioritize diverse objectives was exacerbated by differing interpretations of what was happening in the country from within the mission. This created tensions within the leadership.

Severe intercommunal conflict in the state of Jonglei, around Pibor, in 2011 had provided an early test on UNMISS's commitment to its protection of civilians role. That violence was a consequence of tension between the Lou Nuer and Murle communities that followed escalating tit-for-tat raiding in which cattle and people were taken. Both communities come from a marginalized periphery of South Sudan, which had seen little development. The larger Nuer community could leverage its more prominent political position to attract resources whether aid, development or military. The Murle, however, had no such influence. However, sympathy for the Murle among their fellow South Sudanese could be difficult to come by. The Murle are often maligned as a *bogeyman* based on their perceived predilection for abducting children during raids[27] and appearing almost magically and in force and without warning deep in their enemy's territories.[28] Spiritual leaders play an important role in both communities. Among the Murle, the *Red Chiefs* can mobilize youths organized around age sets to action according to a divined purpose. Among the Lou Nuer, prophets play a similar role, and the important prophet Dak Kueth was implicated in mobilizing the White Army in 2011.[29] In contrast to the reputed stealth of its foe, when the White Army attacked, it was by mass force that destroyed entire villages in 2011 and 2012 and threatened to wipe out the entire Murle.[30]

As violence erupted in Jonglei, UNMISS was presented with a challenge as to how it would define its protection of civilians role in practice and how it would separate itself from its predecessor mission that had largely avoided involvement in mediating such internal disputes. According to staff interviewed in the mission at the time, it was notably during an absence in country of the newly appointed SRSG, Hilde Johnson, that there was a critical reorientation in response to the crisis. The mission's D/SRSG (RC/HC), Lise Grande, was described as being eager to intervene and pushed the mission to be more responsive. This included reorganizing mission structures to permit more devolved and responsive military decision-making and was a driving force behind the decision to deploy peacekeepers more intensively to respond to the crisis. As one UN official described the operation:

> We had UNMISS troops deployed by helicopter in the middle of a rainy season, and then marching for 30, 40, 50 kilometers over several days on patrols and being extracted. . . . It was a sort of thing one thought peacekeeping was going to be until you really *discovered* peacekeeping.[31]

Another former member of UNMISS recalled the operations as being a starting point for more defined divisions within the mission:

> I remember her [Grande's] advisors at the time were like, 'Holy shit, this is what the mission could be doing, and it's what the mission has to be prepared to do because there are clouds on the horizon.' This is when you start to have two distinct camps among the internationals form in Juba. There are the optimists and the pessimists. It really comes out of the Pibor War in 2011 and 2012.[32]

While there were those within the mission that credited UNMISS's actions at that time as saving lives and providing a model for proactive peacekeeping, there were others who worried about the actual and reputational harm of placing poorly resourced and supported peacekeepers in highly uncertain operating environments. From SRSG Johnson's subsequent recollections of the operations in Jonglei, it is clear she felt more ambivalence. While she stands by the decision to intervene, she also complained about the lack of resources and concern for the personal implications of being associated with failure:

> We seemed to be set up for failure. And I knew that I would be the one accused before the Security Council if we failed.[33]

Specifically, she expressed concerns for the negative optics as subsequent media reporting focused, unfairly in her opinion, on the inability of the mission to prevent some of the violence. UNMISS was accused of 'standing idly by,'[34] and the risks that had been taken provided little returns regarding the standing of the mission.

> I knew that it was almost impossible to refute this account without appearing defensive; an impression of a failing Mission festered. I had learnt another lesson.[35]

Grande left the mission in July 2012, and, as challenges to UNMISS increased, the mission appeared to increasingly avoid tactical and confrontational political postures that seemed risky in their ability to expose the mission to conflict. That was particularly evident in its relationship with the government.

When disarmament campaigns targeting the White Army in Jonglei turned violent in 2012, UNMISS was accused of not only failing to intervene but turning a blind eye to government abuses and even supporting the campaign.[36] Even when faced with significant provocation by the government, UNMISS avoided confrontation. In December 2012, the SPLA shot down a clearly marked UNMISS helicopter. The government maintained that the incident had been an accident and never investigated or held anybody to account. Though there was an official UN protest, the incident did not significantly disrupt UNMISS support to state-building activities or create a serious rift in its relationship with the government. As UNMISS shrank from confrontation generally, it also increasingly aligned itself with government security forces in line with its state-building mandate. That had implications in the way that the mission understood its rules of engagement. According to a 2012 report:

> Several interviewees [UNMISS officials] stressed that no UNMISS peacekeeper ever has – or ever would – shoot an SPLA soldier to protect a civilian being abused by that soldier.[37]

The lack of possibility of confrontation with the UN appeared to embolden the national security services. In the six months prior to the outbreak of violence in December 2013, there were sixty-seven serious violations by the government of the Status of Forces Agreement (SOFA) signed with the UN. This included incidents of harassment, threats, physical assault, arrest and detention of UN staff. In one incident, a female member of UN staff was 'severely beaten' by members of the presidential guard following an alleged traffic violation.[38] The lack of strong official response from the SRSG or change in mission posture, particularly when colleagues were being victimized, was characterized as morale sapping by multiple former UNMISS staff that I talked to.

Several people interviewed for this book highlighted the difficult role that Johnson, and all SRSGs, occupy, in trying to maintain consent from the host government in a fraught context such as South Sudan. It reflected the earlier dynamic that the United Nations Mission in Sudan (UNMIS) had faced in its relationship with Khartoum and the aggressive gamesmanship of the latter that always seemed bent on achieving the most advantageous position. Consent of a host government remains a core principle of traditional peacekeeping, and they suggested that avoiding confrontation served as a strategy to maintain it. However, the costs were considerable. A trend towards non-confrontation encouraged the perception that an intervention, militarily or politically, by UNMISS was unlikely, regardless of the threat to civilians.

Framing the problem

By 2013, UNMISS faced becoming weighed down by its own decision-making structures. When the operations had taken place in Jonglei at the end of 2011, they had done so to the backdrop of an organization in its relative infancy. Many senior staff positions remained unfilled with power highly centralized around a relatively few, but highly motivated, individuals who were nonetheless willing and able to filter expert opinion from a broad range of sources within a framework that was focused on emergency responses. However, as the mission matured, decision-making forums proliferated within the constraints of a rigidly hierarchal organization. The consequence was an unsustainable burden of inputs from junior departments on senior decision-making components. In Juba, a Mission Leadership Team (MLT) format effectively had to be abandoned as a decision-making forum when a growing number of participants insisted that they be involved. Johnson retreated to a more streamline Principal's Management Team (PMT) with only four or five of her senior staff.[39]

At the same time, Johnson championed a state-based system for the mission that was supposed to devolve decision-making in a way that might best support operations at the local level. However, all aspects of human resources and programming remained based on a centralized and hierarchal system that meant any significant decision-making continued to be made through the SRSG's office or even in the offices of DPKO and DFS in New York. Significant discretionary funds, other than those attached to relatively small Quick Impact Projects (QIP), did not exist. Without any power to support a symbolically devolved structure, the system never achieved its aims. What was created instead were 'shallow partnerships' between UNMISS officials and subnational authorities that became a raison d'être, justifying the former's professional existence, even though such relationships were accompanied by little to no influence.[40] A structure that was technically decentralized but actually centralized only created complexity that confused and overburdened reporting channels. As one former UNMISS official described the situation:

> In other words, [in 2011] there were less people, less bureaucracy, less senior staff who demanded they had to be consulted, discussed with, or that this area was their responsibility to slow things down. Then, of course, I think the state coordinator structure and the setting up of areas of responsibility was hugely problematic. . . . As the mission structures were being set up, it became less flexible. Decision-making became far more difficult.

Several people interviewed for this book suggested that Johnson's response to trying to navigate a self-defeating and complex decision-making structure, which was partially of her own making, was to increasingly rely on her own cognizance. Decisions looked less consultative and much more as if they were 'done in her own head'.[41]

The reliance that Johnson was perceived to have placed on her own framing of the problems of the country were viewed with alarm by some. Before becoming SRSG, Johnson had served as Minister of International Development for the Norwegian government as well as a deputy executive director of UNICEF in New York. As a minister, she had been a part of the 2005 CPA negotiations. In 2011, she published a book about her experiences during that process. In it she detailed how, after the agreement was signed, she went to John Garang's house with a bottle of Champagne to congratulate him, the situation being sufficiently familiar that the pair spent the evening telling stories and jokes. After attending Garang's funeral a few months later, she called on his successor Salva Kiir, meeting him in his house to reassure him of support.[42] Before, she had even taken up her role, there was a sense from some within the mission that Johnson's perspective was focused on political relationships and state-building, rather than peacekeeping operations, that better aligned with her professional background. There was also a suspicion that she had a preconceived favourable opinion of many of her interlocutors.[43]

While those relationships undoubtedly helped Johnson gain access to political leaders, the increasing contempt with which the government treated the mission suggests that they did not come with a corresponding level of influence. Johnson's tendency to overvalue those relationships created widespread cynicism on how she treated information from sources that she regarded as trustworthy. Johnson was reported to have once said about the politicians in Juba, 'They never lie to me. They know that I know them too well'.[44] As the journalist and author Peter Martell more perceptively noted, 'She thought leaders on all sides were her long-time friends, and so trusted what they would tell her. They lied'.[45] In early 2013, UNMISS received reports of the movement of Mathiang Anyoor from the north to the capital. Most were reported to only be able to speak Dinka and not the language local to the part of the country in which Juba is based, or the Arabic and English languages that serve as a lingua franca. At the time, the militia were referred to in the Dinka language as *Dot Bany* (rescue the leader) or *Gel Bany* (protect the leader). It was only after 2013 that the militia would be more commonly known as the Mathiang Anyoor, named after a poisonous brown caterpillar. Based on discussions that Johnson had at this time, there were estimated to be between 2,000 and 3,000 in a training camp owned by the president, just outside of Juba.[46] In a subsequent enquiry conducted in 2014 by the African Union, estimates of the actual force ranged between 7,500 and 15,000.[47] As stories of the gathering militia emerged, Johnson called on Kiir. On being told that the men were an 'essential' addition to his already-considerable bodyguard, Johnson was sufficiently mollified not to take the matter further.[48] In September, Kiir began making public speeches reminding largely Dinka audiences of the Nuer violence against their community in the 1990s and called on them to be ready to defend themselves. In one speech he declaimed, 'The "Tiger" has now taken out its claws and is ready to crush their faces. Blood will flow.' The *Tiger* was a reference to Kiir's nom de guerre from the civil war. Again, Johnson confronted him, this time over the inflammatory potential of such language. However, she appears to have accepted that he had heeded her admonishment.[49] So confident was Johnson in the effectiveness of her political approach that she did not publicly raise the issue of either the militia or inflammatory speech publicly with the UNSC. Instead, in the UNMISS report delivered to the UNSC in November, directly before the outbreak of war, she expressed 'cautious optimism' and commended the president for the 'smooth transition' in government following his decision to fire his cabinet and oust the vice president.[50]

The wrong place at the wrong time

While Johnson overvalued her political relationships, she appears to have undervalued the potential of the mission to use its military peacekeeping components to positively influence stability in the country. She had never worked in an operational capacity in an emergency context, let alone as head of a peacekeeping mission. In 2011, individuals who had more experience of emergency contexts and were more empowered by a structure that was still relatively light had helped push UNMISS into a more robust peacekeeping intervention in Pibor. By 2013, those individuals had either left, such as Grande, or were subsumed in chaotic clamour trying to be heard by senior decision-makers in an increasingly complex administrative structure. For Johnson, the correctness of a more robust peacekeeping posture was never clear. Since she left the mission, she has expressed confusion of whether the right of UNMISS to intervene even existed in 2013. In reference to the events in Juba, she has stated:

> As the fighting within the security forces spread into neighborhoods, civilians of
> Nuer origin were in danger. For UNMISS to have intervened in the conflict by

using force in a situation of active combat between two belligerent forces, would have required a new mandate from the Security Council.[51]

That assertion is a needlessly narrow reading of the mission's mandate that unambiguously outlined UNMISS's duty regarding 'taking the necessary actions to protect civilians under imminent threat of physical violence, irrespective of the source of such violence'.[52] However, Johnson's tendency to overstate the mission's lack of authority makes sense when considered along with a broader decision-making framework that created uncertainty over the appropriateness of tactical options, particularly when they risked reputational damage and/or might undermine a preferred political or state-building strategy that was tied to maintaining a good relationship with the government.

When Johnson did make more robust peacekeeping decisions, it was under pressure. In spring 2013, the SPLA launched a security operation against SSDA/CF insurgents in Jonglei that drew much of their support from the disaffected Murle community. During those operations, the government was accused of abuses against civilians on a large scale and deliberately allowing communal violence in the state to proliferate.[53] Johnson's account of her arrival in New York at the end of June to brief the UNSC bristles with the indignity of the public nature of accusations that UNMISS had been neglecting its responsibilities:

> Members of the Security Council were told the UNMISS leadership could not be trusted – we were 'too close' to the government.[54]

Under pressure from the Council, Johnson flooded Jonglei with peacekeepers over the next few months. However, the lateness of the operation meant that its usefulness ended almost as soon as it had begun. The peak of the violence had passed. Lower levels of conflict generally associated with the period from September to November, because of mobility constraints during the rainy season also contributed to a general winding down of the violence. By October, the SPLA had officially withdrawn from operations. However, the response left critical hotspots like Juba chronically undermanned as peacekeepers remained in Jonglei even after the threat diminished. As one UN official described the tactical layout:

> You had lots of pinpoint presence on the ground, which meant the mission was fixed and it had small presences all over the place. There were those of us who were saying, 'Look, you're fixed. You need to remain flexible,' but I think it's fair to say she [Johnson] was under massive amounts of pressure just to get people out there [to Jonglei].[55]

In December 2013, as the yearlong political crisis was reaching a crescendo, UNMISS's tactical footprint in Juba consisted of a mere 120 soldiers capable of operating outside of its bases.[56]

Two perspectives

In trying to properly account for Johnson's decisions in 2013, it is important to understand that more optimal choice alternatives were available than those she ultimately made. Even if UNMISS's capabilities were weak, the operations in 2011 showed how they could be deployed proactively and achieve, at least partial, successes. A more confrontational posture of UNMISS could have injected more risk into government decision-making that might have inhibited it from aggression towards civilians and hostility towards peacekeepers. Furthermore, Johnson had a platform to speak publicly about the political situation in South Sudan and shape the perspective of the UNSC in such a way that could have focused international attention on clear signs of escalation that would have increased scrutiny on the government. It also would have strengthened the argument that a robust peacekeeping presence in Juba was required and she might have managed a more flexible deployment of peacekeepers to make such a posture possible. However, the extent to which Johnson appeared to ignore or marginalize pertinent information that would have increased the prominence of these options as rational choices became more pronounced throughout 2013.

At the start of 2013, following the government reshuffle and firing of SPLA staff, several senior UNMISS officials from different departments started to write a report. They had heard persistent rumours that the events represented a more serious schism among the South Sudanese political elites. One of the officials who was involved recalled:

> When just over 100 generals were essentially reshuffled. [a UN official], and I came up with a matrix, essentially. We sat down and started going through every single journal, background, relations, obviously ethnicity, and to try and understand what was happening in this. Then we started getting contacts both from within the Presidential Guard from Nuer, people like [Peter] Gadet. He started reaching out to us, and we started getting quite nervous. We tried to raise this to senior management. [a UN official] wrote a warning note for JMAC [Joint Mission Analysis Centre]. [a UN official] went to the head of civil affairs to raise it up. I wrote a brief to the JOC [Joint Operations Centre], the chief JOC at the time. Every one of us, I think, got a phone call and an email to

basically telling us to shut up in slightly more polite terms, but not that much more polite.

The UN official was told that the situation is 'all under control', though was never given details as to what that meant. In October, UNMISS did write a code cable to New York about serious rifts within the SPLA along Nuer and Dinka lines, creating the possibility of a schism in the national army that reflected some of the points in that initial investigation, but no public statement or change in posture followed.[57] This was despite the fact that, as noted earlier, the president had been amassing a large militia force near the capital and had been using hate speech publicly. It is unclear as to whether the information about the tensions within the SPLA ever reached the UNSC. However, on the ground UNMISS officials continued to privately express alarm about the situation. As one senior UNMISS official described the situation at the time:

> Everyone knows something is up. The red lights are flashing everywhere . . . you had the vast majority of national staff saying something is going badly wrong, all indicators point to violence.[58]

Another analyst, who was working for an NGO, echoed a similar sense of foreboding:

> There was a good six months' notice. . . . I remember that November when I was here, I wouldn't even go out at night anymore in Juba, it was a distinctly uncool feeling going on in the city. Everything was on edge. I was like this place is going to explode. It was palpable. There was so much tension going on.[59]

A South Sudanese analyst, who fled the country with his family days before violence erupted in expectation of conflict, underlined widespread feelings of apprehension in the capital in the lead-up to December:[60]

> The situation had already started to build up [by October], and anyone who was focusing on South Sudan at the time would have known that South Sudan is heading towards crisis, especially, since the President dissolved the entire government.[61]

However, there were also wildly divergent perspectives. The same UNMISS official who talked about red lights flashing also suggested:

> You had a lot of the long-term international watchers including the diplomatic community saying, 'No, they've just got independence. They will pull it back from the brink.'[62]

Other interviewees suggested that the view that the country would 'pull it back' was pervasive among certain international *experts*, who had earned their informal titles either because of their historical experience working on the country during the civil war of independence or else because of their authoritative positions in the diplomatic or UN community. As one expatriate who was employed as a government adviser described it:

> There was a cast of characters that have been around with those groups from the CPA days. Obviously, the narrative in the CPA days was that they [the SPLA] were the goodies. So, people had invested a lot morally and emotionally in a group of people and found it very hard to accept they've been let down by them.[63]

Within this group, the interviewee included Johnson. Analysts who were working outside of this inner circle expressed frustration at the difficulty of penetrating the bubble that had formed around them. As one described the situation:

> I think there were enough people raising the flags but there was an absolute unwillingness and disbelief and then a group of us briefed the SRSG, the diplomats, and we were outright just brushed aside. There was really no desire for a conversation about anything different and part of that conversation was about how this government's not okay, this party [the SPLM] is not okay. It was breaking through the CPA barrier of 'these are the victors, and they are deserving victors, and they're the good guys.' There was a vast sense of a lack of desire to accept any alternative reality.[64]

In interviews for this book, discussion of Johnson's character proved divisive. However, words such as 'intelligent' and 'conscientious' were used by supporters and detractors alike. She could engage with the issues in a way that was compassionate and was, at least initially, able to accept challenges to her own decision-making. However, one UN staff member, who was also the most adamant defender of Johnson, conceded that there was a 'paradox in her personality' that created blind spots in the way she viewed the context.[65] Specifically, she was susceptible to accept more positive assessments of the intentions of individuals she regarded as 'friends'.

The view from the inside

The UN's focus from the headquarters in New York in 2012 and 2013 was not on South Sudan. In 2012, the UN was launching a highly contentious mission in Syria. A damning report about its inaction in the conflict in Sri Lanka had been released. The extent of UN impotence in the Democratic Republic of Congo (DRC) was creating uncomfortable headlines, and the scandal of its cover-up in the spread of cholera in Haiti was also reaching a crescendo. When the UNSC and UN Secretariat were roused to pay greater attention to South Sudan, it was only after a sustained public pressure campaign in New York, because of UNMISS's failure to prevent government abuses in Jonglei in 2013. Even then, however, the extent of concern amounted to an ill-fated reconfiguration of UNMISS. No additional resources were forthcoming that might have suggested broader concern about the future of the country. In South Sudan, international diplomats were concentrated on issues that seemed more pertinent to their immediate investments, which at the time involved leveraging their aid assistance to create influence in the new state. The former Canadian ambassador observed that the diplomatic corps watched much of the unfolding crisis in 2013 with only 'detached disinterest'. Their priority in late 2013 was instead on the more mundane negotiations of a new aid compact.[66] This high-level disinterest was exacerbated by expatriate officials in Juba, who were focused on narrow considerations within their respective fields rather than the broader context. As one international worker, employed by a Troika country to advise the government, described the atmosphere:

> The trouble is, and I was a classic example of someone who didn't think it would happen because I didn't see what I didn't want to see. I was on a nice long-term program working five weeks on, three weeks off, with most people getting paid quite well. I didn't want to think that that was all going to stop. . . . I think the UN staff is like that as well because they like to think things are just going to go on and on because basically, it's a bread-and-butter job for most of them.[67]

A broad international indifference, along with an unwieldy organizational decision-making, exacerbated Johnson's tendency towards developing strategy based on a more limited and informal circle of experts, whom she had known since her work on the CPA in 2005, and she still trusted to be accurate and relevant. She struggled to properly understand the views of some of her more sceptical colleagues who framed the country in an emergency modality that she was less comfortable with. Interviewees suggested that she had often disagreed with D/SRSG (RC/HC) Grande, who, unlike Johnson, had prior experience of fragile contexts and seemed more willing to see the parallels in the country. Johnson also found herself at odds with other staff who did not share her permissive attitude to the government. At the start of 2014, when another well-respected and experienced official of UNMIS and UNMISS, who persistently challenged Johnson's understanding of the context, was told to leave the country by the government, Johnson did not resist and supported the official's removal on safety and security grounds.[68] The lack of pushback was characteristic of her leadership. However, the de-facto expulsion also contributed to the perception that Johnson had little interest in vigorously defending a diverse range of views within the mission. As one UN official reported based on their experiences with the mission in 2013:

> She kept all of the real decision-making power in her own executive office. In the era of Hilde, the JMAC, JOC, and so forth, were very disempowered. They had no tasking authority. They had no information. They were consulted only when it was time to drop the quarterly SG's [Secretary General's] report. They were really outside the room. The whole mission was run from Hilde's executive office, and that was her and maybe four or five people.[69]

Conclusions

The expectations on UNMISS at its inception in 2011 were broad and confusing and created significant uncertainty with decision-makers as to how they should interpret the world and their role in it. Within that uncertainty, Johnson leant on a bounded rationality. Her *values* were visible in her preference for political and state-building strategies and the personal relationships that she highly prized. Those would have broadly aligned with her self-conception as to what a successful peacekeeping diplomat was and would have been *appropriate* to a peacekeeping culture that valued the maintenance of consent through harmonious relationships with a host government. She also acted in a way that was appropriate by showing wariness of interventions, public or tactical, that the UNSC might have felt were their preserve. A light tactical touch was also appropriate to the UNSC's commitments that were evident in their minimal resourcing of the mission. She was responsive to hierarchal *interests* as were exerted in pressure from the UNSC to move soldiers into Jonglei. However, it also indicated a willingness to defend the *organizational myth* when that was threatened by the negative perceptions associated with further inaction in that state in 2013.

The way that the bounded rationality influenced decision-making shows a preference to acting according to embedded beliefs that created bias, rather than prompting a search for more optimal solutions. The way that Johnson used information to support an increasingly unviable interpretation of the country is indicative of a *confirmation bias*. She showed a preference for information that confirmed a preferred political and state-building focus, reorganizing the mission to better deliver on those aims. That understanding led her to ignore information that should have prompted more confrontation with the state and led to a better understanding of the conflict as existing in an emergency setting. Critically, she chose to believe the promises of SPLM elites that they did not intend to instigate conflict, even when a more rational examination of the evidence suggests that that conclusion was highly unreasonable.

A fully successful peacekeeping intervention in December 2013, outside of its own bases, was unlikely based on the mission's capabilities. However, UNMISS could have responded in the lead-up to that period more robustly through its public platforms as well as proactive tactical deployments in a way that might have discouraged government attacks on civilians. However, experiences that would have given Johnson the confidence to deploy peacekeepers tactically in a high-risk environment were not strong. Her personal knowledge of such tactical operations was exceptionally limited before she took up her position with little operational field experience. Her first encounters with such operations in 2011 and into 2012 were not wholly positive. Subsequently, she tended to prioritize choice alternatives that avoided confrontation and focused efforts on building relationships with government officials. Those strategies more closely aligned with the confidence-building approaches she will have been familiar with, including in her approach to the CPA negotiations. That this constituted an *availability bias* is based on her pursuit of such strategies even when escalating aggression to her mission by the government suggested that they were ineffective. Non-confrontation encouraged the perception that UNMISS would not intervene in a situation of a serious attack on civilians by the government, increasing the likelihood of an event such as that which occurred in December 2013.

Johnson also exercised a *substitution bias* in her apparent tendency to stick with understandings of South Sudanese officials she had developed during the CPA. These had taken on a stereotypical quality that led her to mistakenly characterize the actions of the likes of Kiir as those belonging to a flawed but trusted friend. It transpired that they were not her friends, at least in the way that she likely recognized friendship. This created a tendency to take the information that she was offered on face value rather than with more rational circumspection.

Johnson's tendency to develop choice alternatives firstly within a broader diplomatic bubble that shared her views, and then more systematically within a small component of her mission, created *inside views* that offered greater certainty around her decision-making. As divergent views were marginalized and decision-making increasingly concentrated in a small section of the senior hierarchy, junior adherence to the leadership's strategic vision contributed to a *groupthink*, leaving decision-making increasingly unchallenged.

Johnson's lack of comparable experience, when assessing her own tolerance for risk within an emergency context, will also have been a source of considerable uncertainty. That uncertainty will have encouraged *risk aversion* when considering higher-risk strategies such as the deployment of peacekeepers, even when such deployments lowered the likelihood of future aggression by providing a proportionate response to belligerent violence. She will have relied on technical experts within the UN military to create certainty and empower her to decide on such deployments. However, given the known reluctance of troop-contributing countries (TCCs) to take on high-risk roles in peacekeeping contexts it is likely that their own *risk-aversion* will have created a technical assessment that supported Johnson's own disinclination to use them in tactical responses. Attacks and harassment of UNMISS staff in 2012 and 2013 will have diminished even further the tolerance for risk by demonstrating the readiness with which the government would resort to violence against UN personnel.

The eruption of the conflict in December 2013 meant that within a few weeks international attention became focused on the country. The bounded rationality became more complex as interests of the UNSC and UN Secretariat began to exert themselves more comprehensively. The appearance of a UN peacekeeping mission caught unawares was a blow to an organizational myth that had already been battered by poor UN peacekeeping performance and scandals in other parts of the world over the previous two years. Johnson now faced having to account for these considerations more fully as she contemplated the decisions in and around the most violent attack on UNMISS, which occurred in April 2014.

UNMISS under attack

April 2014

I arrived in South Sudan for the first time in March 2014. It was not my first time in a warzone, having spent four years in Afghanistan. However, this was my first time working in a peacekeeping mission. My first impressions arriving at the UN's base, next to the capital's airport in a part of Juba called Tomping,[1] was as to how poor the mission seemed. Afghanistan had given me a warped sense of what an overseas military operation looked like. A single US base there could have twice as many soldiers as existed in the entirety of the United Nations Mission in South Sudan (UNMISS). Their soldiers were well catered for with some of their main bases hosting fast-food restaurants such as Burger King or TGI Fridays that had been shipped in with the rest of the military hardware. Attack helicopters, drones and futuristic tiltrotor aircraft crowded runways around Kandahar, providing a glimpse into what power could be brought to bear by a modern military. By comparison, an UNMISS base was considerably more spartan. A functional cafeteria, a basic gym and a ramshackle bar were generally the extent of its luxuries. UNMISS's air assets consisted of a handful of ageing and unarmed Soviet-era aircraft.

The other base in Juba was UN House, located on the other side of the city and about thirty minutes' drive away. UN House was an impressive show of commitment to the country, being a large complex of modern and permanent looking offices. But the decision to build it so far from the airport had been another ill-fated show of faith in the country's future stability. With the war carrying on apace, UN House had largely been abandoned save for those military and police elements responsible for protecting the large protection of civilians site (POC site) that now existed there. The returning UNMISS civilian staff, who had been evacuated from Juba in December 2013, were largely being squeezed into Tomping. The situation was difficult. The base had been built on an area of swamp that annually threatened to reclaim it during the rainy season. Flooding and the malaria that came with it were significant problems. The overcrowding limited options for accommodation. Converted freight containers were a standard means to house UN staff. Those that were well beyond serviceability were made do for new arrivals such as me. The container that I shared was sparingly populated with two cots and two metal cabinets. The floor was warped, and a rapidly ageing air conditioning unit heaved cool air inside only through seemingly great effort. The roof leaked mercilessly when the rains came. The strategic deployment of duct tape was the only recourse to keep out the water.

The operations centre within which I worked was in another prefabricated building, which the engineers had at least sufficiently prioritized so that it was mostly watertight. In my first weeks, I watched a mission frantically still finding its footing. The room was a constant stream of information. UNMISS bases in places like Malakal and Bentiu in the north were sitting on the front lines with a constant back and forth between the belligerents taking, losing and retaking control of the towns. The fear that eventually the guns would be turned in the direction of the UN bases was a constant threat. Logistics to keep the UN's bases supplied had become increasingly complicated. A UN supply boat came under attack on the Nile during one of my shifts. In another incident, a UN road convoy was found, in violation of its own rules, to be transporting weapons and ammunition, inviting accusations from the government that the UN was supplying rebels. Denial of movement by the government and rebel forces alike became a fact of life even as the mission frantically was trying to preposition enough supplies around the country before the next rainy season arrived.

In the operations room, everyday seemed like some emergency existed. Within that environment, and my limited understanding of the country, what happened at the UN base in Bor in Jonglei State in April therefore seemed like just one more crisis to contend with. On the day it happened, updates streamed through the radio that people frantically relayed to other parts of the mission and to New York, though apparently not to any end. However, within a short time, it was over. The operations centre caught its breath and moved onto the next problem. It was only when I went to Bor the next month that I realized the magnitude of what had happened there, and the horror I felt that it was forgotten so quickly.

In this chapter, I will describe the events leading up to the attack of an armed group, including uniformed members of the government security services, on the UNMISS POC site in Bor. I will discuss how the myth of the POC sites and UN Secretariat's dissatisfaction with its role in those sites is likely to have created a particular environment for decision-making. I will also discuss the aftermath in which the incident quickly disappeared from the organization's institutional memory undermining its positive potential in influencing future decision-making. In the conclusions, I will suggest that Johnson's own values, and the UN Secretariat's interests, undermined the focus on external threats to the civilians that had sought protection on its bases. The subsequent bias meant that information that provided clear warnings was not properly absorbed into decision-making. This undermined UNMISS's capacity to ensure a strong posture that might have discouraged the attacks. The behaviour of UNMISS in the aftermath discouraged understandings about the incident that could have led to more optimal responses to similar events that took place in the following years.

Background

Following the violence in Juba in December 2013, conflict spread to other parts of the country as Nuer contingents of the army mutinied to join Machar's hastily improvised military, the Sudan People's Liberation Army in Opposition (SPLA/iO). The towns of Bentiu, Malakal and Bor were significant flashpoints as large strategic points on or close to dividing lines between traditionally Nuer and Dinka territories.[2] Retributive actions by Nuer soldiers against Dinka civilians soon followed. In an incident at a small remote UNMISS base in Akobo, Jonglei, on 19 December, two UNMISS soldiers were killed when they were vastly outnumbered by a mob of armed Nuer attacking and killing nineteen Dinka civilians sheltering there.

In Bor, less than 150 kilometres north of Juba, Peter Gadet led mutinying soldiers to take the town on 18 December. When the SPLA retook it within a week, an estimated 20,000 men from the White Army joined Gadet. In a harrowing echo of the massacre in 1991, the resultant battle led to widespread attacks on Dinka civilians and pushed thousands across the Nile to a displacement site near the town of Minkammen. On 18 January 2014, Gadet's forces were pushed out a second time following a joint operation by government forces and the Ugandan People's Defense Force (UPDF), which had intervened on the government's behalf. This time, the Nuer parts of the town were destroyed, and thousands of Nuer civilians were chased into the nearby UNMISS base. As in other parts of the country, this temporary response to an immediate threat of violence led to the creation of an UNMISS POC site.

During the fighting, tensions around the UNMISS base at Bor were high. At the airfield next to the UN base, four US soldiers were wounded as they attempted to evacuate international workers from the town in December. The base was struck at least three times by indirect fire during fighting. The UN in Bor became a focus for government ire when Minister of Information Michael Makuei visited the town on 19 January, the day after the SPLA retook the town a second time. The UNMISS state coordinator acquiesced to a visit by Makuei to the POC site the following day. However, when Makuei arrived with a heavily armed bodyguard, an altercation ensued as the state coordinator denied him entry. The minister responded by threatening to withdraw flight safety assurances from UNMISS (effectively cutting off peacekeepers from Juba), and personal threats were made to the UNMISS official by members of Makuei's entourage.[3] Johnson deemed the threat on the life of her state coordinator to be sufficiently serious that within forty-eight hours he had been evacuated from the country.

The government used the incident to publicly berate UNMISS. Kiir denounced their presence in the country as partial and the government orchestrated anti-UN demonstrations in the capital.[4] UNMISS patrols were threatened by SPLA officers that they would be shot if they tried to enter Bor town.[5] Over the next month, the SPLA were reported to have attempted to enter the UN POC site at least four times.[6] Incidents of harassment by government forces were reported against anyone leaving the site including incidents of abduction, rape, maiming and killing, including occurring in front of UN peacekeepers. UNMISS received reports that non-Nuers had been warned by uniformed armed men to, 'leave the POC site before the government attacked it'.[7]

By April, the opening phase of the conflict had calmed somewhat in Bor. The continued presence of the UPDF and a better-organized SPLA had pushed the SPLA/iO threat far from the town. The number of civilians sheltering at the UN POC site had shrunk to about 5,000, mostly Nuer civilians.[8] Protecting the UNMISS base were at least a battalion of UN infantry soldiers, equipped with small arms, light weapons and armoured vehicles. A section of military police and a company of military engineers were also stationed there.[9] In total, at least 500 UN soldiers would have been present on the base in April 2014.

On 15 April, Machar's forces, operating about 400 kilometres north, took the town of Bentiu in Unity State. The aftermath was bloody with at least 200 civilians reported murdered by the SPLA/iO.[10] The civilians in Bor POC site greeted the news of an SPLA/iO victory with loud celebrations, angering some of the now-homogenous Dinka community that lived in Bor town.[11] On 17 April, a group of between 100 and 300 men travelled through Bor carrying signs protesting the presence of the civilians in the UNMISS base.[12] UNMISS were warned at 9.30 am about the protesters, and a team of UN Military Liaison Observers (MLO) drove out to reconnaissance the group.[13] Intelligence received by other parts of the mission suggested that the group were armed and uniformed personnel were involved. However, the information was reportedly not communicated to staff guarding the site.[14] As the protest approached, UNMISS requested the state governor to intervene but no action from the government was taken.[15] As they arrived in the vicinity of the base, most of the group bypassed the main gate, moving straight to the other side of the compound where the POC site was situated. As they walked past the main gate, two men on a motorbike drove up to it, handing a letter to the security officer on duty. When asked who they were, they responded, 'Fuck you! You will see!'[16]

Despite an opportunity to respond at an early stage, 'APCs [armoured personnel carriers] were not deployed preventatively as the crowd approached'.[17] In making their way to the rear of the base, the protesters walked past a contingent of SPLA stationed on the road.[18] They were not stopped or impeded, despite ongoing UNMISS requests for the government to intervene. For approximately 1 kilometre, the group walked past the northern and eastern perimeters of the base, allowing time for additional assessment of the threat by UNMISS.

At 10.55 am, a group of twenty to thirty men climbed over the berm perimeter of the UNMISS base bordering the POC site without significant challenge from the UNMISS soldiers guarding it. The small dirt berm had been recently eroded by rains, meaning that it had become easily scalable.[19] Once inside, the men opened the main gates to other attackers. Eyewitnesses recalled that the UNMISS soldiers stationed there provided no effective defence. Many of the soldiers retreated from their fortified positions to armoured vehicles parked nearby, while others ran from the perimeter altogether, retreating to the main base.[20]

On entering, the attackers began shooting indiscriminately at civilians. The attack was unhurried. The perpetrators had time to loot the site, ransack shelters, and abduct women and children.[21] During the incursion, the attackers interrogated some of the few Dinka internally displaced persons (IDPs) who were resident at the site through intermarriages. Another report described two attackers arguing over who should have a woman as their 'wife'.[22] While the majority of those killed by the attackers were shot, machetes were also used indicating that the incursion was lightly armed. The UNMISS mobile team that had been following the protest since the town repeatedly requested a force response to stop the attack, warning, 'if we don't respond immediately, there will be many dead on our hands'.[23]

UNMISS officials suggested that despite incessant requests to return fire from more junior officers, the battalion commander of the troop-contributing countries (TCCs) delayed action:

> He was on the phone to his national headquarters, and ultimately relinquished when the fight had dissipated and ordered the perimeter guards to open fire.[24]

An armed response from UNMISS soldiers inside the APCs already positioned at the perimeter came thirty minutes after the attack had begun.[25] Reinforcements from the rest of the battalion were slow to mobilize and reach the perimeter. A Quick Reaction Force (QRF) was unable to unlock the main gate that had been closed as the protest initially approached.[26] Once outside, they were impeded by the same SPLA contingent on the road that had allowed the protest to proceed to the POC site without hindrance.[27] A second QRF struggled to travel the short distance within the base as it was reportedly impeded by civilians fleeing the attackers.[28]

By the time the incident was over, at least fifty-three people were reported to have been killed, including eleven children. Three of those were believed to have been perpetrators, though from subsequent reporting it is unclear how they were killed, and it remains likely that civilians defending themselves, rather than UNMISS, may have killed the attackers.[29] A further ninety-eight civilians were treated, largely for gunshot wounds. Eleven women and children were reported to have been kidnapped. During the attack, men in South Sudan National Police Service (SSNPS) uniforms were credibly and consistently reported as having been involved, including one of the dead attackers.[30]

The UNMISS Human Rights Department report on the incident concluded: 'There are reasonable grounds to believe that the attack was planned in advance'.[31] The report does not mention who it believes planned the attack but the failure of the SPLA to intervene, and its role in impeding UNMISS trying to respond, as well as the involvement of the SSNPS, strongly suggests government complicity. While it officially condemned the violence, the government minister Michael Makuei blamed UNMISS for encouraging the initial 'provocation' and used the incident to issue a thinly veiled threat to other civilians sheltering on UNMISS bases:

> Anybody who celebrates successful operations being conducted by the rebels against the government is a rebel, and we cannot continue to accommodate rebels inside UNMISS compounds.[32]

'Posture, posture, posture'

The most glaring failures in Bor in 2014 were tactical and indicative of pervasive structural issues related to the use of TCCs in high-risk scenarios in peacekeeping missions. There was a clear lack of drills to ensure a proper escalation of action to a foreseeable threat. There was also a lack of training of TCCs to carry out POC duties, including understanding their obligations to engage with lethal force to protect civilians. There was also a hesitancy of TCCs to act outside of their national chain of command. However, notwithstanding the tactical failings, the incident at Bor occurred within a decision-making mission framework that had not made physical security at POC sites its main priority. This encouraged lax approaches to security and bias that undervalued information about credible threats.

By UNMISS's own reporting, 'Rumors of an impending attack on the POC site [at Bor] had been gaining momentum several weeks before the attack took place.'[33] Yet there is little evidence that the leadership in Juba were alive to the potential risks. This may be partially explained by the chaotic environment that Juba HQ was operating in. It struggled to properly understand priorities that were beyond reacting to immediate and highly visible threats. Military staff in Bor lamented a sense of strategic blindness complaining that at the time there was 'no downwards flow of information at all' from the JOC in Juba.[34]

When asked by an UNMISS official in the immediate aftermath of the attack on Bor what he thought had gone wrong, the D/SRSG (RC/HC) Toby Lanzer was reported to have replied, 'posture, posture, posture'.[35] While he may have been referencing the failure of the TCCs at Bor to establish a force presence in their area of operations, his statement could have equally applied to the strategic leadership of UNMISS in the months preceding the incident. UNMISS's political position in Bor looked weak following the confrontation with the minister of information in January. While Johnson saw the evacuation of her state coordinator as a pragmatic precaution, others saw his removal as acquiescence to another de facto expulsion and yet another sop to a government intent on marginalizing the mission's ability to play a meaningful role in the country.[36] The official's removal was the third such expulsion of UNMISS staff over the past year and the latest in a pattern of intimidation described in the previous chapter that had existed since before the outbreak of war.[37] The extent to which Johnson had come to disregard the utility of escalating protests against the government can be seen in her withering recollection of the expulsion in her subsequent memoir in which she suggests, 'There was no point in protesting the accusations, for this would just escalate the tension.'[38] Non-confrontation and risk aversion continued to dominate UNMISS decision-making.

The POC sites myth

If Johnson struggled to find a strong public position against the government, it might be assumed that within her bases she had a strong interest in the more practical elements of careful vigilance and robust defence. Bor was one of six POC sites that existed in April 2014, and at the time cumulatively held about 70,000 people. The opening of UN bases to protect civilians became associated with a story that reflected the UN's own organizational myth and Johnson's perception of herself. As she suggested in 2014, only a month after the attack on Bor,

> I would not be able to face the mirror if I were not to say, 'Open the gates.' It was a very strong commitment on my part. Keeping the gates closed was not an option. I did not want that to happen under my watch.[39]

As suggested in the previous chapter, 2012 and 2013 had been replete with examples of international failures of the UN's mythologized purpose. In Johnson's actions in December 2013, it appeared that she had provided much-needed evidence that UN peacekeeping remained connected to its people-centred mythology. However, Johnson's relationship to those events is more focused on the value of the myth than the act of protection. She embellished her and the UN's role in establishing the sites. Her own D/SRSG (RC/HC) Toby Lanzer remembered their formation differently when interviewed for a report on POC sites by Michael J. Arensen:

> We never 'opened the gates,' it was an attitude that if there are people under threat, under stress, jumping over the fence, which was what the vast majority were doing, we will welcome them and we will protect them. So, opening the gates was an attitude that we would assume our responsibilities to protect civilians.[40]

The perimeters around the two UNMISS bases in Juba in December 2013 were large and porous and manned by soldiers that were not inclined to use force. By the time that Johnson was reported to have given the order to 'open the gates', the gates were already reported to be open and civilians were moving inside the perimeter.[41] Johnson's instruction only served to give an official blessing to something that was already taking place.

More broadly, the UN did not welcome its new role protecting civilians as enthusiastically as Johnson suggests. The concept of POC sites were not new to UNMISS, and policy documents had already been produced for the emergency eventualities within which they might be necessary in South Sudan in April 2013. However, those documents had envisaged a situation in which POC sites were a temporary solution to civilians under immediate threat. It was assumed that individuals seeking UNMISS protection would be able to be moved on within seventy-two hours of their arrival. Preparations for longer-term facilities, including the registration of individuals for the purposes of delivering humanitarian services were to be actively avoided in the original strategy.[42] Even the use of the terminology of *POC sites* was supposed to avoid connotations of an *Internally Displaced Person (IDP) site* with more long-term responsibilities.[43] Pressure to maintain the temporary nature of the sites therefore existed from the outset.

Circumstances, however, meant that months after the violence in Juba, and with the war raging across the country, UNMISS was still protecting civilians. The UN Secretariat, through statements by the Secretary General, suggested a simmering resentment about their role in its official reporting. In the Secretary General's report in March 2014, he references the 'huge strain' of the POC sites on the UN and the anxiety associated with 'uncharted territory' that they represented.[44] UNMISS's concerns about its new role were not unfounded. Societal problems and anti-social behaviour that existed outside of UNMISS were transported inside, and potentially intensified within the trapped and traumatized communities. Rule of law functions fell to an unprepared United Nations Police (UNPOL), which had been deployed in the country to support state-building activities. The mission had no adequate guidelines as to how to process lawbreakers within the POC site, where handing them over to the national authorities could not be safely done. Makeshift jails in the sites were hastily constructed out of metal containers that became suffocatingly hot in the extreme South Sudanese heat. UN Formed Police Units (FPUs) had to be deployed using riot gear and tear gas to break up fights within the sites.[45]

Aside from the rule of law dilemmas, the protected civilians lived in appalling conditions often within metres of air-conditioned UN offices and residences. The hastily constructed sites had become their own humanitarian crises, with poor infrastructure creating serious health and safety concerns. With the onset of the rainy season, flooding became so serious in the POC site at Bentiu that children were drowning in the huge pools that formed inside the base.[46] Poorly constructed latrines were collapsing in other sites creating outbreaks of preventable diseases. In April, Médecins Sans Frontière (MSF) launched blistering attacks against perceived UN failings, urging 'the UN leadership to remember that protection means more than just corralling people in a guarded compound'.[47]

If publicly UNMISS continued to bask in the glow of its actions *opening the gates,* internally its attitude to the POC sites increasingly framed them as a problem that outweighed their symbolic importance. Within the UN bases, some UN officials that now lived side by side these overcrowded and desperate POC sites expressed suspicion about their new neighbours. As one researcher remarked following a visit to a UN base:

> I think from the very first, I was struck by how much the residents of the POC felt like pollution. I remember going around the POC just after it was created, and [a senior UNMISS official], just talking about how they would bring trash in, there was dirt, they were going to bring unwanted, nasty people in, terrorists maybe, bandits, who knows?[48]

I ended up spending eight months working in Bor, and during that time, I often felt the relationship between the UN staff and civilians seeking protection within the base, to be one of suspicion and conflict. Staff meetings were frequently taken up with interminable discussions on how to stop 'trespassing' of civilians in parts of the base that had UN offices and accommodation. These became even more frequent after a spate of burglaries of UNMISS accommodation by some residents of the POC site.[49]

Officials from the UN Secretariat in New York were also reported to be fretting about the reputational damage that could be done were it found to be violating basic human rights.[50] Focus in the first part of 2014 was therefore largely on the threats to the POC sites from inside. An internal guidance note sent by Department of Peacekeeping Operations (DPKO) to UNMISS the week before Bor was attacked was entitled *Note of Guidance to UNMISS on the Security of the IDP population in POC sites*. It was entirely directed on how to counter threats posed by the civilians inside the sites, regarding crime and other anti-social behaviour. There was no mention in the document of potential external sources of threats or perimeter security.[51]

Politics as protection

If the UN Secretariat was focused on what was happening within the POC sites, the focus of the UNSC was not even in the country. For the first few months of 2014, international diplomats had been working in the stations to which they had been almost entirely evacuated. They were not idle, but their efforts were focused on peace talks in Addis Ababa and the prospect of reaching a quick political resolution through a hastily convened Inter-Governmental Authority on Development (IGAD)–mediated process. The regional East African body had played an important role during the negotiation of the CPA and was seen as a natural convening organization for the new peace process. A cessation of hostilities agreement was reached in January, and major donors invested millions of dollars to its mediation and monitoring mechanisms. Its collapse within days of its signing only intensified diplomatic efforts. The United States played a leading role under the leadership of the US Envoy to Sudan and South Sudan, Donald Booth. Yet Booth saw the problem as framed by its regional dynamics. He expressed concern that a war in South Sudan could draw other countries into an East African proxy conflict.[52] The fear was not unfounded. Uganda, a long-standing ally of the SPLA, had intervened on behalf of Kiir, while there was strong evidence that Sudan had supplied weapons to its former ally, Machar. These developments were particularly concerning given the long-term US goal of isolating the influence of Khartoum. Elizabeth Shackelford, a state department official working as part of the South Sudan embassy, noted that in early 2014 'Addis was where the special envoy's office was focused. What was happening elsewhere was of minimal concern.'[53]

Johnson's preferred focus was also at the political level. While she had been given no role in Addis, she framed her function in the country as a meso-political one and argued that her primary means to attend to the protection of civilians was through political action. This was in line with a protection of civilians strategy that had been in place for UNMISS since the previous year, in which the 'Tier 1' activity was defined as 'protection through a political process'. The provision of 'protection from physical violence' and the maintenance of 'protective environments' were 'Tier 2' and 'Tier 3', respectively.[54] Despite the dramatic change of circumstances and the huge increase of threats of physical violence against civilians, the order of these priorities remained unchanged in 2014.[55] An argument could be made that a tiered organization of strategy does not necessarily denote a hierarchy of concerns. However, it is distinct from the language of *pillars* for example, which denotes equal standing of priorities. The attachment of a numerical value to each tier further underlines its relative importance. The idea that the UN would have been unaware of the nuances surrounding its use of language is unlikely.

The ordering of UNMISS's strategy did not correspond to a matching of proven capabilities to known problems in a way that a rational actor might have otherwise decided. If the experiences of 2013 had shown anything, it was that UNMISS had little political leverage to protect civilians. Following the humiliating expulsion of its staff in early 2014 and constant complaints by the government of partiality, its political capital effectively disappeared. Given the amount of activity on the South Sudan conflict by the international community, that aside from the United States and other Troika countries included the diplomats of most of South Sudan's East African neighbours, the likelihood that Johnson could add value seemed unlikely. On the other hand, the spontaneous creation of the POC sites showed a concrete means for UNMISS to make a demonstrable impact on objectives set out in its mandate. A more optimal determination of how UNMISS should structure its activities at this time would have prioritized its activity around securing these sites.

However, a prioritization of POC site protection not only sat awkwardly with Johnson's lack of available operational experience, but the UN Secretariat was eager to avoid the perception of the organization as primarily functioning to provide such a service. In an organization staffed by politicians and diplomats, a politics-based strategy was comforting when viewed from New York. In contrast, static protection peacekeeping operations was a source of uncertainty and risks. In the years that followed, the UN consistently restated its desire to see the 'primacy of politics' in its peace operations and has downplayed its own tactical capabilities in key documents such as the *Report of the Independent High-Level Panel on Peace Operations*[56] and *Declaration of Shared Commitments on UN Peacekeeping Operations*.[57]

The aftermath

While much of this chapter has focused on the events preceding and during the attack on Bor, the most significant decisions may have ultimately taken place in its aftermath. At approximately 3.00 pm on 17 April, several hours after the attack had ended, UNMISS officials re-entered the site to begin to document the crime scene.[58] At about the same time, the UNMISS state coordinator instructed a 'clean-up' to begin, stressing the importance of moving civilians that had fled to the more secure sections of the base, reserved for UN staff, back to the original site. This had been instructed to take place by nightfall. UN officials described a scramble to collect evidence as bodies were hurriedly moved. The next morning, the same investigating UN officials were given only two hours to collect evidence from additional examinations of the bodies before they were taken to be buried.[59] A mass grave was dug approximately 100 metres outside of the base. Forty-six bodies were buried there, marked by four wooden crosses.[60] When an investigation team from the AU arrived only a few months later and asked UNMISS to view the grave, the foliage had been allowed to grow so thick around it that the crosses were sufficiently hidden to make it impossible for officials to identify the location.[61]

The sense that the memory of the tragedy, and even evidence that it had taken place at all, was allowed to disappear from the organizational memory was more than simply a product of the chaos of the aftermath. The kind of public highlevel board of inquiry that would have been normal for such a serious loss of life on UN premises was never conducted according to those interviewed.[62] Internal reports by the UN Department of Safety and Security (UNDSS) and the military Force Headquarters (FHQ) did take place. However, the thoroughness of those investigations was questionable. Key civilian UNMISS staff who were present at the site during the incident expressed surprise that they were never interviewed as part of these investigations. The resultant reports were also not widely distributed, even internally. I was unable to see a copy but one UN official, familiar with the events of the attack recalled his reaction at reading one of these documents for the first time:

> It was whitewashed, it was unbelievable. . . . I don't know what the underlying motivation is. I mean, the UN has a hard time criticizing itself but [exasperated exhalation of air]. I was shocked when I read that thing, because it was so not true, so fabricated.[63]

A public report on the incident was released nine months later. However, carried out under the auspices of UNMISSs' Human Rights Department, the focus was on the actions of the attackers than the responses of UNMISS. A UN official I spoke to struggled to account for the lack of impact that the incident at Bor seemed to make on mission strategy:

> It doesn't have the historical resonance, I guess. Frankly, because it was, I don't know how significant, like in terms of a strategic event, maybe it just wasn't that important. I don't know. It's tragic. Maybe it fell of the radar, right?[64]

The incident at Bor could have served as an opportunity to honestly reflect on the mission's shortcomings and reorient UNMISS's strategy with greater focus on physical security of civilians to avoid being compromised again. Instead, Johnson appears to have viewed the incident as anomalous and only obliquely significant in its impact on the broader political situation. In her memoir of her time in South Sudan, the incident is dealt with in a single page. In it, she brushes over UNMISS's failures. Instead, she highlights how the president had 'told me how angry he, personally, was' on UNMISS's behalf. She also described how the incident affected the political process because it represented a 'game changer for international engagement'.[65] The ever-present lens of personal relationships and political strategy were again most prominent in her analysis.

Johnson did not mention UNMISS's inability to translate clear warnings into action, a lack of care around physical security infrastructure and the poor state of readiness of UN soldiers. During research for this book, there was no indication that the UN had deliberately sought to cover up the event. The pervasive sense was that it simply did not seem important, providing additional evidence that the UN did not see its role in physically protecting the POC sites as its priority. With no worthwhile reflection on the incident at Bor, and no lessons drawn, those faults were left unaddressed. The mission subsequently failed to repulse two more attacks on POC sites that it guarded in separate incidents in 2016,[66] each resulting in a significant loss of civilian life. When media pressure forced the UN to conduct more wide-ranging and public investigations into those incidents, they found a similar set of failings as had occurred at Bor.

Conclusions

By 2014, a cohesive shared understanding of the context of South Sudan would have seemed even more remote than it had been the previous year. The chaos caused by the disruption of the conflict meant many UNMISS staff had been evacuated. Bases in some parts of the country were abandoned, and access was severely constrained in the face of a high tempo of violence. Capacity was turned towards emergency roles, particularly coming to grips with the influx of tens of thousands of civilians seeking protection. External networks of information gathering were also significantly degraded with diplomatic, humanitarian and media organizations facing equally severe disruption to their information gathering and analysis capacities. That capacity was further stretched by the mission having to face multiple threats simultaneously and having to construct meaning around which of those threats should be prioritized. The effect of this uncertainty would have meant an ever-greater reliance within the mission on the absorbed beliefs and understandings that comprised the bounded rationality of decision-makers and provided a means to bridge knowledge gaps and deal with uncertainty.

The tragedy at Bor was a consequence of tactical failures of UN peacekeepers stationed there. However, Johnson's strategy of non-confrontation, including refusing to protest the expulsion of her staff, continued to create evidence that would have informed a government assumption that the UN would not respond to provocations. Johnson's concentration on her own *values* meant that she continued to see herself as a political player than the leader of a military peacekeeping mission. The escalation of violence in 2013 also brought the *interests* of the UNSC to the fore. Their focus was on a state perspective in which the political peace process, rather than a physical defence of civilians under UNMISS's care, was of greater importance. If the POC sites had been an initial boon to the UN's *organizational myth*, they quickly became a burden. The UN role at the sites was undesirable and created a tendency within the UN to be inward-looking by viewing them as a problem, rather than core to the mission's priorities. Johnson's actions were *appropriate* in her reflection of a framework that was both politically focused and avoided perceptions of the protection of the POC sites as its main priority.

The way in which the organization failed to prioritize evidence of clear and credible threats at Bor that might have engendered better preparedness appears more rational when viewed within the decision-making framework of the bounded rationality described earlier. A *confirmation bias* would have meant that even though clear and explicit external threats were available, the framing did not exist to ensure that they would have received the attention of senior staff that were focused on other concerns. This included an overvalued need to address threats from within the POC sites, undermining an ability to properly evaluate external threats. It also meant that focus was on a misplaced priority to be responsive to the broader political context, even when UNMISS added little value to that process. A *substitution bias* likely existed in the tendency to attach a negative stereotype to residents of the POC sites in ways that also would have made it more difficult to give priority to threats against them.

The failure to conduct an appropriate investigation and share its findings within the organization also looks like a *confirmation bias*, in which the mission avoided the creation of knowledge that they knew would undermine the organizational myth and the preferred interests of the mission's leadership, Secretariat and UNSC. The incident at Bor was therefore incorrectly characterized as an anomalous and unpredictable event. That set up the foundation for a long-standing *availability bias* as the mission struggled in future years to reference available evidence, sufficiently prominent in its mindset, as to why it should be more concerned with physical security at its bases.

Another behaviour that may have affected the way that UNMISS chose to interpret the incident at Bor can be attributed to a sunk-cost fallacy. By 2014, UNMISS had spent almost $3 billion. In return, twenty-five peacekeepers had been lost[67] and the country had been allowed to slip into a devastating civil war. The ambiguous success of *opening the gates* represented a minor consolation to the UN's organizational myth. A rational accounting of UNMISS's performance would have been that its strategy and investments up to that point represented a colossal waste, necessitating a significant rethink of its strategy. However, the avoidance of an open enquiry into either the failure to pre-empt the outbreak of violence in December 2013 or the attack at Bor allowed the UN to avoid recognizing its failures. Some changes to the mandate were made in 2014, particularly suspending UNMISS's state-building role. However, UNMISS did not rethink the main components of its protection of civilians strategy. Instead, that strategy, including its focus on the primacy of politics, became even more prominent in broader institutional thinking. UNMISS incorrectly maintained the value of their strategy up to the point that it inhibited the pursuit of different and more optimal approaches. Whereas the tragedy at Bor could have been a wake-up call, it was allowed to disappear from the organizational memory.

UNMISS's incorrect assessment that its approach in South Sudan had not been fundamentally flawed outlasted Johnson's departure in July. The UN Secretariat played a role in fostering that mistake. While Johnson's tenure as UNMISS senior representative of the Secretary General (SRSG) was privately seen as disastrous by many in New York, her actions remained *appropriate* by the standards of the UN. Thus, no proper account was ever made of her mistakes. Any public inference that she had been a failure was avoided as she was subsequently awarded a seat on the highly influential *Independent High-Level Panel on Peace Operations*.

In the chapters that follow, I shall describe how even as Johnson's successor was charged with rectifying the perceived mess that she had left, there was no fundamental change from her strategy. The lasting significance of Bor became less a representation of UNMISS failure and instead was a cautionary example of the risks of hosting POC sites. Peacekeeping efforts continued to be less focused on creating a robust defence of the civilians within UN bases, and more focused on strategies to close them to better focus on priorities that were perceived to align better with the organizational image, and the professional self-conception, of decision-makers within the UN. That tendency towards an irrational understanding of the available evidence increased the likelihood of suboptimal operational strategies.

The battle for Unity

April 2015

By the summer of 2015, I had left my job at the United Nations Mission in South Sudan (UNMISS) to take up a new role with the South Sudan NGO Forum, working as their conflict and security analyst. The new job gave me an opportunity to work outside of the restrictions of the UN and across a much broader remit. It also gave me the chance to see the context from the perspective of the NGO community. From within UNMISS, NGOs were viewed with a strange mix of admiration, suspicion and condescension. The *admiration* was a result of the knowledge that NGOs were mobile and active in the country in ways that UNMISS could only dream off. They were not subjected to the same punishing access restrictions that the government had placed on peacekeepers. Nor were they shackled by a rigid security and safety regime that could undermine attempts by UN civilians to do work outside of their bases. Objections by the UN Department of Safety and Security (UNDSS) to risky movements could scupper time-sensitive investigations and deterred UN staff from going to areas that had not been cleared by security assessments. The willingness of a troop-contributing country (TCC) to support a mission that required a force protection could represent another inhibitor of movement. In contrast an unarmed NGO could deploy quickly to areas that UNMISS could not or would not. Also, in comparison to UNMISS, NGOs were much more embedded with the communities that they served and consequently often had better information than the UN managed to get through its own networks that were more likely to be fixed to official structures.

UNMISS's *suspicion* of NGOs stemmed from the perception that the frequent criticism that the mission endured from them was unfair. The likes of Médecins sans frontières (MSF) had been an irritant to the mission since its beginning, creating protests from UNMISS that not only did expectations put on the UN exceed its capacities, but that NGOs lacked sympathy for its difficult position in relation to the government. The *condescension* came from the largely unwarranted belief that UNMISS sat at the top of a hierarchy of interveners. As many within UNMISS understood it, NGOs responded to a narrow humanitarian aspect of what was happening, while the UN existed to create order within international peace, security and development arrangements. NGOs, particularly in South Sudan at the time, were also often staffed by younger professionals at the start of their career adding to the perception that they were more junior, idealistic and naïve. UNMISS was also charged with preserving space for humanitarian delivery, creating a paternalistic sense of the responsibility, regardless of their ability to positively deliver.

My experience with the NGO community belied the caricature. It had its own problems. The overrepresentation of international staff and the risks thrust upon national workers were among the most problematic. Nonetheless, the level of dedication, willingness to be responsive to the context and enthusiasm for their work often provided a stark comparison with some UNMISS staff. Among NGOs there was a similar tendency to stereotype UNMISS. For them, the peacekeeping mission often felt like an uncaring behemoth of overpaid bureaucrats who cared little for the country and seldom left the comfort of their own bases. However, that also ignored the many extraordinary and dedicated individuals who I had worked with and who were committed to trying to achieve the best they could in difficult circumstances.

These attitudes created identities out of professional affiliations that became bound to rites and rituals. Generalizations of how individuals from these two tribes dressed, spoke and acted were formed to *other* in a way that created satisfaction around differently affiliated individual's professional self-conception. In coordination meetings between UNMISS and NGOs, disagreements over policy too often became emotional and combative as each side sought to defend their group's perspective in a way that was simultaneously an attempt to win the argument while affirming distinct values and a corresponding identity. That difficult relationship predated the outbreak of the war. However, in the summer of 2015 and the crisis in Unity, it reached its lowest point.

In this chapter, I will discuss Johnson's departure and Ellen Margrethe Løj's arrival as the new Special Representative of the Secretary General (SRSG), and the expectations which accompanied the change in leadership. I will suggest that Løj's previous experience gave her a specific set of values that influenced her decision-making and her leadership style. This led to an even greater commitment to systemic UN interpretations of the context and an even more isolated perspective than had existed under Johnson. I will also discuss the role of the UNSC and its attitude to the conflict that appeared increasingly partial as the government launched massive new offensives. I will suggest that UNMISS's response to an escalation in the conflict was deficient in ways that cannot be accounted for by capability gaps alone. In the conclusions, I will suggest that SRSG Løj's framing within a diplomatic and peacebuilding framework, which suited her own values as well as the interests of the UN Secretariat and UNSC, constituted a bounded rationality that again disincentivized more optimal, timely or confrontational decision-making.

Background

In Johnson's farewell statement in July 2014, she went to great lengths to emphasize the extraordinary and unprecedented nature of the events of the previous eight months. She repeated the refrain 'never before' three times to describe the 'explosion of violence, the hurricane'. But she left with the assertion that the worst might be over:

> And it is only when you have weathered the storm, and you are in somewhat calmer waters, that a captain can dock and hand over to someone else. That is the case with me now.[1]

However, if there were 'calmer waters' to be found in July 2014, they would have only seemed so compared to the extremities of violence that had recently taken place. The country remained territorially divided with both sides entrenched in well-defended positions, indicating the likelihood of a protracted conflict. Attempts to reach a political resolution had achieved little. A cessation of hostilities agreement between the parties in January was breached within days, and a peace agreement in May similarly collapsed less than two weeks after Johnson left the country. The numbers of civilians seeking protection from UNMISS continued to rise, reaching 100,000 in July.[2] UNMISS's capacity to carry out operations beyond the immediate vicinity of its main bases remained limited. Having closed most of its smaller bases following the attack on Akobo in 2013, its tactical footprint had shrunk, further limiting its access in the country. When UNMISS ventured out on patrol from those bases that they retained, they regularly faced roadblocks and harassment. What patrols took place often had a performative aspect to them, involving a movement along a single road within short proximity to a main base. Nonetheless, it fulfilled reporting requirements that measured quantitative success in patrolling through the number conducted.

A UN official who worked in civil–military cooperation between humanitarians and UNMISS suggested to me that the lack of a conversation about measuring the impact of patrols meant that those that took place during this period were meaningless.[3]

The implications of the lack of freedom of movement were nowhere more evident than in Unity State. The town of Leer in southern Unity was the birthplace of Riek Machar and became a predictable focus for Sudan People's Liberation Army (SPLA) operations in the early stages of the war. Violence in the area had created widespread displacement and significant humanitarian needs. Southern Unity became the most food-insecure area in the whole country with all parts considered either in crisis or in emergency phases by the end of 2014 under the integrated phase classification.[4] Yet, despite these needs, the restrictions on peacekeeping movement meant that no UNMISS patrols took place in southern Unity between December 2013 and May 2015, and humanitarian services in the area were provided without peacekeeper support.[5]

The new captain

There was a gap of two months between the departure of Johnson and the arrival of her successor, Ellen Margrethe Løj.[6] The gap was unfortunate. During that period, not only did the latest peace agreement collapse but another UNMISS helicopter was shot down, this time by the SPLA/iO, killing four of its staff. While it seems unlikely that the presence of an SRSG would have altered the outcome in either instance, the lack of UNMISS leadership during these critical incidents would have further undermined the stature of the mission in the country. The reasons for the gap are unclear. Several interviewees suggested that the UNSC had privately lost faith in Johnson and were impatient to see her leave. In the hurried search for a replacement, they sought a different direction more likely to adhere to orthodox peacekeeping approaches. As one official described the situation:

> I think Løj as a person was brought in as a direct response to Hilde, much more hardnosed and true to UN concepts. They brought in a bureaucrat who had experience in New York and the Council and in UNMIL. . . . [Johnson] was a political animal, viewed herself as a political animal, and a lot of it was done in her head personally and depends on personal relationships. Løj was much more, 'sit back, use the structures.'[7]

If Johnson was a politician in her attempts to situate UNMISS policy around her own interpretations, Løj was the consummate diplomat. Her career up to that point showed that she was invested in the established international peace and security architecture. She had represented Denmark on the UNSC and was closely identified with her support to the reform process of UN peacebuilding mechanisms. She helped establish, and was co-chair, of the first informal consultations of the Peacebuilding Commission and stated a strong belief in the role of peacebuilding within peacekeeping strategies.

> I think I cannot underline strongly enough the importance of peacekeeping and peacebuilding going hand in hand. They are two sides of the same coin. If we don't urgently work on building the peace while we keep the peace, then we will not achieve our ultimate goal, namely sustainable peace and prosperity.[8]

Between 2008 and 2012, Løj was able to see how peacebuilding could be effectively incorporated into a peacekeeping mission when she was appointed as SRSG of the United Nations Mission in Liberia (UNMIL). That was possible because of the close relationship she had with the host government. In Liberia, she enjoyed a strong relationship with President Sirleaf Johnson, and the increasing stability of the post-conflict country provided Løj with positive affirmation for a collaborative strategy focused on peacebuilding outcomes. The perceived success of UNMIL, represented a rare *win* for UN peacekeeping[9] and created a positive halo around Løj's performance and her strategies. Between 2012 and 2014, she additionally served as a member of the Board for the Centre for Humanitarian Dialogue, again focused on diplomatic and peacebuilding work.

Forging relationships

If Løj favoured a peacebuilding strategy of engagement with individuals who had official standing, through their participation in legitimate government structures, the reality of the South Sudan government's violent excesses in 2013 and 2014 complicated such engagement by UNMISS. Continued UN support of the state, which had been a core part of the UN's mission in the country after independence, was quietly set aside. In 2014, the UNSC authorized a new UNMISS mandate. The laundry list of state-building activities that had weighed down the mission since 2011 disappeared. In its place were four priorities of which the protection of civilians was the primary role. Under pressure to address the ambiguity that Johnson had felt undermined her capacity to intervene against the government between 2011 and 2014, the UNSC strengthened the language around the use of force to protect of civilians. UNMISS's other three priorities included monitoring and investigating human rights, creating the conditions for delivery of humanitarian assistance, and supporting the implementation of the Cessation of Hostilities Agreement.[10]

Løj from the outset distanced herself from the shift in focus of the mandate. At her first public press conference as SRSG in October, she acknowledged the change. However, she also insinuated that such a change bore little reflection on how UNMISS felt about the government:

> Let me say that the mandate for the Mission is solely in the hands of the members of the Security Council, it is the 15 members of the Security Council who decide what the mandate of the mission is. We will not be consulted on the mandate.[11]

Løj also distanced the mission from the political machinations of the international community that Kiir and his allies regularly railed against as perennially unfair in its treatment of the Juba government. She ruled out, for example, UNMISS's involvement in the peace process taking place in Addis Ababa:

> Let me say that I hope very much, and I support the Security Council's call for a peace agreement, the negotiations as you know are taking place under the mediation efforts by the regional organization IGAD, so we are not involved in that.[12]

A diminished political role did not also lend itself to greater focus on the practical considerations of securing the Protection of Civilians (POC) sites and improving the mission's tactical posture in the country. In her first weeks, Løj took more substantive steps to normalize the relationship with the government around the POC sites. She sent a draft memorandum to the government on mechanisms for the transition of criminals within the sites to national authorities in what seems to have been an initial attempt to regularize their status and undercut the perception that the POC sites existed as parallel to the state.[13] She also echoed government concerns that the POC sites harboured opposition supporters and SPLA defectors. In November, as part of an UNMISS press release, she claimed:

> I have no doubt that in the Protection of Civilian sites there are many people who support the opposition, or that there are many who are former soldiers, who defected from the army. That's a fact.[14]

In the same press release, she criticized civilians in the POC sites, calling on them to do better at respecting their civilian nature. In the following month, UNMISS organized a series of well-publicized weapon searches and weapon destruction ceremonies within the sites.[15] Løj's actions and statements may seem prudent in their attempt to placate a sensitive government that viewed the POC sites with suspicion. However, humanitarians fretted that the new SRSG's attempts to show sympathy to a government perspective risked legitimizing inflammatory language that had previously been used to justify attacks on POC sites including at Bor.[16]

Despite the mandate change, UNMISS also continued to provide symbolic material support to the government. This included capacity building of security services around protection issues as well as building security infrastructure, such as the construction of at least three guard posts for security forces in Juba.[17] No such support was offered to the SPLA/iO.

Løj's strategy was a transparent attempt to reforge links between the South Sudan state and the structures of international peace and security. The presumed hope would be that once accomplished, those structures would build confidence and encourage normal state behaviour. Aside from whether such a strategy would work, Løj struggled to create those links that were critical to her strategy. If Johnson's personal relationships had ultimately been misplaced, they at least gave her access that Løj struggled to replicate. Her first meeting with President Kiir was reported to be frosty by UN officials,[18] and her subsequent meetings were sporadic, often weeks apart and unproductive. Despite the setbacks, she persisted. As one UN official commented:

> She definitely wasn't an optimist, but somehow there was this ego thing that like tomorrow they're going to wake up and realize that we're doing a lot of good stuff and this meeting will go better. I don't know it's just this weird expectation.[19]

Løj had less time for forging similar links with the opposition. Her contact with the SPLA/iO was even more sporadic; and in an early and much publicized decision, she denied a request by the Inter-Governmental Authority on Development (IGAD) to support a transportation of SPLA/iO as part of the ongoing political process.[20] Løj also did not re-establish any bases, even of a temporary nature, inside territory held by the SPLA/iO during her tenure.

Løj's inside view

By 2015, UNMISS's footing in the country looked surer. It had begun to move back to its offices at UN House and the emergencies that, for a while, were occurring almost daily subsided. However, fighting in the country continued at a sufficient pace that information continued to be received in fragments that policymakers demanded be absorbed rapidly by harried analysts. Competition between departments undermined attempts to produce a coherent narrative. The UNMISS Joint Mission Analysis Centre (JMAC) played the primary role in synthesizing cross-mission information to inform decisions. However, former JMAC staff complained to me that they had to rely on personal relationships and goodwill to access information held by other departments and consolidate it into a mission perspective.[21] Staff from those other departments countered that JMAC's presentation of information to senior leadership as its own, even when another department had given it to them, diminished their own value in the eyes of the UNMISS leadership.[22] JMAC was also accused of over-classifying its analysis meaning that whatever it produced was only seen by the most senior members of the mission. There appears to have been a constant anxiety of being 'left out' of decision-making processes that undermined individual's professional self-conception.[23] An incentive therefore existed to find perspectives that appealed to the mission leadership in a way that was more likely to echo than challenge leadership positions, in a way that would have created the illusion of participation.

Another obstacle to the appropriate absorption of information was the relative lack of analytical staff, or lack of willingness to prioritize analysis, in departments outside of JMAC. One official described the struggle they had with one UNMISS department in trying to access their information:

> They were furiously working up all these reports, daily reports, weekly reports, monthly reports. It was report central, sending them all in and then going to Juba and then talking there to the human rights team and being like, 'Where are all these reports? Where is all of this information going on the cases and on the follow-up of the cases and on-trend lines and all of this stuff and this analysis?' They were like, 'Well, we have a problem with our reporting.' That was often an explanation that I would hear from them is that, 'Oh, we don't have the capacity to really write decent reports. We're working on that, we're overhauling and restructuring our reporting function.' That was one thing that I heard for three years.

Without capable analysis, reporting would have been more susceptible to those interpretations that senior management chose to make of them. Løj's management style also exacerbated a tendency of departments to favour information that supported her views rather than existed independently of her opinions. In an interview with Joel Gwyn Winckler, a staff member of Løj described her decision-making process when she led UNMIL:

With Doss [Løj's predecessor in UNMIL] we all were gathering around him as a team and consider[ing] the aspects together and collaboratively. Løj wants to see things with her own eyes and wants to make up her own mind. Her staff here [in UNMIL] is more the support who should pave the way for her.[24]

Some junior staff in UNMISS at the time reported that Løj could be 'invisible', rarely engaging with them and even undermining forums within which more junior staff had found relatively empowering means to provide inputs without referring to their department heads.[25] This included instructing the team responsible for consolidating early warning analysis in the mission to remove early response recommendations from their reporting. More senior staff, particularly from the military parts of the mission, disliked that component of the mechanism that narrowed their control of defining operational response alternatives.[26] Løj was more responsive to those feelings than the perceived value of an early warning mechanism tightly attached to early response.

As Løj developed her own interpretations of the context, it was within a familiar environment. Many of her senior team had worked with her previously at UNMIL. A UN official suggested to me that a cluster of senior officials who had previously worked together is not unusual in the UN system and may have been especially comforting to Løj as she struggled to grip the complexities of the mission:

It's very common with these missions. When she came to UNMISS, she brought her people from Liberia with her whose entire careers were pegged to her success. That's how you get that group thing at the top. I think she was just so far outside of her scope that she didn't really know what to do without it.[27]

Løj was reported to be a 'voracious reader' and willing to at least 'listen to all sides of an argument'.[28] However, she also had a reputation for trying to aggressively shape discourse in a way that corresponded to her assumptions about the role of the UN. This was particularly evident in her relationship with humanitarians who worked alongside the mission. One humanitarian working for an NGO characterized the relationship as

combative and it tended to be a little bit – What's the word I want? Almost like a rubber band reaction, where it was just like we would push back on something and then you just get this complete shutdown. There wasn't a lot of room for like, 'All right, let's negotiate. Let's find a middle ground.' It was like, 'Oh, you don't like that. Okay, you're now kicked out of the POCs [POC sites].' You'd just be like, 'What?' It's just a massive overreaction.[29]

A UN official interviewed defended the SRSG's reputation on her interactions with humanitarians but conceded:

> If they [humanitarians] came at her with stuff which wasn't sympathetic to UNMISS' point of view, she used to steamroll them. I saw one poor guy from MSF, she let him speak for five seconds, and just ran through him.[30]

This combative approach also extended to her attempts to shape public discourse to negate criticism of the mission. Journalists and researchers complained that under her their access to the POC sites became more restricted. UNMISS could deny entry to journalists, time limits were set on how long they could spend there and chaperones could be required.[31] Even research questions could be vetted by senior leadership before they were put to UNMISS officials in a perceived attempt to limit staff interactions with the press to set 'talking points'.[32] Løj was also much less inclined to provide interviews or attend press conferences than her predecessor.

Peace, but first war

In 2015, the peace process was still dominated by the United States. While there is no question that the United States had expressed frustration at both parties to the conflict, their political interests were partial. Their ally, the Ugandan President Yoweri Museveni, had unambiguously come down on the side of the government sending the Ugandan People's Defense Force (UPDF) to South Sudan to help the SPLA push the SPLA/iO away from capital. The United States had additional reason to be wary of Riek Machar, whose only material support came from its long-standing foe, Omar al-Bashir. At an early stage, the United States openly explained its partiality. In May 2014, Kerry clarified the US position as follows:

> we do not put any kind of equivalency into the relationship between the sitting president, constitutionally and duly elected by the people of the country, and a rebel force that is engaged in use of arms in order to seek political power or to provide a transition.[33]

In 2014, the United States blocked efforts by France and the UK to get the UNSC to agree to an arms embargo in South Sudan.[34] This allowed the government to make huge purchases of arms that included small arms and light weapons, hundreds of armoured vehicles, the country's first attack helicopters and even an air-to-ground attack jet.[35] In contrast, the SPLA/iO found their already-meagre weapons supply slowly cut off as the United States used its sanctions regime to dissuade Khartoum from further involvement in the south. While US frustration with Kiir's government and its tendency to target civilians was palpable,[36] their actions suggested official tolerance for some escalation of military action by the government, likely to force the opposition to reach a quick agreement.

Even though the UK and France had misgivings over the failure to obtain an arms embargo, the importance of the diplomatic relationship with the United States vis-à-vis the fate of South Sudan meant that they did not vigorously protest their ally's position. The maintenance of a pre-existing EU arms embargo on the country may have sufficed as a satisfactory symbolic moral position.[37] China's interests also aligned at this time with the United States. It maintained a relationship with the South Sudan government through its economic involvement in the country, particularly in oil.[38] In the initial stages of the war, China had invited military personnel from the government to the country and allowed large arms shipments from its state-owned defence company, Norinco.[39] China's narrow interests also found expression in UNMISS's mandate. The section that dealt with UNMISS responsibility to protect buildings and infrastructure crucial to the protection of civilians included, 'schools, places of worship, hospitals' and 'oil installations'.[40]

No escape in Unity

By early 2015, the government's build-up of armaments meant that by spring, a large-scale government offensive looked imminent. In March, the International Crisis Group wrote:

> The SPLA has been gaining ground since May 2014 thanks to major arms purchases, improved tactics and the influence and presence of the Ugandan army. Many in the SPLA increasingly see little reason for concessions to the SPLA/iO. . . . The government feels an urgency to push for victory, as a looming financial crisis threatens its fragile coalition, much of which is built upon patronage networks running short of cash.[41]

In that same month, UNMISS sent a code cable to New York, having identified large deployments of freshly supplied government security services in forward positions in Unity State. They assessed the likelihood of coordinated military campaigning as 'probable'.[42] The potential impact on civilians of any escalation of conflict was significant. In 2014, Kiir had handed over command of the SPLA to Paul Malong. Malong had a fearsome reputation as the architect of the Mathiang Anyoor militia that had been heavily implicated in perpetrating the massacres in Juba in 2013.[43] As SPLA chief, Malong had overseen the partial integration of that militia into the regular SPLA.[44]

When government operations began in Upper Nile state in March, the SPLA/iO showed themselves incapable of withstanding the now-better-armed-and-supplied SPLA. It was only the surprise defection of a key SPLA-allied militia from the Shilluk community that prevented a total collapse of the opposition in Upper Nile.[45] Attacks on civilians in Upper Nile were significant. However, areas under attack were either connected to stronghold SPLA/iO territory or else bordered other countries to which civilians might escape as refugees, such as Sudan and Ethiopia. A concentration of fighting in the vicinity of Malakal also meant that civilians could more easily seek protection within the UNMISS POC site.

When the offensive reached Unity State the following month, the avenues of escape for the civilians there were fewer. As the government launched the predicted offensive from all sides in April 2015, civilians were left with four hazardous routes of escape. To reach the safety of the UNMISS base in Bentiu, they needed to travel north through at least 100 kilometres of government-controlled territory in which informal militias made up of armed cattle herding youths had been armed and given licence by government security forces to rob, murder and rape civilians fleeing the fighting. The militias largely came from the Bul Nuer community from western parts of Unity State that was the only Nuer community to have remained loyal to the government in 2013.

If the route to the POC site appeared too risky, a civilian might find access to a boat and pay the cost of travel. They could then travel north along the Nile to reach an opposition stronghold in Jonglei and then potentially travel to safety in Ethiopia. They might also travel south to the isolated Panyijar County, which the SPLA/iO maintained a fragile hold over, and where the large number of people in need competed for limited humanitarian services. Finally, they could hide in the swamp, and the many islands near the fighting that offered natural protection. However, on the islands they were exposed to harsh living conditions without access to humanitarian services. Drowning while either escaping along the Nile or hiding in the swamps represented a significant danger that alone would kill hundreds.

On 25 April, the SPLA moved from Mayom and Bentiu in the north, with local armed militias in their wake. The SPLA were also boosted by the remnants of the Bul Nuer-dominated South Sudan Liberation Army (SSLA), which had reached an accommodation with the president shortly before the outbreak of the war. From the west, they attacked from Maper in Lakes state. In the south, SPLA boats shelled the port of Taiyer. Thousands of homes were reported to have been destroyed in coordinated attacks on civilian centres. The displaced brought a litany of horror stories about the initial offensive and the attacks they sustained as they travelled to the POC site. UNICEF reported in mid-May that, according to eyewitnesses they had interviewed,

> Whole villages were burned to the ground by armed groups, while large numbers of girls and women were taken outside to be raped and killed – including children as young as seven.[46]

According to UNMISS's own public reporting released in June:

> This recent upsurge has not only been marked by allegations of rampant killing, rape, abduction, looting, arson and displacement, but by a new brutality and intensity, including such horrific acts as the burning alive of people inside their homes.[47]

During the offensives of the SPLA in Unity, a conservative estimate of the number directly killed was 7,165, the vast majority of which were civilians. An additional 829 were believed to have drowned while trying to escape in the swamps. Furthermore, 4,155 children were separated from their families, and 890 people were reported to have been abducted.[48] Without a secure base from which to operate, all humanitarian services were evacuated from southern Unity in May, leaving 300,000 people without access to life-saving aid and likely resulting in a significantly higher mortality. At least 100,000 heads of cattle were plundered, representing the community wealth of the entire southern Unity.[49] Throughout the violence, over the course of several months, I witnessed the humanitarian community make continued and increasingly exasperated calls for UNMISS to intervene, at least to create an area in which they might more safely deliver vital humanitarian services. Meetings degenerated into personal attacks and the gap between the peacekeeping and humanitarian tribes became a gulf. Humanitarians accused UNMISS of being indifferent. UNMISS accused humanitarians of being unreasonable.

A peacekeeping response?

UNMISS had been aware since March that an offensive was likely. Once it started, it could access almost real-time information about threats against civilians from the huge numbers fleeing the violence to their base. Between April and August, the number of people seeking protection from UNMISS in Bentiu rose from 50,000 to more than 120,000.[50] However, UNMISS's reaction to the incoming information was slow.

On 15 May, UNMISS sent a letter to the authorities requesting that they allow unhindered civilian movement for those fleeing the conflict and allow humanitarians to access the contested areas. The government denied that they were hindering civilians, provoking strongly worded statements by IGAD, the UNSC and the UN Secretary General. Under pressure, the government issued a decree instructing the armed forces to lift restrictions on movement and allow humanitarian access. There is no evidence that the decree was ever enforced but, in a meagre concession, UNMISS was granted limited access to parts of southern Unity.

Between 23 and 28 May, the mission conducted a patrol to Leer as part of *Operation Unity*. Subsequently, a response plan was developed in which it would establish a static presence through a temporary operating base (TOB) in Leer, primarily to allow the distribution of humanitarian aid in the affected area. However, implementation of *Operation Unity II* was persistently delayed. Eventually, after near-constant fighting between April and August, the government wound down its campaign in southern Unity. The de-escalation coincided with Kiir signing a peace agreement heralding an official pause in SPLA campaigns. However, it would still not be until November, more than six months after the fighting began, that UNMISS finally deployed the Leer TOB. Despite having interviewed several people involved with aspects of the planning of *Operation Unity II*, there was a general inability to pinpoint the exact reason for the delay. One UN official I interviewed offered technical issues as a possible reason:

> It seems that the main delay with setting up the Leer base were the problems with road accessibility to the area, combined with the prolonged lack of serviceability for the appropriate air asset, the Mi-26, for transferring materials required for setting up the base.[51]

Another interviewee involved with the humanitarian response claimed that objections also arose from the civilian side of UNMISS with unnamed 'political issues' as well as bureaucratic problems such as the insurance of air assets.[52] While technical and bureaucratic reasons may have provided official excuses for the delay, it was generally agreed that there was organizational hesitance and especially a lack of enthusiasm within the military. The research done for this book was replete with stories about individual TCCs and officers who were enthusiastic supporters of a robust and broad interpretation of UNMISS protection of civilians responsibilities. The Mongolian contingent in Bentiu, for example, were frequently singled out for praise and consistently showed bravery in high-risk situations around the base. However, the more common story told about UNMISS military was that its components were often reluctant to participate in operations outside of the bases in which they were stationed. The ongoing conflict and government harassment when UNMISS tried to leave its bases made the establishment of a TOB in Leer look highly risky. In the period between the start of the 2015 Unity conflict and the deployment of the TOB, UNMISS reported sixty restrictions on its movement, almost entirely by the government.[53] However, hesitancy by the military often far exceeded the risks that they encountered. One UN official described meetings about military patrols in Unity at this time:

> I remember being in meetings where they basically talk about an entire patrol of armed peacekeepers, like half a battalion. A couple of hundred guys with armored vehicles and automatic weapons basically being turned around by a barefoot SPLA teenager on the side of the road.[54]

In a report to the UNSC in November 2015, the Secretary General refers to the issue of 'troop reluctance' as a key factor undermining the ability of UNMISS to carry out its tasks.[55] However, neither Løj nor the UN Secretariat appear to have taken any action to address the issue. Nor was there any suggestion that UN leadership sought to intervene in any other way that might have unblocked the various obstacles that created delays in the deployment of the operation. In 2017, UNMISS would carry out a similar operation in a similar set of circumstances with only a few days' notice (see Chapter 9) suggesting that the issue was not capability based.

Complete and utter failure

Humanitarian frustration with UNMISS during the summer of 2015 was not only about inaction in Unity but also a broader sense of abandonment. Despite the presence of the mission, South Sudan overtook Afghanistan in 2015 as the most dangerous for aid workers.[56] In contrast, between Løj's arrival and the deployment of Op Unity II, there had not been a single UNMISS fatality because of conflict, making it one of the safest peacekeeping missions in the world.

UNMISS was also persistently reluctant to use its political heft to protect civilians and create space to allow humanitarian delivery. When Løj reported to the UNSC in May 2015, her characterization of the violence was partial in its apparent even-handedness. She portrayed the situation as fighting between equals in which both sides bore equal responsibility for the crimes against civilians.[57] Her portrayal contrasted sharply with the mid-term report from the UN Panel of Experts that was leaked over the summer and was more unequivocal in its criticism of the government that by virtue of its role as aggressor and it its overwhelming position of strength was much more often the perpetrator in violence against civilians. A member of that panel reported that the moment was notable for a change in their relationship with Løj:

> When we came in, I would say that UNMISS was very welcoming. Ellen Løj was definitely instrumental in that. She made it very clear. She received us herself and spoke to us. She was very clear about her intention to have a very good relationship with the Panel of Experts . . . 'What do you need to know? Where do you want to go? Who do you want to meet within the mission? What kind of contacts can we facilitate with the government, with non-government, with the opposition?' Doors wide open. That was our first trip there. That was very clear. Then things changed drastically. . . . Obviously, our midterm report was quite critical of everything that was going on. That really changed the relationship with UNMISS. Our interpretation was that that came from Ellen Løj very much herself.[58]

In the following months and years, UNMISS was reported to have been less forthcoming in their support to the panel, in terms of both their administrative support and their willingness to talk about sensitive subjects. In trying to explain the change the expert suggested:

> For her, maintaining a good relationship with the government was key and the priority, and everything else had to give way for that priority. The association with us just became too troublesome for her, too disconcerting because we were clearly a critical voice, and the government didn't appreciate that.[59]

That attitude was also evident following the expulsion of her D/SRSG (RC/HC), Toby Lanzer, in June 2015, after he publicly decried the humanitarian plight of civilians in Unity.[60] In July, his deputy was also seriously assaulted by government security services in her own home, forcing her to also leave the country. In a continuation of Johnson's avoidance of confrontation, UNMISS's response in both instances was shockingly quiet.[61] In June, UNMISS indirectly criticized the government through the report on violence in southern Unity that it issued through its Human Rights Department.[62] However, the SRSG's office avoided any direct criticism in the press leaving the humanitarian community with the impression that Løj had no interest in using her platform to influence the crisis in Unity. As one humanitarian noted:

> She was never a voice on protection. It never struck me that she was speaking up or pushing back. It just felt like she was completely absent. I think it is telling that at no point during my time with the protection cluster did we feel that we could go to her for support on protection issues.[63]

At the end of the year, comments made by MSF to *The Guardian* newspaper surmised the feelings of confusion felt around UNMISS's refusal to act or speak as a 'complete and utter failure'.[64] In contrast to her low-key engagement with the press throughout most of 2015, Løj lashed out at MSF in an op-ed in the same newspaper, claiming the criticism as 'entirely unjustified'. She praised the successes of UNMISS that included the hosting of the POC sites and the eventual establishment of the base in Leer in November. She made no mention of the suboptimal performance that related to either of those activities. In relation to UNMISS's position in the country more generally, she complained:

> To imagine that, in a context like this, a UN mission can be in all places at once, is both unrealistic and unreasonable.[65]

As with her predecessor, a focus on tactical weaknesses rather than areas of strength defined UNMISS's posture. This was despite the improvements that had been made to the mission since 2013. UNMISS had been given a more streamlined mandate and an additional 5,000 peacekeepers (an uplift of more than 60 per cent from its pre-war capacity). Despite this there was no discernible improvement in its performance. It was not that UNMISS failed to be everywhere, but that UNMISS was nowhere outside of the fortified perimeters of its main bases.

'Why are we investing?'

The difficulty with explaining a lack of enthusiasm from the senior leadership for intervening in Unity can be better explained within a bounded rationality in which the disincentives to action outweighed the incentives. As suggested previously, Løj was keen to improve UNMISS' relationship with the government and avoid actions that challenged its institutional legitimacy. UNMISS POC sites continued to look like an obstacle to that. At the same time, the UN Secretariat persisted in it attempts to extract itself from its role at the sites. As a UN official who worked closely with her suggested to me:

> She was under lots of pressure not to make them [the POC sites] permanent structures and minimize them for a whole host of reasons and a lot of political pressure from just about every angle. . . . She took very much the political position supported by the Council, supported by New York [the UN Secretariat] of, 'Let's try and minimize these protection sites. Let's try and make them temporary in nature.'[66]

In 2014 and 2015, Løj brought in rules on the extent of services that could be offered within the sites, and the durability of the materials that could be used in building shelters.[67] When a donor contributed to a humanitarian push to improve the dire conditions of Bentiu POC site in early 2015, one UN official noted her displeasure:

> The Dutch had put in a lot of resources to expand Bentiu and did a lot in terms of urban planning. She [Løj] really didn't like that. Now maybe someone practically speaking might say, 'Well, you got these people you don't know how long they're going to be around, let's at least have a decent facility for them, but her thing was, 'Why are we investing?' Not 'we' but even this Dutch donor at the time, I think it was the Dutch, 'investing all of this into making what, in the end, she didn't want to be an incentive for people to come.'[68]

In May 2015, even as the necessity of the POC sites was at its most vital because of the horrific violence in southern Unity, she warned the UNSC that the POC sites were at risk of becoming

> magnets that attract people looking to avail themselves of the services available in the camps, rather than those needing physical protection.[69]

Løj signalled a perspective that aligned with a known organizational priority to avoid new POC site responsibilities. At the start of August, UNMISS refused to allow fleeing civilians inside the gates of its base in Yambio in Western Equatoria following fighting there.[70] This *closed gate* strategy marked a significant change in the UNMISS operation, though no such change had been communicated from the mission to its humanitarian partners in the country. In my role at the NGO Forum, I can recall expressing dismay as NGO staff had also been left on the outside in Yambio, unable to seek the protection of the UN. If there was a new UNMISS policy that affected the security contingency plans of NGOs, which often relied on evacuating to UN bases, there was an obligation to share it.[71] The answer from my interlocutors in the JOC was a somewhat embarrassed explanation that there had been no change in policy and a reminder that UNMISS had no obligation to accept civilians on its bases, if it could provide protection outside of them. The fighting in Yambio turned out to be minor, and there was no subsequent disaster, but it provided further evidence of a hardening of the UNMISS posture and an unwillingness to be sucked into new protection responsibilities. The establishment of a TOB in Leer at this time, while people were still fleeing violence in large numbers, would have guaranteed that people would seek UNMISS protection there, necessitating the de facto opening of yet another POC site. That would have critically undermined the success of UNMISS' strategy at that time.

Beyond the perceived burdensome nature of another POC site, Løj would have also been aware of how negatively an intervention in Leer, especially one that might have created another POC site, would have been perceived by a government she was desperately seeking approval from. That need became acute in the summer of 2015, as a viable peace agreement finally became a possibility. The likelihood of moving from an emergency peacekeeping modality to a peacebuilding one would have seemed tantalizingly close. Furthermore, the peace agreement had been heavily endorsed by an international community that was increasingly desperate to find even a modicum of diplomatic success in the country. In that instance, the uncertainty of how a risky intervention in southern Unity might derail diplomatic efforts in Addis Ababa would have meant that UNSC pressure on Løj to provide a more aggressive deployment to protect civilians would have been limited.

Conclusions

The lack of a timely response by UNMISS in Unity appears irrational when compared to the expected outcome of the mission's new mandate with a more robust protection of civilians component. Løj's implication in her op-ed at the end of 2015 that taking six months to implement a solitary response to an attack on civilians, despite having access to 12,000 soldiers and a powerful diplomatic platform, represented an optimal answer to a mandated priority lacks a strong evidentiary base. Against similar constraints in 2017, UNMISS managed a comparable mission to Aburoc (see Chapter 9) in a matter of days. Capability and resource constraints are insufficient to explain the delays. Without a proper investigation into the management decisions in 2015, it is impossible to say exactly why those delays took place. However, the disincentives to action far outweighed the incentives when considered within the bounded rationality that Løj existed. That would have encouraged decision-making hesitancy.

Løj's *values* supported a belief in the institutions of peace and security and meant that she would have shown deference to UNSC *interests*. In 2015, those interests included an openness to an escalation in conflict as a necessary evil to bring about peace negotiations. The value that Løj placed on her relationship with the government would have aligned and incentivized a focus on choice alternatives that avoided confrontation while also granting them a freer rein to conduct security operations. Increased trepidation from the UN Secretariat that it was being pulled into ever-expanding protection of civilians roles would have been a source of additional *interests* that undermined certainty around an intervention that created a high possibility of a new POC site.

Løj's values were based on a respect for the power of international peace and security, diplomacy and the efficacy of peacebuilding. Her available experiences from Liberia and New York and the success that she associated with such approaches would have loomed large in her mind and created an *availability bias* that created less urgency around an intervention that was confrontational and undermined government legitimacy. A *substitution bias* is visible in her unsuccessful attempts to ingratiate herself with South Sudanese government officials. She struggled to incorporate information that her counterparts were something other than the stereotype of the type of officials that she had successfully worked with previously. This was despite evidence provided by repeated failures to create relationships with those officials, as well as continued belligerence by the government and attacks and restrictions on UN staff. Only a *confirmation bias* that supported focus on information that underplayed the seriousness of the situation or created uncertainty around the extent of civilian casualties and human rights abuses could have legitimated the failure to intervene in what was otherwise a clear example of war crimes on a mass scale.

Decisions based on bias, created within a bounded rationality, was more likely given *inside views* that appeared to be strong in UNMISS decision-making during this period. Løj showed a preference for hierarchical decision-making over flat structures, a lack of tolerance for narratives that diverged from her own perspective, and propensity to have staff with whom she was familiar with in her inner circle of decision-making. The concentration of decision-making among a small group of individuals similarly aligned in their values would have made it less likely that challenging perspectives would have a sufficient platform to create more varied choice alternatives, including those that related more closely to practical elements of overcoming practical obstacles to achieve an intervention in Unity.

Risk aversion would also have been a prominent factor in decision-making around the Unity offensives. Løj appears to have been no more confrontational than her predecessor. The low casualty rates of the mission at a time of high conflict, as well as reports of poor patrolling performance, suggest that there was little appetite for tactical risk-taking. This is unsurprising given that Løj, as her predecessor, had little experience of operational roles within an emergency environment and she appears to have taken no action to address the tactical shortcomings of the mission that might have better positioned UNMISS to more appropriately respond in 2015. The context of leading UNMIL in a permissive post-conflict environment would have been little use in confidently making decisions that placed peacekeepers in the way of significant harm of the considerably riskier environment of South Sudan. The ensuing uncertainty would have encouraged *risk aversion* to Løj, compounded by reliance on the advice of military planners and TCCs that, as highlighted earlier, had their own reasons to be risk-averse.

Decision-making was also structured in a way that made *groupthink*, which reflected rather than informed senior decision-makers, more likely. Competition between different departments, and low analytical capacity within some departments, will have incentivized staff to emulate perspectives known to be popular among the mission's leadership in a way that created greater certainty around their preferred choice alternatives.

Løj's full-throated defence of her decision-making in December 2015 was a denial that any of these biases existed. For Løj, the challenges of the context sufficed to explain the perceived failures. In her view, UNMISS had provided an optimal answer to the challenges that year and was performing as well as could be expected. The failure to fully account for problems in decision-making, and a desperation to justify a world view that made sense in the accepted bounded rationality, meant that UNMISS again ignored critical problems. As a result, 2016 would be a disaster year for UN peacekeeping that would again bring worldwide attention to the country.

UNMISS under attack . . . again

February 2016

After the peace agreement was signed at the end of August 2015, there was a fall in violence. To those who were looking for it, the lower tempo of conflict was evidence of the success of the political agreement, the possibility that the worst might be over and a situation in which finally there was a peace to build. A contrary view held by me, and many within the humanitarian community, was that the agreement was critically undermined by a lack of good faith on either side and the fall in conflict looked more like a tactical breather. By the time the agreement was signed, gains from the government offensives in Upper Nile and Unity in 2015 had slowed as easy targets diminished and the militias that had been supporting the SPLA retreated with the plunder that they had gained over the preceding months. The peace agreement also coincided with a period of the year that was normally associated with lower levels of conflict when the culmination of the rainy season constrained mobility. At the same time, focus was shifting that suggested that even as large operations in Upper Nile and Unity were being scaled down, new arenas of conflict were emerging in areas that had hitherto been relatively unaffected by the war.

In addition to the violence in the Equatorian region of the south, described in the first chapter, there were increasing incidents around Wau in Western Bahr e Ghazal. As in the Equatorias, these also related to tensions between some of the local community and the perceived encroachment of neighbouring Dinka communities supported by a partial government administration. The local community were comprised of the Luo and the Fertit. 'Fertit' is a catch-all term to describe a diverse number of communities that largely inhabit areas of Western Bahr e Ghazal. Their identity has become more cohesive through intense competition with neighbouring Dinka communities. Many Fertit have stronger cultural and communal ties with northern Arabic groups; during the Second Civil War, some fought the Sudan People's Liberation Army (SPLA) and attacked Dinka civilians as part of the Army of Peace (Jaysh al-Salam), and later through other Khartoum-supported militias. At independence, Garang's 'Big Tent' policy of reconciliation extended to these communities in the west, but tensions persisted. In 2012, violence erupted during protests when the government moved the administrative centre of Wau County from the city of Wau to the much smaller town of Baggari, in a move that was interpreted among many Fertit as a way to marginalize their influence in the most important urban centre in the region. Those tensions festered during the civil war after 2013. The national security services became increasingly aggressive to perceived dissent, and when Dinka pastoralists moved into Western Bahr e Ghazal at the end of 2015, the SPLA were partial in defending the rights of the cattle herders at the expense of the local community. A self-defence force known as the *Fertit Lions* emerged, aligning itself with Machar's SPLA/iO.[1] The incidents in the Equatorias and Western Bahr e Ghazal were sufficiently large that they offered clear and worrying signs of protracted conflict taking root in those areas. They were also evidence that opposition to the government was spreading, creating an expanded scope in the geography and number of individuals involved in the national war.

At the start of 2016, I did a presentation for senior diplomats using the rising number and scale of incidents in these areas to suggest that, along with the inherent weaknesses within the peace agreement, a return to an expanded version of the war over the forthcoming months was more likely than not. The presentation was met with a mixture of scepticism and resignation. The sceptics suggested that the carefully prepared data, graphs and maps that I used to support my argument did not elevate my analysis out of opinion. They spoke more warmly about the assessments of their diplomatic peers who at that time were directly engaged in the peace negotiations and had an abundance of anecdotal reassurances that contradicted my more quantitative assessments. Those who were more resigned were those who had been in the country longer and were leerier of being caught out in the way that they had in 2013. However, even among those with a more realistic outlook, the peace agreement had become 'the only option', regardless of how bleak its prospects were. That perspective was privately and publicly reiterated constantly during this period, presumably as an attempt to create a zero-sum imperative that diplomats hoped the belligerent parties would be forced to accept. However, their gambit lacked conviction, and time and again the international community accepted damaging compromises to the process that suggested there were almost no circumstances in which they would abandon the agreement or confront the signatories of it in a way that might cause them to abandon it. As the situation in 2016 unravelled, it became increasingly difficult to distinguish between whether saving *the peace* or saving *the peace agreement* was the priority decision-making frame of senior decision-makers.

In this chapter, I will examine the willingness of UNMISS to also overlook the flaws of the Agreement for the Resolution of Conflict in South Sudan (ARCSS) in preference of an overly optimistic interpretation of the potential of the agreement to positively impact the context. Consequently, by 2016 it was already quietly downgrading its commitment at the protection of civilian (POC) sites including in Malakal, where tensions were rising to create a high likelihood of localized violence. When an attack on UNMISS took place there in February, the staff were unprepared and made another series of poor decisions. In the conclusion, I will suggest that these mistakes existed within a context in which UNMISS decision-makers, operating under a specific bounded rationality, continued to make emerging threats to civilians a peripheral concern. A lack of urgency among more junior UNMISS officials to fix deficiencies at the protection sites mirrored senior reluctance to invest further in the POC site concept, in a display of groupthink.

Planning for better days

Barely a month after the signing of the peace agreement, Secretary General Ban pre-empted a successful outcome for the peace process and made recommendations on the future of the UNMISS strategy in November 2015. He suggested that UNMISS had

> an opportunity to rescale the perimeter security provided by the military so that a portion of the resources can be diverted to achieve greater projection to areas of displacement, return and resettlement.[2]

The findings were based on a 'troop-to-task' review but the logic behind the conclusion is unclear. As the failure in Unity showed, UNMISS had been effectively limited to its bases in the period prior to the peace agreement. Despite the qualified success of finally establishing the Leer temporary operating base (TOB) in November, UNMISS had yet to show significantly improved mobility. Violations of the Status of Forces Agreement (SOFA) remained high with restrictions persisting on the United Nations Mission in South Sudan's (UNMISS's) land, air and river operations. The assumptions of the strategic review appear to have been based on a hope that the mission's relationship with the government would improve significantly under the agreement. It did not, and access constraints remained in place. Moreover, the demand for protection at its bases had dramatically increased in 2015. During the year, the number of people on the sites doubled to 200,000.[3] Viewed from a rational actor perspective, this might have provided evidence that the sites required greater focus and attention especially as in most instances those rises closely correlated to attacks on civilians in nearby areas. With a sustainable peace yet to be practically secured, the POC sites remained important. However, from the UN perspective, that was focused on reduction of its exposure at the POC sites, the rising numbers were less rationally perceived as evidence of an increase in humanitarian pull factors as people sought services, as seen during Løj's submissions to the UNSC, the previous year (see Chapter 6).

In support of the UN's preferred narrative around the POC sites, a myth developed that portrayed them as the reason for UN failure in the country. An increasingly common refrain from UNMISS staff was that it was the POC sites, rather than its own reticence or government obstruction, that prevented the mission from proactive deployments such as that which failed to take place in Unity. UNMISS staff complained that 40 to 45 per cent of its forces were tied to the protection of POC sites severely limiting its ability to project force.[4] The number does not correspond to any publicly available documents or observations made of the POC sites at the time. About 40 to 45 percent of UNMISS forces would suggest that in 2016 about 5,000 soldiers were dedicated across the five main POC sites at a density of approximately one peacekeeper to every forty civilians. However, anyone who has stood on a berm at the perimeter of one of the sites can attest to how thinly guarded they were. Reports from the time suggest that watchtowers were on occasions left empty, even at sites where armed intrusions were regularly taking place.[5] Incursions by armed men from outside the site could not only happen without detection but there could be lengthy intervals before military personnel responded to critical incidents. At an incident in Bentiu in May 2015, it took forty-five minutes for UNMISS to respond to a breach by armed soldiers.[6] Furthermore, if the number cited is to be believed, it creates even more questions about the failure of UNMISS to prevent attacks at POC sites as occurred in 2014 and 2016 given the extent of personnel dedicated to them. In those instances, eyewitnesses should have seen hundreds of UNMISS soldiers abandoning their posts rather than the few dozen that they reported on each occasion. Publicly available planning documents submitted to the UN Secretariat in 2014–15 put the actual proportion of UNMISS military capacity dedicated to POC site protection at a more modest 11 per cent.[7] That planning figure even fell in absolute terms the following year, despite an uplift in soldiers and the doubling in size of the sites.[8]

These numbers that were included in planning documents need to be qualified by the fact that they were prepared in advance of the year to which they apply. A criticism of the way that peacekeeping is structured is the way in which a mission is forced to create budgets, and corresponding strategies, far in advance of an implementing year even in environments that are highly changeable. In an interview, one UN official complained about the pressure on UNMISS to be constantly planning when flexibility and discretionary budgets were needed:

> I think for me it was bound up with the fact that the missions always feel so forward-looking, even though they tend to be in crisis mode. Everything is about, okay, so where are we going to be in two years, three years, four years, what's the plan?[9]

The planned numbers are evidence of a constant pressure to make overly optimistic assessments about a future that showed the potential for UNMISS success. However, the numbers also correspond more closely to the observed reality that suggests UNMISS was regularly fielding lower levels of soldiers to protect the POC sites than it sometimes claimed.

A tendency to downplay the need for UNMISS to protect the POC sites from external threats can be seen in other aspects of its planning. In a tabletop exercise to rehearse against threats to Malakal POC site in September 2015, two scenarios were discussed. In both, the only threat to civilians was that posed by the civilians themselves. The first involved a violent protest by internally displaced persons (IDPs) and, the second, the possibility of intercommunal fighting within the site.[10] While these were realistic scenarios, an independent UN investigation later found that contingency planning by UNMISS in Malakal was consistently targeted in a way that did not give appropriate credence to the full range of threats.[11] In reliving its mistakes from Bor, UNMISS gave greater weight to those internal threats that had become more prominent in its imagination than the external threat that the POC sites had been created in response to.

UNMISS also showed ambivalence to the POC sites in its attitude to maintaining perimeter security infrastructure. When the Bentiu POC site expanded in May 2015, the construction that Løj was alleged to have privately opposed, UNMISS disputed its responsibility to pay for the perimeter security infrastructure during the summer of 2015, even as violence in Unity created urgency around the work.[12] Fencing around portions of the site would not be completed until 2016. At Malakal, humanitarians also reported that the mission had 'become lax in repairing fences', despite having a military engineering capability responsible for such repairs.[13] In 2016, UNMISS further demonstrated its desire to limit its exposure to new responsibilities at the POC sites. When tensions between the Fertit community and the SPLA led to serious violence in Wau in June 2016, as many as 20,000 people fled to the UNMISS base in the town. As they had done in Yambio the previous summer, UNMISS kept its gates shut. Too scared to return to their homes, the civilians camped next to UNMISS, forcing the mission to set up a perimeter around them. While the site looked much like any other POC site, UNMISS insisted on the convoluted title *Protection of Civilian Area Adjacent to UNMISS* (Wau POC AA site). While notionally still under UNMISS's protection, by siting the civilians outside of its base, UNMISS placed civilians in an area that was initially physically and legally less protected. The change in nomenclature is also notable given that the term *POC site* was already meant to convey impermanence.

Evidence from those involved in civil–military coordination suggest that with a hardening of attitudes in the mission, the frequent turnover of military staff meant that incoming personnel in 2015 and 2016 were even less sympathetic to humanitarian perspectives. A humanitarian staff member responsible for negotiating civil–military coordination noted a particular change in the lead-up to 2016:

> You have these troop rotations on the military side. During my time, I think I was working with three different chiefs of staff and two different teams on the UNMISS side. What we were able to do, and how we were able to coordinate really was just was dependent on the personalities who were occupying these positions. The first year we were pretty good, at least on influencing the military, which then subsequently, with the change of personnel, turned into frankly, a major disaster, where we weren't able to reach the military any longer and to have the military listen to our concerns from a humanitarian perspective. That was more I would say, mid-2015 to 2016.[14]

Fault lines in Malakal

The signing of the peace agreement in August 2015 had been marked by bad faith. President Kiir had refused to sign at the official ceremony in Addis Ababa. He only signed a week later at a fraught and confused ceremony in Juba, at which hardliners like Michael Makuei stormed out in disgust.[15] Paul Malong also expressed his opposition, and Kiir was forced to attach an addendum of reservations to the agreement. Ceasefire breaches took place within days of the signing. Many of those initial breaches took place close to Malakal in Upper Nile, where tensions had been simmering since the government was denied a key strategic victory against the SPLA/iO earlier in the year. The government's bitter failure came following a defection by a militia comprised of members of the Shilluk community. They had abandoned the SPLA cause following the murder of one of their senior commanders by a militia from the neighbouring Dinka Padang.

The long-standing rivalry between the Shilluk and Dinka Padang related to competition over dominance of territories in Upper Nile. For the Shilluk, their claims to land around the White Nile related to a kingdom that had existed for the better part of 300 years between the fifteenth and nineteenth centuries. A Shilluk King remains a significant leader that connects that community to its historical claims.[16] However, more recently the Dinka Padang through its closer communal and patronage ties with the government had been better able to press its own claims in parts of Upper Nile, especially along the east bank of the Nile, that it sees as its preserve. In May 2015, Shilluk forces known as the Agwelek, and led by the formidable Johnson Olony, marched on Malakal, which lay at the heart of the contested claims between the two communities. After occupying the town for a short time, the SPLA pushed the militia back to within a few kilometres. After the signing of the peace agreement, skirmishing around positions close to Malakal continued and were the subject of heated early discussions under the Transitional Security Arrangement (TSA) in September.[17]

The government stoked further tensions when it unilaterally redrew the boundaries of national states in a way that was not only a major breach of the peace agreement but also limited Shilluk influence in Upper Nile. The contested Malakal was placed in a state that was overwhelmingly Dinka Padang. In December, a Dinka Padang SPLA Commander was appointed as governor of the new Eastern Nile State to which Malakal now belonged. Almost immediately the opposition accused him of militarizing the area, recruiting and mobilizing Dinka Padang militia groups, and then manoeuvring those forces close to Malakal to instigate fighting with nearby SPLA/iO positions.[18] UNMISS also started receiving reports of Dinka civilians being transported by the government to parts of Eastern Nile State, in a pattern of behaviour that was later described as 'population engineering' by the *Commission on Human Rights in South Sudan*.[19] On 1 February 2016, the Eastern Nile State purged the administration's new civil service of Shilluk and Nuer, depriving many of the people who still lived in Malakal, albeit within the confines of the POC site, the livelihoods that connected them to the area. By February, the remaining substantial links among non-Dinka to Malakal was largely within the UNMISS POC site.

The powder keg

If political and military tensions outside were moving ever closer to the Malakal POC site, the situation inside it was equally tense. Whereas other POC sites had seen some reductions in the number of residents in the last months of 2015, the continued tensions in Upper Nile meant that in Malakal the numbers remained close to its peak of 48,000. This was more than double what it had been at the start of 2015.[20] As a consequence, the site became dangerously overcrowded with only approximately 10 square metres available per person, about a third of the internationally accepted standard.[21] When a fire broke out in January 2016, as many as 1,000 shelters were destroyed, increasing pressure on the residents. Malakal POC site was also unique in the mix of communities that made up its population. As well as the Nuer and Shilluk, it housed the only significant population of Dinka civilians under UNMISS protection. Although the communities lived separately, the tight conditions inevitably led to regular conflicts that had to be diffused by UNMISS, sometimes by force, including the deployment of riot police and tear gas.[22]

Following an increase in clashes between the SPLA and SPLA/iO close to Malakal in the first week of February, again in breach of the ceasefire agreement, the SPLA began blocking access to the POC site. UNMISS internally reported to New York that it had begun to see increased SPLA movements close to the site.[23] Médecins sans frontières (MSF) staff also reported increasing tensions along with a growing number of weapons confiscations at the site gates.[24] Humanitarians were sufficiently concerned about this new escalation that they requested UNMISS, on 8 February 2016, to produce a risk mitigation plan. UNMISS is alleged to have declined the request.[25]

The breach

On 16 February, two men, believed to belong to a Dinka Padang militia, attempted to enter the POC site. Following a search by UN security guards, they were found to be smuggling rifle magazines into the camp. As UN police questioned them, SPLA waiting just outside intervened. They assaulted UN staff, allowing the men to escape. On hearing about the incident, Nuer and Shilluk camp leaders expressed concern to the UN about weapons within the Dinka section. However, no follow-up actions appear to have been taken. Tensions were reported to be high on the site during the rest of the day, and UNMISS deployed security guards and Formed Police Unit (FPU) to intervene in an altercation between Shilluk and Dinka youths in which sticks and stones were used as weapons.[26]

On the morning of 17 February, UNMISS security reported a breach in the perimeter fence which was being controlled and kept open by Dinka residents. A group of SPLA soldiers were reported to be congregated by it. Additional deployments of UNMISS military were made along the perimeter nearby, but they did not secure the breach and the hole was not repaired.[27] An altercation in the evening between Dinka and Shilluk youths triggered more violence. Gunshots were heard at 10.30 pm. UNMISS withdrew the FPU from the POC site to reinforce the main base. An emergency crisis management team (CMT) was convened at midnight with the eventual decision that armoured personnel carriers (APCs) be deployed at flashpoints. However, fighting persisted and escalated. At 2.30 am, grenades were thrown inside the Nuer section of the site.[28] The soldiers inside some of the APCs showed an unwillingness to move in areas that were affected by fighting, including refusing to accompany an UNMISS fire truck responding to a fire.[29]

During the morning of 18 February, UNMISS reported that Dinka civilians were leaving the POC site through the breach in the perimeter fence. The CMT reconvened at 8.00 am and decided to continue 'robust patrols'. There is no evidence that the team sought to secure and/or repair the breach or establish that their soldiers understood their responsibility to engage with lethal force against imminent threats to civilians. At 9.30 am, UNMISS held a meeting with the state governor and SPLA sector commander. UNMISS were criticized by government officials for their failure to protect Dinka civilians in the previous day's violence. At 10.00 am, UNMISS reported SPLA soldiers entering the breach. UNMISS sentries posted less than 10 metres away abandoned their positions. Soon after, fighting inside the POC site resumed with an even greater intensity. SPLA soldiers were witnessed to have been involved in the fighting while also carrying jerrycans of petrol and fashioning Molotov cocktails. They subsequently burned down large sections of the site. In total 3,700 family's shelters were destroyed as well as multiple humanitarian facilities.[30]

During the morning, an MSF clinic was dealing with 'mass casualties' on the main base.[31] In front of a gate leading from the POC site to the main base, a large crowd of several thousand had gathered. UNMISS were reported to have kept the gate closed and deployed a tank to reinforce it, preventing IDPs from escaping the violence. Humanitarians were reported to have repeatedly asked UNMISS to open the gate,[32] while civilians were described as, 'pounding on the gate, begging to be let through'.[33] The mission only relented when the fighting got closer and desperate IDPs began to climb the fence at about 12.00 pm. Only at 1.41 pm, when a few SPLA soldiers tried to enter the UNMISS main base, were peacekeepers ordered to fire on the intruders. According to the subsequent Board of Inquiry, officers refused to carry out the order without written authorization. The UN sector commander sent an email to all UN military confirming the rules of engagement and ordering the soldiers to use all necessary means to respond. That was then reconfirmed by the D/SRSG (Political), who was the officer-in-charge, in the absence of SRSG Løj who was out of the country. UNMISS finally returned fire at 3.45 pm, almost sixteen hours after the first shots. In the end, it took only forty-five minutes for UNMISS to re-establish control and force the intruders out of the site.[34] Approximately thirty civilians were reported to have been killed, and a large section of the site was destroyed. However, the extent of the immediate investigations in the aftermath of the violence seems to have been even more cursory than those that took place in Bor in 2014, and the final death toll was likely higher.

The investigation

Unlike at Bor in 2014, an international journalist had been on site during the attack. As the incident took place, UNMISS asked that he leave and return to Juba, denying him the opportunity to report on the violence. The journalist told me that UNMISS staff helped him avoid UN security, to allow him to gather information for his report:

> There was one security guy who for these five days kept trying to find me. I was hiding more or less because I basically didn't respond to the request to me to leave. I just hid for five days, which as you know, is not really possible to do without help from everybody at the UN. Everybody was helping me out and it was really fascinating, people on the ground in Malakal trying to get the information out to me, giving me everything that they had and the [UNMISS] spokesperson's office, trying everything they could to suppress the information from getting out.[35]

The attempt to limit the journalist corresponds to a general tightening of restrictions as to how UNMISS's story was externally communicated. The willingness of UNMISS staff to help the journalist contravene those restrictions is indicative of the extent to which individuals, with divergent opinions felt marginalized from their own organizational priorities.

As the story became public, the Secretary General convened an investigation. As had been the case in Bor, UNMISS had had more than enough soldiers to defend the perimeter. With at least two infantry battalions and additional companies of engineering and other military units, there would have been more than 1,000 soldiers capable of withstanding the lightly armed incursion that took place.[36] However, the situation in Malakal again casts doubt on the level of personnel that UNMISS claimed it routinely dedicated to perimeter defences. The subsequent investigation criticized UNMISS's posture and tactics, describing many of the same failures that had taken place at Bor less than two years previously. The investigating team highlighted the lax attitude to perimeter security, both patrolling and physical, and misconceived priorities in its tabletop exercises. They berated command decisions, particularly regarding the delayed use of force. They also accused UNMISS of being aware of the threat and yet not reacting:

> In relation to security/intelligence information, the Board found that the Mission has a relatively comprehensive early warning system in place. However, the translation of that information into appropriate and/or timely actions remains elusive.[37]

From those sections of the report that were made public, the investigators avoided commenting on the role of UNMISS's management in setting the decision-making environment. That avoidance of public criticism of its senior civilian staff is consistent throughout official reflections on decision-making mistakes within the mission.

Notwithstanding the many valid tactical recommendations of the report, its larger contribution to the strategic direction of the mission was its failure to offer an interpretation of the context that was fundamentally different from that already being pushed by the UN. The Board of Inquiry provided as its first recommendation that the UN immediately 'review the concept of Protection of Civilian sites . . . so as to avoid creation of false expectations'. This fits with UNMISS's belief, persistently stated in 2015, that its capabilities were incompatible with its role at the POC sites. Internally, the UN amplified that component of the report. On the same day the findings of the review were released, on 17 June, Bank Ki Moon circulated a separate memo to the UNSC prepared by Department of Peacekeeping Operations (DPKO), providing an overview of the negative peacekeeping experience of the UN at the POC sites. That document, entitled *Challenges, lessons learned and implications of the protection of civilians sites in South Sudan*, was a restatement of the recommendations of the strategic review it had presented in November 2015 that had sought to find ways to decrease, rather than strengthen, UNMISS commitment to protecting the POC sites.[38] As happened with Bor, the main takeaway of the tragedy was to reinforce the existing belief that the POC sites themselves were to blame for the UN's failure. That will have diminished the urgency to address the other tactical failings that related to reasonable expectations on the mission's capabilities and highlighted in the investigation.

Conclusions

The signing of a peace agreement in 2015 provided confirming evidence to preferred understandings within an organizational bounded rationality. For Løj and her *values*, it would have created the possibility of space for the kind of peacebuilding and state-building support that better aligned with her available experiences of peacekeeping missions and a corresponding withdrawal of continued involvement in the problematic POC sites. Likewise, for UN Secretariat *interests*, it created the first steps to normalizing the situation in the country and allowed it to publicly argue for its withdrawal of resources from the POC sites. These values and interests were evident in statements made by the UN in late 2015 and evidence of UN obstruction or lethargy when considering improvements to perimeter security at the sites.

Through a *confirmation bias*, the lack of UNMISS mobility in 2015 was incorrectly explained through interpreting its role in perimeter security as evidence of a burden that prevented it from carrying out operations outside of its bases. That showed a disinclination to focus on other reasons for their lack of mobility, of which troop reluctance and government obstruction were much more significant. The official planning records suggest that UNMISS overstated its troop commitment to the POC sites and that forces were available for operations outside of its bases but were not utilized. However, in trying to make the belief *real*, evidence of the importance of the mission's role in the protection of civilians struggled to gain prominence in the leadership's understanding of the context. The mission overstated the pull factors of humanitarian services associated within the sites. It was unable to appropriately absorb the information that suggested that its only significant role in the country of protection of civilians was its static protection of the POC sites and that this role continued to be vital, and its necessity was even rising in places like Malakal.

An *availability bias* meant that the mission could not properly reflect on its past failure at Bor, having marginalized the importance of that incident in UNMISS mindsets. Lessons from that earlier incident had not been properly absorbed into the organization to create urgency around resolving known weaknesses in perimeter defences or respond proactively to escalating threats that were repeated in the incident at Malakal. In Malakal, the time lag between the start of the incursion and the response was considerably longer, suggesting that the performance there was even more suboptimal than it had been at Bor.

Evidence that these leadership perspectives were impacting more junior-level staff can be seen in a hardening of attitudes that were less sympathetic to humanitarian perspectives. This can be seen in the squabbles that emerged around perimeter security infrastructure in Bentiu, military staff less amenable to coordinate with humanitarians as well as a lack of responsiveness to contingency planning in Malakal. This created a combative relationship with humanitarians that mirrored leadership attitudes and made it difficult for the mission to accept external guidance on how better to perform its protection role at the tactical level. This *groupthink* can also be seen in the rebellious actions of some UNMISS staff in the aftermath of the violence in Malakal in helping a journalist. Such dissent had become more likely as marginalized staff felt incorrect perspectives had become so dominant, as to make challenging them within the system meaningless.

A more significant cost to decision-making from the way that the UN subsequently interpreted the events of February 2016 was a deepening investment in a sunk-cost fallacy. Notwithstanding the criticism of tactical elements of the mission, the report into the disaster in Malakal largely avoided discomfiting conclusions that their senior strategic decision-making structure was critically flawed. Focus on the concept of the POC site seems likely to have encouraged an erroneous focus on the object of the task, rather than the organization's failure to fulfil reasonable expectations of its performance. The full importance of lessons that could have been learned from Malakal were missed as can be seen in its continued reluctant attitude in the establishment of the Wau POC AA in June. UNMISS stuck with an interpretation in which the POC sites, and by extension the need for a generally robust protection of civilians' posture, were increasingly unnecessary as superficial progress in the peace agreement was achieved. That mindset was critical to the catastrophe that followed only a few months after the attack on Malakal.

Peace fails

July 2016

In June 2016, I joined the International Organization for Migration (IOM) as their South Sudan conflict analyst. The transition brought me into an organization that existed somewhere between the worlds of the NGOs and the United Nations Mission in South Sudan (UNMISS). Although, at the time, IOM was not a fully integrated agency of the UN,[1] it operated much like other UN humanitarian agencies such as the World Food Programme (WFP), the United Nations Children's Fund (UNICEF) or the United Nations High Commissioner for Refugees (UNHCR), and was part of the UN family of organizations. Beyond the absence of soldiers and armoured vehicles, these agencies could be distinguished from their sibling peacekeeper mission through the blue lettering on the vehicles that they drove, compared to UNMISS's black. This cosmetic difference signifies a more fundamental distinction between the two sets of actors. The so-called *UN blue* humanitarian actors not only solely work on humanitarian activities but also are guided by principles of humanity, impartiality, neutrality and independence. *UN black* peacekeepers are also impartial. However, they are not expected to be neutral, to allow them the ability to execute their mandate. Nor are they necessarily guided by independence. Not only are they subject to the instructions of the UNSC, but they operate under principles of consent that can constrain the way they act in relation to the host government.

Operationally, distinction between these two sections of the UN has implications. Each must use its own transport and is not permitted to travel by the other's vehicles. A myriad of guidelines cover what circumstances other assets could occasionally be shared. With the increased prominence of the protection of civilian (POC) sites, where peacekeepers and humanitarians worked side by side, these became more important as well as contentious, leading to arguments such as those that surrounded the construction of Bentiu's perimeter fence. However, organizational pressure within the system also existed to push the *blue* and *black* together. UN humanitarians and peacekeepers operate under the same staff security architecture, administered by the UN Department of Safety and Security (UNDSS). The various leaders of the UN also sat together on the UN Country Team in which it is likely that shared understandings of the context were developed. And while the Special Representative of the Secretary General (SRSG) could not instruct humanitarians, they were nonetheless the Secretary General's representative and thus occupied the most senior role in a system to which UN agencies belonged. A 'One UN' policy, aimed at delivering system-wide coherence, has more recently been used to justify a blurring of distinctions including through the role of the triple-hatted D/SRSG (RC/HC), who exists as both humanitarian and peacekeeper. During my time in New York, I heard senior UN leaders within the Secretariat refer to the principle of distinction only in disparaging terms. Their perception was that it chiefly existed as a means for UN humanitarian agencies to maintain independence from Secretariat control. Any senior staff asserting the importance of distinction would likely find a cool reception at UNHQ, including within the Secretary General's office.

In South Sudan, the cultures of individual UN agencies depended greatly on how they were run locally. Some heads of UN agencies showed a high level of deference to UNMISS perspectives and shared a disdain for continued support within the POC sites. In IOM, I was fortunate that the senior leadership continued to prize their independence, showed less deference to a UN system that they were being absorbed into and were much more keen to be responsive to evidence from the ground. IOM maintained a Level 3 (L3) emergency status when others deferred to the decision of the UN-led Inter Agency Standing Committee (IASC), in May 2016, to stand it down. An L3 is reserved for the most serious humanitarian crises, and, within the UN system, allows agencies to circumvent some human resource and procurement rules and guidance that can slow an emergency response. IOM made the most of the flexibility that the designation allowed, especially in its recruitment processes that were freed from the usual stringency of normal procedures. Specifically, it was more likely to directly hire staff that had previously worked in the country, usually with NGOs, and had proven experience of the context. This contrasted with other agencies that relied on hiring from within their system individuals that were technically proficient but often came from outside the country and had less understanding of the context. I was hired under such circumstances, and at IOM I was given free rein to conduct analysis as I saw fit. Over 2016, this allowed me to develop an interpretation of the conflict that diverged widely from that offered by senior UNMISS officials. This chapter is an attempt to explain that divergence.

In this chapter, I will discuss in greater detail how UNMISS became increasingly tied to an overly optimistic interpretation of the 2015 peace agreement. Decision-making minimized the urgency of easily actionable contingency planning and ignored threats that suggested a catastrophic breakdown in violence was likely. When that did take place in Juba in July 2016, UNMISS leadership had become so fixed on a single understanding of the context, encouraged by UNSC and UN Secretariat interests, that it was unable to properly evaluate the implications of new information that suggested an escalation of the national conflict would follow. In the conclusions, I will suggest that a fixation on the peace agreement and legitimacy of the government, as part of a bounded rationality, created bias that undermined Løj's ability to react to changes that were taking place. Even as the situation worsened and the appropriateness of the peacekeeping strategy began to be at variance from an understanding of the context that was observed by most other actors, a sunk-cost fallacy had taken hold within the UN that made it difficult for her to deviate from the suboptimal strategies that the mission had pursued up to that point.

The insubstantial peace

By August 2015, international diplomats had been negotiating off and on in Addis Ababa for almost twenty months. In that time, significant bills were being accumulated at the expensive hotels that were chosen as the venues for negotiations, as well as generous per diems for the representatives. The cost for the first year alone was reported to be $20 million.[2] International diplomats grumbled that their investment, both political and material, had generated little. They pointed with frustration to the narrow interests of regional powers and the intransigence and ineptitude of the South Sudanese negotiators.[3] By 2015, what could be agreed upon was adapted from a boiler plate of the kind of international agreement that satisfied a low-enough bar to get warring parties to lay down their weapons.[4] Critical elements were missing, and the Agreement for the Resolution of Conflict in South Sudan (ARCSS) lacked 'oversight mechanisms' and was 'ambiguous on matters of security and de-mobilization'.[5]

That lack of oversight was exacerbated by a UN that showed limited interest in taking a significant role. Løj remained true to her promise the previous year that UNMISS did not intend to insert itself into the process (see Chapter 6). There is little evidence that UNMISS representatives sought to shape the agreement in a way that its mission might effectively complement the proposed peace strategy. When a suggestion was tabled that a UN force play a security role in a demilitarized Juba, the UNMISS representative was reported as flatly rejecting the proposal citing the limitations of their mandate.[6] It was likely with some relief that the government also ultimately rejected the proposal. Instead, the role of UNMISS was reduced to one of logistical support to the IGAD-sponsored Joint Monitoring and Evaluation Commission (JMEC) and its operational component, the Ceasefire and Transitional Security Arrangements Monitoring Verification Mechanism (CTSAMVM). Financial and human resources support to JMEC and CTSAMVM was provided by the United States, Germany, the UK, Norway, Denmark, China, Japan and the European Union. However, the IGAD mechanism lacked the kind of organizational depth in expertise, resources and political clout that the UN possessed. Despite this, they were asked to police a peace agreement that would have been challenging for even a large, experienced and well-equipped peacekeeping force.

A long-standing tenet of the peace negotiations had been that the capital should be demilitarized save a few hundred personnel to act as bodyguards for Kiir and Machar. At the last minute, the government rejected the principle of demilitarization. Under pressure from the offensives in Unity, Machar let the demand go and put off the discussion about how militarized Juba should be until after the agreement was signed in August 2015. Under the subsequent Transitional Security Arrangement (TSA) agreed in October, almost 5,000 soldiers were agreed as being allowed to be in the capital during the transitional period.[7] About a third would be from Machar's SPLA/iO and the rest from the government. While IGAD sought to clarify that additional government security services in Juba, which included armed police, wildlife services and even the fire brigade, should be disarmed, there was no mechanism to ensure that that took place. Equally, CTSAMVM had limited means to confirm that additional military forces belonging to the government stayed outside of the capital's 25-kilometre exclusion zone. There was no way to know how many armed men were in Juba during the transitional period, leading to widespread scepticism of the workability of the TSA. In a document that I wrote while still with the NGO forum, and circulated to organizations in South Sudan that included UNMISS in October 2015, I suggested:

> It is unclear how this number of armed men can be successfully monitored let alone contained, should hostilities break out again. Already Juba, under the

auspices of a peace agreement, may be looking less secure than it had been during war.[8]

As armed SPLA/iO began arriving in Juba in April 2016, supported by UNMISS, regional diplomats started to express concern. In a leaked cable from April 2016, the Kenyan ambassador suggested that the SPLA and SPLA/iO, 'are competing on the military front, trying to outdo each other by amassing troops and armaments around the capital' with the consequence that Juba was 'more dangerous than ever'.[9]

What mechanisms did exist to create discipline in the implementation of the peace agreement were treated with contempt. The government was reported to not be complying with even minimal levels of monitoring of its forces. It was also accused of regularly harassing peace monitors including illegally detaining them and obstructing access.[10] The most brazen attack by the government on the peace monitors came in April, when government security services interrupted a meeting of international diplomats in Juba. At the meeting, they attempted to arrest the deputy head of JMEC, accusing him of 'misrepresenting' the government. A human chain of diplomats around the hapless official offered only temporary protection as he was expelled from the country soon after.[11]

A war by any other name

As suggested in the previous chapter, there was an overall fall in the conflict following the signing of the peace agreement in August 2015. However, this was the result of the end of large-scale military campaigning in areas that had represented the frontlines of the conflict since 2013. By 2016, smaller outbreaks of violence were occurring in areas that had hitherto been regarded as peaceful and under government control. CTSAMVM declared that the violence in the Equatorias and Western Bahr e Ghazal constituted a widespread disregard for the terms of the ceasefire. By March 2016, it described the conflict as 'spreading'.[12] The government furiously contested CTSAMVM's interpretation. It stressed the law enforcement nature of its operations in the country against 'criminals' that were not covered by the ARCSS and harassed monitoring missions that tried to visit these areas.[13] Progress on the technical elements of the agreement was also difficult. Vital committees tasked with negotiating the transitional arrangements became bogged down in wrangling over their composition.[14] Kiir unilaterally changed the national administration, by increasing the number of states from ten to twenty-eight in a move IGAD declared a significant violation of the peace agreement that had been based on power sharing within ten states.[15] The change in state administration also stalled substantive conversations in the various committees between the SPLA and SPLA/iO with the latter complaining that the changes represented an attempt to engineer a more favourable arrangement from the implementation of the peace agreement by the President.

Looking for green shoots

While the UN acknowledged the problems that existed in the political process, it remained non-committal on its broader implications. In both Secretary General Ban's reports in the first half of 2016, he highlighted 'positive developments' and 'noticeable progress' in the implementation of the ARCSS. Referring to the spread of violence to other parts of the country, Ban noted in June that the situation was merely 'tense' with the presence of unnamed 'armed groups' primarily to blame.[16]

The UN's taciturn public posture undermined the starker warnings about the state of security in the country. Ban's failure to connect the violence with the broader political context also ignored the UN's own panel of experts that explicitly linked the armed groups in the south and west to the command structure of the SPLA/iO and supported the JMEC findings that the conflict was spreading in the country.[17] A refusal to be drawn into a narrative of ongoing conflict, during a supposed transitional period to peace, also reflected pressures on staff within the mission in Juba. One UN official remembered the period as one in which

> Everybody was pushing this line of peace, peace, peace, peacebuilding. It was lonely to be that voice of dissent saying that everybody else you're listening to is wrong because they're just relaying the messaging that is coming from effectively government counterparts who were towing the SPLA line.[18]

The publicly positive line was also echoed among diplomats, reflecting a desperation by the international community to show success around policies that it had committed ever-greater political and financial resources to. Machar had initially refused to return to the capital complaining that under the arrangements of the TSA it was 'suicidal'.[19] For that astute observation, he was roundly condemned by the United States, which accused him of prolonging the conflict.[20] The government's willingness to receive Machar had been equally underwhelming, and it was only another intervention by the United States pushing JMEC to table a 'take it or leave it' proposal to the conflict parties that Machar unenthusiastically returned and the government unenthusiastically received him.[21] Diplomats hailed his return a milestone that they took some credit for, and 'a palpable mood of optimism' existed for a while among ambassadors in the capital.[22] Ban proclaimed to the UNSC in June Machar's arrival, and the technical start of a thirty-month transitional period, as the primary success of the previous six months. However, Machar's presence in Juba not only raised tensions but he became an obstructive presence in the implementation of a peace agreement already mired in arguments.[23] A more rational accounting of Machar's return should have noted decreased political will and increased risks of violence. The pressure to implement a peace agreement without reference to the context in which it was taking place was making a return to war more likely.

Considerable risk

Reports from interviewees suggested that UNMISS staff were aware of the emergence of a more dangerous phase in the implementation of the peace agreement. However, in characteristic style, it struggled to articulate knowledge of those threats into action. One senior staff member said that she had seen documents from UNMISS JMAC that 'clearly set out' likely scenarios of large-scale violence in Juba.[24] Even SRSG Løj, notwithstanding her publicly bullish views of the peace process, was privately expressing doubt. In an internal communication to Department of Peacekeeping Operations (DPKO) on 1 July 2016, she suggested that the risk of the peace process collapsing was 'considerable'.[25] However, the full extent of such concerns was never heard in public submissions to the UNSC. Nor did they lead to any significant change in posture.

Contingency planning around known threats did not take place. Increased patrols were not deployed proactively. The responsibility to engage with deadly force to protect civilians was not reiterated. Contingency plans to protect humanitarian compounds were insufficient. UN House in Juba was notably unprepared, without adequate medical facilities or proper perimeter security infrastructure around the POC site. Perhaps most critically, the UN continued to remain on the political sidelines and did not publicly intervene to warn of the likelihood of an impending conflict. One UNMISS official offered the explanation that the mission found it increasingly difficult to properly evaluate the significance of information about specific threats:

It was like all of the elements are in place for this to combust and go completely sideways, but they had been in place for weeks and weeks without combustion. I feel like a sense of latency certainly developed.[26]

July

On 16 June 2016, government security services shot at Machar's convoy inside the city of Juba. The following week, dozens of civilians were killed, and 70,000 people were displaced following violence in Wau in the west of the country.[27] The president cancelled the country's Independence Day Celebrations due to take place on 9 July. On 2 July, a senior SPLA/iO officer was shot and killed by government security services in Juba. On 7 July, five security services officers were killed during a shootout between SPLA and SPLA/iO at a checkpoint in the city. In two more separate incidents that day, the head of UNESCO was shot, and security services shot multiple times at close range into US embassy vehicles carrying the US Charge d'Affaires.

On 8 July, UNMISS were still not in a high state of readiness. When the SPLA and SPLA/iO clashed outside the Presidential Palace, UNMISS's three most senior leaders (Løj and her two D/SRSGs) were attending separate meetings elsewhere in the city. Much of the UN's efforts on 8 July were spent trying to get those leaders back to base through various government roadblocks, a process that took more than twenty-four hours to complete.[28] A member of the SPLA/iO claimed to me that a call was placed from inside the palace, where Kiir and Machar were sheltering together, requesting that UNMISS intervene. The official suggested that the request was declined.[29] Once the skirmish died down, Machar hurriedly returned to his base close to UN House. Sporadic fighting followed him including the use of small arms fire, mortars and rocket-propelled grenades. On 9 July, there was a lull. In the public part of the official UN investigation into UNMISS during those few days, there is no mention of any tactical or political action taking place at this critical moment. In contrast to the undermanned UNMISS that had been in Juba in 2013, in 2016 the mission now had four infantry battalions and multiple auxiliary companies based in Juba, equipped with light weapons, and armoured vehicles.[30] Yet as the fighting from the presidential palace appeared to spread to other parts of the city, UNMISS's tactical deployment remained essentially unchanged from December 2013. Its peacekeepers were largely confined to base.

On 10 July, the SPLA launched a massive offensive against Machar's headquarters. The extent of the coordination suggested that significant planning had gone into the operation. The SPLA deployed tanks, attack helicopters and its only jet plane. Once the main thrust of that assault ended, the SPLA turned their forces on the rest of the city to destroy perceived pockets of resistance. What followed was large-scale attacks on civilians and their property[31] as well as wholesale looting of humanitarian compounds. WFP's main warehouse in the country was systematically looted by the SPLA, which removed 4,500 tonnes of food and fifty vehicles (enough to feed and move a small army). In total, almost $29 million of food and equipment was taken from the humanitarian community.[32] The SPLA also attacked a compound housing humanitarian staff know as *Terrain*. The report found that successive UNMISS military contingents refused to deploy to the compound less than a kilometre from UN House, despite persistent requests for help.[33] One person was murdered and five gang-raped at the site after the SPLA forced their way into the panic room. The last survivors were only extracted when private security guards were deployed to the compound the following day.[34]

While UNMISS failed to deploy outside, their ability to adequately defend the perimeter of their own base again proved insufficient. The subsequent UN investigation found that the arrangements for physical security around the perimeter of its headquarters had been inadequate with security posts unable to withstand even small arms fire. Peacekeepers again abandoned their positions, and the resultant incursions inside the POC sites killed as many twenty civilians. Two Chinese peacekeepers were also fatally wounded when an RPG was fired at an APC inside the compound. The peacekeepers could have survived their injuries had the base been equipped with an adequate medical facility. However, despite the base being the country's largest, and responsible for protection of one of the biggest POC sites, there was no medical facility with blood transfusion or surgical capacities to attend to the dying soldiers.[35]

After the fighting dissipated from 13 July, assessments were made on the human cost. Tens of thousands had been displaced. While many of those fled to the two UN bases in the city, others concentrated at humanitarian compounds which were left unprotected during the violence. In the first month after the fighting, the UN documented 217 incidents of sexual violence.[36] Some of those incidents were reported to have occurred within sight of UN peacekeepers manning the perimeter of UN House, but they did not intervene.[37] Initial reporting suggested at least 300 people were killed[38] of which 73 were confirmed to have been civilians.[39] However, no reliable assessment exists for the extent of either sexual violence or fatalities, and the respective number in both instances is likely to considerably exceed reporting.

I had first-hand experience of UNMISS's response to protect humanitarian delivery when peacekeepers arrived at the IOM compound, about 600 metres away from its Tomping base, nine days after the start of the fighting and long after the violence had stopped. When they were told that they were not needed, it provoked an angry response with the commanding officer saying that he would report IOM to the SRSG for preventing them from 'doing their job.'

'This is what we're dealing with now'

It is unclear at which stage of the fighting Machar snuck out of the capital, but it must have been sufficiently early that he slipped through the SPLA's security cordon without detection. Once they realized he had gone, the government pursued him south through the countryside over almost forty days. SPLA/iO forces in Central and Western Equatoria fought a rearguard battle that we only received patchy information about. A chronically ill Machar may yet have died in the jungle had it not been for a rescue mission launched by another peacekeeping mission. When he crossed the DRC border, the UN peacekeeping mission MONUSCO mobilized a helicopter to pick him up and provide urgent medical attention. The reasons for MONUSCO's intervention remain shrouded in mystery but UN staff that I spoke to suggested that Machar had personally reached out to senior staff in the mission who had previously worked in South Sudan.

In attempting to justify its actions in attacking and then pursuing Machar, the government opted for an audacious strategy. As it had done in 2013, it argued that its actions were defensive and blamed the SPLA/iO for instigating the violence, despite the latter being vastly outnumbered and outgunned.[40] In Juba, the government rounded up the SPLA/iO politicians who had been left behind. Through what appears to have been a mixture of incentives and intimidation, they persuaded a group, led by Machar's deputy and occasional rival Taban Deng, to declare themselves the *official* opposition. The government announced that the July violence did not affect the implementation of the 2015 peace agreement and Deng would henceforth speak on behalf of all opposition.

Deng's elevation was almost universally rejected by the SPLA/iO. Even though his flight from Juba had taken a physical toll on Machar, and left him separated from his field commanders, his forces appeared resilient and cohesive. JMEC also publicly rejected the government's gambit and asked Deng to step aside to allow Machar to return.[41] However, UNMISS was more hesitant and avoided a public position. As one of the interviewees reported, the organization was conflicted as to how it should respond:

> I think privately, certainly within my department, we thought the whole Taban Deng thing was a joke of such outrageous proportions that it was just almost impossible to take seriously. The whole thing was just so outrageous. . . . However, the impression that I got was that the understanding in the senior levels of UNMISS was that 'this is what we're dealing with now'.[42]

Within a month Løj appeared to have accepted the official explanation of events and returned to her long-standing attempts to normalize her relationship with the government with a series of technical meetings that started on 18 August.[43] In what appears to have been a *doubling-down* of its 2015 gamble that the government, unpalatable as they may be, could deliver peace, John Kerry announced on 23 August that the United States would accept a change in the leadership of the SPLA/iO.[44] Within a week, IGAD and other key international partners followed and made similar statements.

The fighting spreads

Following the United States' decision to support the South Sudan government, it used its diplomatic energies to marginalize the influence of Machar. Under pressure, Sudan and Ethiopia closed their doors to the rebel leader.[45] A trip to South Africa by Machar for medical treatment ended in effective house arrest in what appears to have been a ploy to keep him as far from Juba as possible.[46] Kenya joined the piling on of pressure by arresting SPLA/iO officials based in Nairobi and deporting them to South Sudan.[47]

The most serious implications of the international community's support of the government's position were that they legitimized its characterization of the security picture in the country. Those who remained outside of the Deng's official opposition, which included almost all the SPLA/iO as well as the considerable number of other groups that had joined them in 2016 in the south and the west of the country, became legitimate targets again. The first target of SPLA operations were the restive parts of the Equatorias where newly affiliated SPLA/iO militias had been pivotal in facilitating Machar's escape from the country. Characteristically, the operations in the Equatorias involved widespread attacks on civilians that devastated the south. Human rights groups documented systematic and large-scale human right abuses around Yei, where I had been at the outbreak of the July violence.[48] An exodus of civilians from the country took place on a scale hitherto unseen. In the six months after the violence in Juba, approximately 600,000 people fled the country, most making their way to refugee sites in Uganda. The violence against civilians became so severe that by November the Secretary General's Special Adviser for the Prevention of Genocide, Adama Dieng, openly talked about the possibility of the situation devolving into a genocide.[49] At the end of November, a visit by the UN Commission on Human Rights in South Sudan accused the government of ethnic cleansing and added that the whole country was on the verge of catastrophe, with the Equatorias as the new epicentre of the war.[50] According to subsequent assessments, the violence that directly followed the breakdown of the peace agreement in 2016 was the deadliest period of the entire war.[51]

The ability of many Equatorians to flee into refugee camps in neighbouring Uganda lessened the requirement on UNMISS to provide protection in these areas. However, pockets of civilians remained caught in the violence. Approximately, 100,000 were reported as trapped inside the town of Yei while fighting raged around it.[52] The UNMISS response was characteristically lacklustre. Seven patrols to Yei were delayed or denied by the government. It appears to have been successful at conducting two others. However, in the section that covered the UNMISS protection of civilian activities in the Secretary General's report in November, UNMISS could report no activities to alleviate the threat against civilians in and around Yei.[53] Officials involved with providing a humanitarian response to the unfolding tragedy expressed frustration at having to provide a competing narrative to that of the UN's in raising alarm at the deteriorating situation in the south. The pressure on the UN to maintain the fiction of a normal peace process undermined attempts to articulate the extreme extent of the actual collapse of the agreement. A staff member in a donor organization at the time, and recorded by Briggs and Monaghan, partially blamed the SRSG for the failure:

> 'This makes our job so much harder,' they said. 'We are trying to tell head-office that there is a war, the SRSG is saying there is no war'.[54]

Løj retires

The second independent investigation that the UN convened in 2016 offered a devastating portrayal of the mission's failures in July. The Executive Summary was unequivocal:

In the weeks prior to the violence, UNMISS and the humanitarian community saw timely and accurate warning signs of the resumption of hostilities in Juba between the Sudan People's Liberation Army (SPLA) and the Sudan People's Liberation Army in Opposition (SPLA-IO). Notwithstanding the early warning that fighting would take place near UN House, the Mission did not properly prepare.

Furthermore, responsibility for those failures lay in its leadership:

> The special investigation found that a lack of leadership on the part of key senior Mission personnel had culminated in a chaotic and ineffective response to the violence.[55]

However, the Kenyan force commander, and not Løj, was fired. The Kenyan government bitterly protested the sacking, ultimately withdrawing its soldiers from the mission. Accusations that he had been made a scapegoat are well founded. He had been in the mission for only three weeks before the violence in Juba.[56] When asked how civilian staff of DPKO again avoided any blame for mission failures, one UN official familiar with the incident suggested:

> It's because there's so much personal ambition involved in these things, everyone makes sure the dirt doesn't stick. When the mission gets investigated, it gets fobbed off on somebody. In 2016, the force commander took the spear. Never mind that that wasn't force commander's failure. He was not a good force commander, a different story, but he was the fall guy for the mission. There was nothing at the top. No questions were ever asked up there.[57]

No public responsibility was ever placed on SRSG Løj or the head of peacekeeping, Herve Ladsous, even though the investigation suggested that the organizational environment was fundamentally flawed:

> The Mission's established culture of reporting and acting in silos inhibited effective action during a period in which swift, joint action was essential. . . . The special investigation found that the lack of preparedness, ineffective command and control and a risk-averse or 'inward-looking' posture resulted in a loss of trust and confidence, particularly by the local population and humanitarian agencies, in the will and skill of UNMISS military and police to be proactive and show a determined posture to protect civilians under threat, including from sexual violence and human rights violations.[58]

The criticisms related to weaknesses that had existed within the mission for years and had played a role in multiple failures of which there was reasonable expectation that the UN should have been aware. However, for the reasons suggested in this book, those weaknesses were repeatedly ignored or underplayed as critical problems. Even though Løj avoided being named in the investigation, she announced her retirement a week before it was published. She was allowed to exit the role without having to publicly defend her role.

Conclusions

By 2016, UNMISS had a large force of peacekeepers in Juba compared to December 2013. They also had opportunities to access a much greater range of experiences based on knowledge of the conflict and its combatants and of how belligerent capabilities could be brought to bear in attacks on UN bases. According to their own analysis, UNMISS was aware of a high likelihood of a breakdown of the ARCSS and a return to conflict in 2016. It even had analysis on how it might take place. Despite this advantageous position, the leadership could not offer any improvement on UNMISS's suboptimal actions in 2013. Preparations were not made, and tactical decision-making during the violence reflected long-standing cultures of risk-aversion and conflict avoidance that were prevalent within the mission. In the lead-up to the violence, UNMISS also avoided public diplomacy that might have put the government on warning. If anything, the gap between its performance and expectations compared to 2013 had worsened.

If improvements in resources, knowledge of the context and expectation of an attack led to no discernible improvement in performance, it lends weight to the idea that flaws in decision-making deserve greater focus. The increasingly pressing requirement to reinvigorate UNMISS tactical readiness does not seem to have become a priority in this period despite evidence suggesting its urgency, including from the recent attack at Malakal. Even easily achievable tasks, such as appropriately hardening its watchtowers and ensuring UN House had a surgical capacity, were not done. While UNMISS's military deserve much criticism for these failures, Løj remains accountable in her overall responsibility. It remains likely however that given her *values* she delegated these responsibilities to concentrate on those aspects of the context that were more relevant to her experiences of peacekeeping. In the first half of 2016, this would have been especially as to how the implementation of the peace agreement related to her preferred peacebuilding framing of the context.

The *interests* of the UN Secretariat and UNSC were also not in improving UNMISS's performance, rather a search for totemic signs of success in the peace agreement that lessened the urgency for the mission to fix its tactical shortcomings. When the United States made the ill-conceived decision to support the government's reconstitution of the SPLA/iO's leadership, UNMISS showed itself as responsive as other nations and regional organizations to that policy decision. Notwithstanding its obligation to advise UNSC members on optimal policy approaches in countries where peacekeeping missions are present, the UN and UNMISS avoided divergence from the United States' preferred strategy. It remains likely that not only was this a sign of deference to a UNSC permanent member but that it was also a strategy aligned with their own values and interests at that time. This was even though, as according to UN officials on the ground, the political fiction on which this strategy was based was 'outrageous'.

These elements of the bounded rationality ensured *a confirmation bias* in which information regarding the success and worth of the peace agreement appeared to be persistently overvalued. UNMISS were aware of the risks, yet the irrational focus on otherwise-insignificant signs of success in the peace process undermined the urgency of corresponding UNMISS action to respond to threats. After the eruption of violence in Juba, UNMISS's subsequent reporting was notable for its avoidance of information that undermined the logic of supporting the government's reconstitution of the SPLA/iO, despite its poor evidence base. At the same time, UNMISS's portrayal of the subsequent violence in the Equatorias was out of step with more accurate descriptions of mass violence that was not only a resumption of the war but also an escalation of its seriousness.

There was an *availability bias* that stemmed from the way UNMISS had absorbed the understanding of its role in 2013. Notwithstanding the parallels with that moment, UNMISS was unable to show learning that might have informed better and more proactive responses. In 2013, what little reflection on the event is known can be seen in the public comments of the UN leadership that suggest that those events were perceived as atypical and unpredictable. The possibility of their repetition was irrationally discarded, preventing the mission from recognizing similarities in the escalation of tensions that should have triggered more proactive peacekeeping responses in 2016. The implications of events in Bor, Unity and Malakal were similarly improperly absorbed into the organization in a way that undermined its ability to understand the potential of proactive responses to early warning.

Without an available comparison, and a corresponding desire to see success in the peace process, the peace process will have looked more like a prototypical situation that could more abstractly be related to recognizable peace and security norms, rather than the specific context of the country. A resulting *substitution bias* would lead decision-makers to see various actors as being more responsive to these norms than they were. The evidence that such responsiveness was illusory, such as the depth of obstruction and bad faith of South Sudanese politicians, was ignored by decision-makers, making it difficult for them to understand the political and military strategies of the signatories that were clearly taking the country back into conflict.

The unresponsiveness of the mission to changing circumstances also seems like an increasingly desperate attempt to justify a sunk-cost fallacy. To defend its own prior decision-making, UNMISS resisted criticism in the months that followed July despite the worsening situation in the Equatorias, which provided an additional indictment of their failure. A change in tactic in 2016 risked exposing years of miscalculations. To recognize the accumulated mistakes of those years would have been personally uncomfortable to decision-makers and a huge blow to the *organizational myth* of the UN. Instead, it went along with the South Sudan government's explanation of events, also endorsed by the United States, which ultimately created a legitimizing environment for a huge escalation in attacks on civilians. It also became difficult to give areas such as Yei the operational priority they required without admitting a mistake in the framing of the violence and the corresponding threat on civilians. By November 2016, it was becoming increasingly difficult to hide the truth of these mistakes. Yet, even with two deeply critical special investigations in 2016 and claims that genocide was becoming a possibility, the UN struggled to articulate a description of the context that matched the observed reality.

Løj achieved some success as UNMISS SRSG, in her ability to bring some cohesion to a mission that had struggled from years of poor administration and the impact of the events of 2013. However, in her failure to grasp the potential of tactical peacekeeping and her attachment to an ineffective peacebuilding framework, she failed. Nonetheless, in her departure the UN again refused an opportunity to institutionally learn from its mistakes. In placing all the blame on the UNMISS force commander, her decisions escaped any public examination. If Løj had underperformed, she had been *appropriate*. Within a year she was re-employed by the UN to lead a strategic review of the peacekeeping mission, the United Nations Multidimensional Integrated Stabilization Mission in Mali (MINUSMA). At the time, MINUSMA was one of the UN's most dangerous missions where the kinetic nature of the conflict created highly tactical challenges.

9

Change in tactics

April 2017

By 2017, I was readying myself to leave South Sudan. It had been a hard few years and the signs of burnout, which will be familiar to anyone who has worked in similar high-stress roles and contexts, were becoming more evident. I drank too much, smoked too much, exercised too little and struggled to make healthy life choices as friends suggested that I had taken on an unwell pallor. The work I produced was still good, but the moment where that was no longer the case felt close. Also, if this book has been critical of those whose overly optimistic perspectives created dangerous biases, then that should not detract from the equal truth that overly pessimistic ones could be just as destructive. I had begun to show signs of a 'normal' reaction to the events that I was documenting. Attempting to keep the anger and sadness that I increasingly felt out of the analysis that I was producing became strenuous, and I occasionally faltered. This was even though in 2017 there were at last some green shoots. I was concerned that that I would not be able to see the opportunities that arose from them.

In this chapter, I will discuss the dramatic changes in UNSC and UN Secretariat interests that occurred at the end of 2016 as well as the arrival of a new SRSG. These changes affected the bounded rationality. Under the new SRSG, David Shearer, a more robust peacekeeping operation took place. When faced with a similar set of circumstances as to those that existed in Unity in 2015, Shearer was more proactive. In responding to available evidence and properly weighting the probability of events, he took action that ended with a result that could be broadly described as a more optimal example of tactical peacekeeping. Shearer's values appeared more suited not only to the role but also to the changing interests of the UN Secretariat and the UNSC, that were more willing to confront the government. The requirements to preserve the organizational myth, that had been severely damaged in 2016, also incentivized more optimal action. However, the circumstances of early 2017 were fleeting, and the system soon reverted to a *normal* bounded rationality. Corresponding bias and enabling behaviours also returned. If Shearer appears to have been more successful than his predecessors, then much can be attributed the fortuitous circumstances that he inherited. UNMISS used that permissive moment to withdraw from most of the POC sites and downplay the need for a continued peacekeeping mission even as conflict was again rising, and related humanitarian emergencies were worsening. An alternative to viewing this period as a peacekeeping success is that, given a permissive environment, he wasted opportunities by prioritizing those tasks that were superficially important within a normal peacekeeping bounded rationality but contributed less to accomplishing UNMISS's mandated objectives.

'None of us can say that we did not see it coming'

While Løj showed consistency in her approach to the end, the bounded rationality within which she was making decisions was changing. As suggested earlier, the horror of the situation in South Sudan was becoming increasingly visible. While the UN continued to offer anodyne assessments of the situation, the United States administration abandoned its previous tolerance towards the South Sudan state in an extraordinary about face. The United States tendency to favour Kiir had always been strained. If it strategically indulged him, that strategy was the source of deep divisions within the United States administration, and it also publicly criticized him. Internally, it was known that United States policy on South Sudan was contested, with John Kerry and Samantha Power more sceptical on the leeway that should be allowed to Kiir than Susan Rice.[1] By late 2016, the massive increase in violence finally made that leeway untenable, and Rice's position undefendable. Power used the opportunity to unleash an extraordinary attack on the government that also implicitly criticized UN inaction:

> We are reminded of all of the warnings that the United Nations missed or saw but chose to ignore in places like Srebrenica and Rwanda in the 1990s. Given the accumulation of warnings, we have lost the right individually and collectively to act surprised in the face of even greater atrocities in South Sudan. None of us can say that we did not see it coming.[2]

Power went on to demand from the UN an alternative and more robust peacekeeping strategy, in which those elements of consent and partnership with the host government that were deemed essential by Johnson and Løj should be cast aside:

Let us not treat the leaders of South Sudan as though they are responsible and credible interlocutors but engage them as the cynical actors whom they unfortunately have shown themselves to be, too often putting their short-sighted personal interests above the welfare of millions of their own people who are suffering. Let us stop asking for permission to carry out a mandate authorized by the Security Council in the interest of peace and security and, instead, start demanding it to unite around that message and mandate. Let us stop acting as if the principle of sovereignty, as critical as it is to the functioning of the international order, gives the South Sudanese Government or any Government license to commit mass atrocities against its own people or fuel a humanitarian crisis that has left millions of lives hanging in the balance.[3]

Beyond the rhetoric, Power announced a proposal for an arms embargo on South Sudan, a move that the United States had previously opposed. She also called for an 'inclusive' peace process, with the face-saving ambiguous inference that Machar should be allowed to return as leader of the opposition, without having to refer to him by name. Kiir also looked to have exhausted what international goodwill he had elsewhere. Following an argument with President Museveni in 2015, the country's relationship with Uganda declined. The death of two Chinese peacekeepers in 2016 and tensions over the administration of the country's oilfields had also soured relations with Kiir's most valuable supporter on the UNSC. The interests of the Council shifted.

New perspectives

Power's diatribe came in the weeks that followed the release of the second special investigation of 2016, which focused on UNMISS failures in July. In the two investigations that had been convened that year, UNMISS was lambasted for its failure to pre-empt foreseeable threats. With the expansion of the conflict in the second half of 2016, and the continued growth in the numbers of individuals seeking protection, the situation looked bleak. Power's comparison of the country to previous UN failures in Rwanda and Srebrenica would have chilled the Secretariat and anyone who believed in the organizational myth of the UN. Along with Løj's departure, several other changes in personnel brought changes to the context of decision-making. Ban Ki-Moon's tenure as Secretary General finished at the end of 2016, and the head of peacekeeping, Ladsous, also departed in early 2017. A new United States administration, which had much less interest in African affairs, created a vacuum of policy on South Sudan that represented another departure from previous decision-making frameworks.

The choice of David Shearer to replace Løj as SRSG was a notable shift. He had never held a position in New York, as his two predecessors had done. Instead, he had experience in humanitarian operational roles in the field, including in emergency and conflict environments that resembled the context of South Sudan.[4] The collapse in faith in the mission and a wholesale change in leadership created a favourable environment for an overdue shift in strategic direction. The 2016 special investigations into UNMISS offered some technical recommendations that a demoralized staff became eager to implement as they tried to separate themselves from the mission's previous missteps. Military staff, particularly, became more proactive than they had been for some time and UNMISS staff suggested that during that time they were 'much more willing to go and try'.[5] In line with these recommendations, Shearer implemented more robust means to physically protect civilians at POC sites, including the construction of better perimeter defences and weapon-free buffer zones around the sites. He also oversaw the creation of more frequent and robust patrolling strategies. Critically, this included instructions that soldiers should assert their right to patrol and stand their ground for forty-eight hours when confronted with an access denial. More training was devoted to ensuring soldiers understood the rules of engagement, and more regular scenario training involving directives on use of force were ordered.[6]

Shearer's leadership style was the antithesis of Løj's. He appeared to eschew her preference for hierarchy, in favour of a flatter structure of decision-making. Interviewees differentiated Løj's 'old school' hierarchical style with Shearer's more 'democratic' approach.[7] One interviewee commented on his arrival:

> We were certainly happy to see someone who came in and spoke the language of proactivity and seemed interested in wanting to know what was going on, and who seemed quite dynamic and keen to engage across the mission.[8]

Others who worked with him described his openness as being breath of fresh air compared to that of Løj:

> He came in, he had great credibility, not to say that Ellen didn't. [But] The way he came in, he came in fresh, he had ideas. He clearly had his background, his credibility had been here, there, everywhere. Also, he is a politician, so he is very good at presenting himself. I think that was really appreciated.[9]

Shearer reorganized components of the senior decision-making team. He elevated the long-standing Chief JMAC to the role of head of political affairs, signalling importance around institutional contextual knowledge. As well as being more engaged across a broader range of the mission, interviewees suggested that Shearer was better at engaging externally. One interviewee noted:

> I think it's the manner of those discussions [about protection of civilians]. Shearer continued those discussions but changed the narrative. I think, given his background he was much more able to communicate with humanitarians and then was able to discuss each [POC] site as an individual entity.[10]

Another key difference with Løj was Shearer's experience in politics, having previously led the government opposition in New Zealand. Much more than Løj he showed confidence in using his public position for political ends. However, in contrast to Johnson, he also seemed more adept at finding a position of constructive opposition. In his first months, he openly and directly criticized the South Sudan government for blocking humanitarian assistance.[11] In March 2017, he wrote an editorial for *Newsweek* with the provocative title, 'Why South Sudan's leaders are to blame for the country's famine'.[12] When UNMISS displayed robust postures against government security services, he pushed his press office to promote the willingness of peacekeepers to make forceful interventions.[13]

Cometh the hour?

The first real test of the new SRSG came at the start of 2017. Following a stalemate in the Equatoria offensive in the south, the government turned its attention back to those parts of the country it had fought over in 2014 and 2015. Fighting in Upper Nile began in late January, with an attack on the town of Wau Shilluk. As with Unity in 2015, the attacking force placed itself between the UNMISS POC site and its target, limiting the ability of fleeing civilians to seek protection from the UN. Civilians from the Shilluk community were instead pushed into the shrinking opposition's territory as the SPLA advanced. As many as 20,000 escaped north along the River Nile to the town of Kodok. On 26 April, the SPLA pushed again, attacking Kodok and forcing up to 30,000 civilians further inland to the town of Aburoc. Beyond Aburoc, the nearest safe haven was sufficiently far that it would be impossible for any vulnerable groups to escape by foot. Coordinated attacks on the SPLA/iO along the entire west bank of the Nile saw their defensive capabilities crumble. Areas like Aburoc represented the few pockets that the SPLA/iO were able to cling to. With government forces regrouping only 30 kilometres away, any advance would take place with little warning. Given the brutality of previous SPLA offensives, the threat against civilians was high. Significant violence against civilians had already been reported as having taken place in Wau Shilluk and Kodok.[14] The potential for a decisive victory for the government meant that further advances to Aburoc were sufficiently likely that a peacekeeping protection mission became warranted.

On 27 April, OCHA published a flash update calling on parties to the conflict to adhere to international humanitarian law.[15] Having already been evacuated from Kodok, humanitarians were concerned about their ability to stay in the insecure Aburoc and provide the vital services required. A protection cluster report from the time starkly noted:

> Without transport to a safer location, food and water, the population, especially the most vulnerable persons, are at serious risk of being abused, raped and killed.[16]

The warnings resembled those that had been produced in the early stages of other government offensives in Unity in 2015 and Central Equatoria in 2016 and which in those instances had led to no pre-emptive deployment by UNMISS. Aburoc was also inside opposition territory into which UNMISS had avoided significant operations. However, on this occasion UNMISS's response was substantially different. Following the attack on Wau Shilluk, Shearer expressed public and specific concern about the displaced population because of the government's operations.[17] Evidence that the government had become inured to the possibility of an UNMISS intervention was shown by the subsequent SPLA advance to take Kodok. UNMISS responded with a military operation.

On 7 May, Shearer announced that he had deployed peacekeeping troops to Aburoc to secure the area for humanitarian delivery, essentially putting peacekeepers in the way of a potential SPLA advance. What had taken UNMISS six months to achieve in Unity in 2015 took a matter of days in Upper Nile. The operation lasted six weeks, allowing humanitarian services enough time to provide life-saving services and support the transport of the most vulnerable out of the hostile area. During the operation, Shearer provided public visibility of the situation there by visiting the site along with journalists. Of the impact of the operation, he commented from Aburoc:

> It's something that we hadn't done before. It's something that our peacekeepers aren't known for, getting in helicopters, flying in at very short notice, establishing a base on the ground in a potentially hostile environment and then getting on with the job of bringing others in to do the humanitarian work. It worked really well here, and it set a precedent and a bit of a model for the rest of our peacekeeping

troops to look at. . . . The bottom line here is that there are hundreds of people alive here today who would not have been alive if we hadn't done this.[18]

Whether Shearer was correct that the operation saved hundreds is debatable. At least one analyst I talked to was sceptical as to whether the threat was as pronounced as was made out and that Aburoc had never been a target. Regardless, the evidence in the moment that there was a civilian population requiring protection created a rational basis for the proportionate intervention that was ordered. Regardless of the outcome, Shearer can claim credit for overseeing a more optimal response than his predecessors had managed in previous similar circumstances.

The UNMISS intervention in Aburoc also came at a watershed moment in the conflict. In the months that followed, enthusiasm within the government for continuing the war dwindled. On 9 May, days after peacekeepers were deployed to Aburoc, Paul Malong was fired as chief of staff of the SPLA in a shock decision by the president. A few months later, he was arrested and forced into exile in a move that showed the waning influence of hardliners within the government. The route back to the peace process was a slow one. It would be another year before Machar formally rejoined it, and he only returned to Juba in October 2018. Violence continued throughout the country but the large-scale offensives that had led to mass atrocities and huge displacements between 2013 and 2017 stopped. Having had its bases attacked at least four times[19] between 2013 and 2016, there were no similar attacks during Shearer's tenure.

The extent to which this positive change can be attributed to the sudden emergence of a more robust peacekeeping operation needs significant qualification. This turning point had been sometime in the making. Malong had failed to deliver a decisive victory against the SPLA/iO since taking control of the SPLA in 2014. His high-stakes gamble to attack Machar in Juba in 2016 had, by 2017, been shown as an unmitigated failure leading to an expansion of the conflict and another economic collapse. In 2017, the SPLA/iO could claim control over a greater amount of territory than they had at any point since the start of the war thanks to a broadening of its base beyond the Nuer community. Malong's security strategy that had alienated many non-Dinka communities was significantly to blame. The strident reaction of the international community following the offensive in the Equatorias was another indicator that the hardline strategies that the Government of South Sudan had pursued up to that point were no longer tenable. The change in peacekeeping posture, which Shearer oversaw in 2017, would have contributed to an undeniable logic that conflict to achieve political goals that favoured Kiir and his allies was no longer effective.

Conclusions

The Aburoc operation took place without any fundamental changes to the mission's mandate. Nor had the resources available to the mission significantly improved. UNMISS still lacked critical tactical tools such as unmanned aerial vehicles (UAVs) and attack helicopters. Following the collapse of the peace agreement, the UNSC had authorized an additional 4,000 soldiers. However, government obstruction and UN inefficiency meant that by April 2017 few had entered the country, and those who had barely made up for the loss of Kenyan soldiers who had been withdrawn the previous year. In April 2017, there were approximately the same number of peacekeeping soldiers available to the mission as there had been in the summer of 2015, during the Unity offensives.[20]

What had changed by 2017 was the bounded rationality within which peacekeeping decisions were made. UNSC *interests* were less indulgent towards the Government of South Sudan. The UN Secretariat's *interests* also shifted as it saw the maintenance of its existing strategy as endangering the *organizational myth* of the UN. Attempts to ignore public criticism of UNMISS were no longer viable given the UN's own investigations and increasing external evidence that contradicted the mission's stated understanding of the context. For the first time, proactive tactical action became incentivized to preserve the organizational myth and support UNSC interests. These elements were more threatened by the spectre of inaction than the perceived risks of maintaining the POC site burden. Consequently, for the first time since the start of the conflict the need to extract the UN from POC sites did not seem like the mission's primary concern. Shearer also brought with him a new set of *values*. He was more at ease with a perspective that understood the operational aspect of the mission as well as using his public platform from a position of opposition.

If there was a new pressure on information, it existed to push the mission towards focusing on being able to show demonstrable incidences of effective or optimal action that reflected the robust and dynamic capabilities that a peacekeeping mission is supposed to have. This necessitated a more serious consideration by decision-makers to create such examples. Shearer's previous experiences and management style would also have been better suited to the creation of such action. Given his operational background, he would have been better able to draw on more relevant available experiences to more confidently explore tactical options to demonstrate robust and optimal action. That would have made him less susceptible to uncertainty that otherwise could have increased the prominence of *risk aversion*. His apparent flat management style would have also meant that he was less susceptible to *inside views*.

A focus on optimal action as desirable over and above the normal concerns of a bounded rationality meant that the need to apply *confirmation* or *availability biases* to interpret information were less prevalent. The use of force in Aburoc appears to have been a proportionate and rational use of tactical capabilities to known threats according to the mission's mandated priorities.

Shearer's flatter management style would likely have also reduced *groupthink* and *inside views*. Having not been associated with previous suboptimal strategies, Shearer would have been better placed to break with a sunk-cost fallacy that irrationally put a premium on maintaining the coherence of previous interpretations of the context. Leadership therefore moved away from an attachment to discredited interpretations and embraced focus on task optimality.

However, a bounded rationality that allowed UNMISS to focus on task relevance in creating decision alternatives for action would not last. It is notable that, notwithstanding the United States change of political tack, they were unsuccessful in achieving an arms embargo in December 2016. While no country voted against the resolution, eight abstained, depriving it of the required number to pass.[21] Even if international opinion had broadly turned against the Government of South Sudan towards the end of 2016, a consensus on a more robust peacekeeping strategy was limited. The attitude of the UN Secretariat to the operation in Aburoc also seemed ambivalent. There was a lack of official celebration when it took place and its mention in the subsequent Secretary General report to the UNSC in June distilled the event to a single underwhelming sentence. The tone belied the unprecedented nature of the operation.[22]

Shearer had sought the operation to be a model of a 'more nimble, mobile, and proactive' type of peacekeeping in the country.[23] Yet, while he appears to have had some success improving the tactical robustness of the mission, the deployment of similar operations was not forthcoming. The new Secretary General, António Guterres, made no mention of a new strategy or tactical posture for the mission. Instead, his reporting on UNMISS to the UNSC looked like that of his predecessor. Description of UNMISS's implementation of activities to protect civilians remained pinned to the three-tier approach that had existed since Johnson and retained the primacy of politics in peacekeeping, regardless of the circumstances.

In my research, I have been unable to determine where this lack of enthusiasm for the Aburoc mission came from. It is possible that its implications were overlooked, given the difficulty of proving causal success from preventive action. However, it is also likely that, viewed from a more *normal* bounded rationality, the operation looked riskier than institutional stalwarts in DPKO were comfortable with. At the same time, it looks like the kind of mission that the UNSC might ordinarily prefer to be consulted on, lest it be interpreted as an intervention against a sovereign government. Kiir's apparent contrition, in marginalizing hardliners and the lowering tempo of conflict in the country, also softened UNSC displeasure with the country. The resumption of the primacy of politics and a non-disruptive peacekeeping mission would have become desirable again, while the value of robust tactical peacekeeping postures in the field would have diminished.

In 2018, the poorly constructed ARCSS was dusted off and an increased number of signatories asked to recommit to a rejigged version. Unreassuringly, the sponsors attached a single word to distinguish the *Revitalized Agreement for the Resolution of Conflict in South Sudan* (R-ARCCS) from its failed predecessor. UNMISS again found itself in a supporting role to a flawed political process. The obsession with shrinking the POC sites reasserted itself, and Shearer was described as again 'under pressure' to prioritize that.[24] If Shearer had struggled to demonstrate the positive effects of robust peacekeeping, he had better luck taking advantage of the lower tempo of violence to extract UNMISS from POC site responsibilities. As a diplomat connected to the UNSC at the time described Shearer's strategy:

> There was definitely that pressure from New York coming from, 'Why can't we get better news? Why can't we hear that things are progressing?' . . . .He needed to bring a story. He was very good at storytelling. Again, I don't mean this in a bad way, I mean this in a positive way, the guy's talented, he knew he had to bring a positive story. He realized that the POC sites was a potential way for him to do that. . . . 'This is where I can go and bring a good news story. I'm going to tell them that we're going to start to look at how we can bring some of these folks back'...He brought this whole story and you could see that from where I was sitting, again, I've known South Sudan for a few years by that point. I'm like, 'That's not how this is going to play out,' but you can see on the Security Council, how member states were like, 'Yes, yes, that's great. Yes, yes, that sounds good, let's do that.'[25]

Under his tenure, and taking advantage of lower levels of conflict, Shearer managed to redesignate all but one of the sites, ultimately withdrawing peacekeeping responsibility from everywhere except Malakal, where continued tensions between communities made such a withdrawal impossible. The move reignited tensions between the mission and the humanitarian community, many of whom felt sidelined from the transition process.[26] One senior UN humanitarian, who I talked to, suggested that he used the credibility from his background in humanitarian operations to pursue goals that ultimately undermined humanitarian goals to benefit UNMISS's interests.[27] Another UN official, who had served under all three SRSGs, suggested that Shearer lost some of the 'energy' that he had arrived with and had been associated with in his early desire to reinvent peacekeeping action. It is possible that familiarity with the context and the reassertion of a more traditional bounded rationality created greater levels of *risk aversion* in his approach.[28] Other staff, who worked for UNMISS, and who had been complementary as to the openness that he brought to the role, came to perceive his management style as performative. They suspected that, as with previous SRSGs, his decision-making was increasingly based on his interactions with a limited number of officials that comprised his inner circle.[29]

What's old is new

When I returned to South Sudan in 2021, Shearer looked successful. The peace agreement had, more or less, held since 2018, and UNMISS was moving out of the POC sites. Yet even as conflict between signatories of the national peace agreement subsided, violence was rising at an exponential rate. Since 2018, civilian deaths because of violence had doubled in each of the three years that followed.[30] While UNMISS sought to emphasize the local or intercommunal components of that violence, those incidents of significance such as in Jonglei in 2020[31] and around Tambura in Western Equatoria in 2021 were often connected to prominent politicians that tied them to national conflict dynamics.[32] The insurgency in the south of the country also persisted under the auspices of an Equatorian-led rebellion known as the National Salvation Front. Both sides continued to fiercely manipulate the peace process, contesting appointments as part of the power-sharing arrangements at every level, in what looked like the revival of the intense rivalry that instigated the conflict in 2013.[33] However, it was Kiir and his allies who were more successful. Machar had re-entered the peace process considerably diminished, and was effectively confined to the capital as Kiir retained control over the most significant state resources. No significant military SPLA/iO force was allowed in Juba, as had happened in 2016. Deliberate delays to the implementation of the unified national forces meant that SPLA/iO forces were literally allowed to starve in the field in makeshift cantonment sites, even as Machar secured high-ranking positions in government for close allies and members of his family.[34] Kiir placed more pressure on those forces by encouraging defections that undermined cohesion in the SPLA/iO that ultimately prompted a serious schism in the summer of 2021.[35] During that split, the SPLA/iO's most senior generals abandoned Machar, complaining that to retain him as leader meant to accept the destruction of the movement. Even as Shearer sought to project success, the country looked as unstable as ever. The vast majority of the four million people, who had been displaced by the conflict since 2013, had not returned to their homes suggesting widespread concern at the continued violence and poor levels of confidence in the future of the country. Critical food insecurity, including famine in some parts of the country, and catastrophic flooding additionally undermined stability.

In this context, UNMISS efforts redesignating POC sites without making progress in supporting security and stability in the country looked like another response to a task that was important from the perspective of a UN-bounded rationality, but less significant when compared to a broader interpretation of its mandated goals to support peace and security. It is noteworthy that the removal of UNMISS from the POC sites did not dramatically change the numbers of people populating those areas who wished to remain close to the UN bases. A South Sudanese activist involved in grassroots peacebuilding complained that UNMISS should have sought to end the POC sites through addressing the reasons for their existence:

> There are many people, who have their home outside. If they also see that there is a space and that the peace is being implemented then all of these people, all of them, everybody, there is no one who needs to stay in the POC. They can actually go to their place. . . . I don't think they feel safe currently because there was a lot of complaints when the status was changed. They said that they were not feeling well if they're going to be left without any protection. What happens if anything happened? It would be a nightmare.[36]

In early 2017, a moment existed that allowed for more optimal action based on an accurate assessment of a broad range of information within a bounded rationality that allowed focus on the practical elements of a task to protect civilians. It does not appear that that moment lasted. As the memory of the success of the Aburoc operation faded, a normal bounded rationality re-emerged in prominence. As the memory of the circumstances of 2016 faded, it is likely that the vividness of available institutional memories, which provided the opportunity to create more optimal responses, also disappeared. Shearer fell into the need to demonstrate peacekeeping success through goals which were less relevant to supporting peace and security in the country and more attached to an organizational bounded rationality.

10

Conclusion

The ten-year anniversary of South Sudan independence was a muted affair. Much of what had been achieved since ending the war of independence lay in ruins, and its communities were more divided than they had ever been. The people in the country had been let down not only by their own leaders but also by the international community and the UN, whose implicit promise to steward the country through its first difficult years was marred by negligence. Their miscalculations were fuelled by an unwillingness to accept the reality of the context on its own terms. Some of the greatest failures were the result of good intentions. The various UN officials referred to in this book undoubtedly believed in the correctness of their approaches. But they struggled to understand their role from outside of a bounded world in which their own values and other's interests, myths and appropriateness did not necessarily exist to create optimal action against the United Nations Mission in South Sudan's (UNMISS's) objectives.

This book is an attempt to provide a means to examine one aspect of the tragic first decade of South Sudan and the way peacekeeping decision-makers created value around different types of information and how that influenced their development of choice alternatives. To do this, I have focused on the cognitive life of the mission and suggested that thoughts and behaviours are a better way of explaining decisions than approaches traditionally taken by academics researching peacekeeping action. I have suggested that decision-makers necessarily distil reality to their perception of relevant facts to develop choice alternatives. I have further suggested that relevance is subjective and liable to relate to those elements that are important to an individual and their relationship with the organization within which they exist. In the UN, and specifically from the perspective of a Special Representative of the Secretary General (SRSG), this is not necessarily focused on practical elements of a mandated task. Instead, individual values, UNSC and UN Secretariat interests, organizational myth and systemic appropriateness are the means through which an SRSG is most likely to understand the world around them.

In situations of uncertainty, the bounded rationality that these elements represent becomes increasingly relevant to replace stable shared understandings. In an unpredictable environment, peacekeepers become reliant on their own organizational understandings to create knowledge. To align knowledge with the bounded rationality, bias encourages preferences around information that confirms beliefs and experiences that relate to elements assimilated within that bounded framework. The inherent capacity with organizations to mitigate bias can become undermined by behaviours that distort framing and anchoring of tasks.

In applying this theoretical framework to South Sudan, I have described the contexts of six decision events that took place between 2013 and 2017 with a focus on the role of the three different SRSGs that served as the heads of the mission during that period. In Hilde Johnson, her individual values were allowed to play an outweighed role in defining the bounded rationality in 2013. Her bias towards framing the context in her preferred political terms, and her tendency to view her political relationships in irrationally favourable terms, undermined her ability to pre-empt and plan for the outbreak of conflict that year. In 2014, UNSC interests were focused on political processes, while the UN Secretariat sought to limit the UN's exposure at protection of civilian (POC) sites. Along with Johnson's preference for political processes, less attention was given to physical security of civilians under UNMISS protection, contributing to failures that resulted in the massacre at its site in Bor. The failure to properly account for that disaster also made the repetition of such mistakes more likely as it undermined the availability of knowledge from previous mistakes within the organization's mindset.

Following Johnson's departure, the UNSC focus on political process involved partiality towards the government and acceptance of its escalation of violence in the country. At the same time, UN Secretariat antipathy to its role in the POC sites deepened. When Johnson's successor arrived, these aspects of the bounded rationality aligned with Ellen Løj's own values. Her self-conceptualization as a diplomat who strongly believed in international governance structures and peacebuilding underpinned her attempts to ingratiate herself with the government, which took on an irrational outweighed importance in her strategy. This created a tendency to view government security actions as more legitimate than the evidence practically suggested and the tendency to understand POC sites as obstacles to peace rather than core to the mission's protection of civilians' objectives. The consequence was that during the violence in Unity in 2015, UNMISS struggled to understand reality in a way that would have prompted more urgent action that could have mitigated the loss of life that occurred.

In Malakal in 2016, the actions at a tactical level demonstrated how emulation of leadership mindsets, in which POC sites had become peripheral to UNMISS's organizational understanding of its core objectives, had become entrenched in groupthink. Later in 2016, the attachment to past decisions created an ever more extreme bias to justify inaction that appeared irrational to most observers who were situated outside of the UN's bounded rationality. That commitment to consistency with previous decisions constituted a sunk-cost fallacy that was guaranteed by a UN Secretariat that persistently refused to fully investigate its decision-making failures, including by ensuring the scope of the investigations excluded civilian management. In promoting, or re-employing bad peacekeeping decision-makers, the UN ensured that their actions appeared appropriate at an organizational level. In 2016, UNMISS squandered a more favourable position than it had had in 2013, to allow an even more suboptimal set of decisions to occur. It stuck with its discredited strategy even as disconfirming information became abundant as South Sudan reached the worst part of its civil war in November 2016.

The extent of the disaster of 2016 was sufficiently visible that UN action looked irrational by an increasing number of external observers. Those bounded elements of interests, beliefs and values were no longer served by adherence to the existing strategy. The disastrous turn of events undermined UNSC and UN interests, imperilled the organizational myth and made decision-makers look professionally incompetent. Greater consideration of those elements of the context that were more practical to the task became increasingly important. Specifically, this entailed addressing the unfettered ability of the government to define the security situation in the country and seek out opportunities in the political and tactical space for the UN to demonstrate successful robustness in its peacekeeping response. The values that David Shearer brought to the role of SRSG also seemed more suited to eschewing unhelpful organizational behaviours that warped the framing of decisions and showed a willingness to absorb information and develop choice alternatives that were based on elements more practical to achieving optimal results. This contributed to success in Aburoc. However, a more normal UN-bounded rationality asserted itself as the memory of the 2016 disaster faded and Shearer sought ways to demonstrate peacekeeping success that the UNSC and Secretariat could more easily recognize.

The consistency of the content of the bounded rationality within peacekeeping in South Sudan, and its tendency to revert to type despite the disruption of 2016, suggests that it is anchored by structural elements that survive the changes in contexts and individuals that comprise decision-making environments. The broader lessons of UNMISS suggest that UN peacekeeping is ill-suited to being reactive to practical concerns in an unpredictable world. In trying to predict the most likely action of UN peacekeepers in any given situation, the static elements of its mindset, which comprise the greater part of its *normal* bounded rationality, provide a better predictor of action than consideration of the practical elements of the task. For a host government, intent on marginalizing the positive influence of a UN peacekeeping mission, this predictability can give rise to set strategies that undermine the effectiveness of UN peacekeeping. The replication of access denials, expulsion of diplomats and bureaucratic impediments that were used by the Juba government during this period, replicated similar strategies deployed by Khartoum during the UNMIS mission.

Towards a better peacekeeping

The implications of accepting the value of a more organizational approach to understanding peacekeeping action have consequences for policymakers. This offers a better alternative to envisaging significant change in practice than through influencing policy norms. Furthermore, it offers a different way of seeing the role of individuals in effecting policy change beyond simple agency. Instead, it recasts officials as cognitively complex beings whose decision-making relate to interests, values and beliefs as well as their relationship to their organization. Better decisions cannot take place without addressing the environment of those individual's decisions.

The conclusion that the application of bias in decision-making within a UN peacekeeping mission, because of bounded rationality, may be systemic and systematic will be an uncomfortable one. The international system that comprises international peace and security architecture has proven itself stubbornly resistant to reform especially where those reforms imply changes that might affect core interests, beliefs and values. However, previous success in peacekeeping reform suggests changes that create better peacekeeping outcomes are possible. The development of an information analysis capacity within peacekeeping missions reached a significant juncture in 2006 with the development of the Joint Mission Analysis Centre (JMAC) concept. Further effort should be placed on not only improving mechanisms to gather and analyse information but also placing that information at the heart of decision-making. This could include ensuring that a mission's Chief JMAC is appointed at a D1 level, thereby making them at least equivalent to other senior staff in decision-making forums in peacekeeping missions. Analytical components of other departments should be strengthened alongside more pronounced managerial expectations that decision recommendations be tied to evidence-based approaches that are based on quality analysis. At all levels of the UN, a generation of managers will need capacity building to understand how such approaches differ from traditional policy approaches within diplomatic settings.

A larger and better information analysis system needs to be developed within the UN Secretariat. From my own experience working in such a role in New York, what information analysis exists largely serves to support decisions already made by senior leaders. That capacity must be reorganized and presented to better challenge orthodox thinking. It should also serve as feedback to field missions on a more honest assessment of peacekeeping approaches based on comparative assessments of tactical and strategic failures. A reinvigorated information analysis mechanism should enjoy some level of independence from other parts of the Secretariat to mitigate those behaviours that might otherwise undermine its impartiality. It should operate as a centre of global JMAC activity and synthesize information affecting peacekeeping operations in a way that can better exploit complementary knowledge.

Some UN Secretariat reforms that have taken place in recent years have been positive. This includes devolving some human resource and financial decision-making from New York to field missions as well as deconflicting the roles of DPKO and DFS in the new Department of Peace Operations (DPO) and Department of Operational Support (DOS). In UNMISS, the tendency for UN Secretariat departments to become fixated on policy issues that had little relation to lived experiences in the field were an unhelpful contribution to developing peacekeeping policy, and their role in defining decision-making contexts at the mission level should be limited.

A less-positive move has been the absorption of administration of the RC/HC system to the UN Secretariat. The D/SRSG (HC/RC) on occasions provided a vocal counterpoint to SRSG decisions. They were willing to be a dissenting voice in the UN system in a way that improved peacekeeping outcomes. Now that the role is administered directly by the UN Secretariat, it will be less likely as there will be implicit disincentives to undermine organizational coherence. The role of a distinct humanitarian voice must be protected to challenge peacekeeping and political approaches in the field that may not be as human centred.

Further work needs to be done on creating a better-equipped cadre of SRSGs. The logic that experienced politicians and diplomats are also equipped to manage military and state-building missions in complex environments is fundamentally flawed. Practical experience of operational roles in emergency or conflict environments should be a minimum standard for any SRSG being considered for an appointment to lead a peacekeeping mission. This will also entail a change in the mindset of how the UN Secretariat and UNSC view the role of peacekeeping. A reluctance to take seriously the tactical capabilities in peacekeeping has reduced some operations to little more than armed political missions, negating the potential positive impact of robust tactical postures. The staff of the UN Secretariat and the diplomats of the UNSC need to take more seriously the operational aspects of peacekeeping, including the minutiae of how it can be effectively used at the tactical level.

Greater effort should be put on considering the kind of team that exists around an SRSG to disrupt inside views and create diversity in the way teams develop choice alternatives. The common practice among UN senior officials to move staff that they are familiar with into their new mission should be overseen more closely. At the same time, flexibility in hiring is required to ensure that an SRSG is empowered to hire staff suited to the context, including from non-UN backgrounds within the country. SRSGs should also be encouraged to manage peacekeeping missions through flatter organizational structures that encourage discussion and diverse views that challenge senior thinking. Field structures need to be better organized to ensure that all departments are properly absorbing information from their officers in a way that can best inform senior-level decisions. An SRSG should also dismantle, as much as possible, information silos that concentrate the tools to make informed decisions within the senior hierarchy. They should engage more fully with external viewpoints even when they may be challenging.

The UN Secretariat can also seek ways to assimilate more challenging and diverse viewpoints into its peacekeeping policy processes. The organization can be sensitive and defensive when criticized, thereby missing opportunities to improve on valid concerns about its performance. The Secretariat continues to be isolated from NGOs and activists who play a marginal role in their work in New York. The tendency to prioritize diplomatic processes over lived experience creates obsessions around totemic policies and practices that are important from a diplomatic perspective but have no practical relevance to a given task. The isolated and inward-looking culture in New York should be challenged to allow a more diverse range of external voices to participate in discussions.

The UN needs to routinely investigate suboptimal decision-making against mandated tasks. The remit of these investigations should relate to a system perspective, rather than the narrow technical remit that reviews and investigations of peacekeeping missions usually entail. An understanding of the flawed managerial systems will likely be painful but necessary. Individuals that conduct investigations should be from a more wide-ranging background than are currently appointed by the UN. The tendency to use retired UN staff, who have an overly sympathetic perspective to the UN, will be less likely to create challenging conclusions that the UN needs to improve. Individuals who specialize in management and organizational behaviour would usefully augment the usefulness of these investigations. Where it is found that a decision-maker has performed badly, the UN needs to be better at firing that official or, at the very least, not rehiring them. The risk of not doing so creates appropriateness around bad actions and reduces disincentives to the repetition of mistakes.

The behaviour of member states, particularly those that are part of the UNSC, could also be much improved. A broader, more representative and more democratic UNSC would likely lessen the tendency for the flawed political perspective of a single nation to dominate strategy. However, it remains highly unlikely that any reform of the UNSC along these lines is currently possible. Nonetheless, the UNSC can better manage how they communicate on peacekeeping matters, to avoid ambiguity that can inhibit an SRSG from confidently identifying certain choice alternatives. That includes ensuring that the UNSC commits adequate and appropriate resources to the peacekeeping missions it requests. It also means ensuring that political obstacles are dismantled so that critical tactical tools that include attack helicopters and UAVs are available where needed.

The UNSC should open its mind to the possibility that a confident, well-resourced and tactically robust peacekeeping mission can have a positive impact on international peace and security when allowed to act according to the priorities within its mandate. There are good reasons as to why member states should relinquish their parochial interests to give peacekeeping missions greater freedom to make decisions more independently. In South Sudan, the fixation on individual state interests became self-defeating. The UNSC prioritization of diplomatic processes at the expense of successful peacekeeping responses likely contributed to the continuation of conflict.

The importance of efficient administration of peacekeeping missions should be taken more seriously. A poorly administered mission is unlikely to be able to effectively implement its mandate. The UNSC should be less willing to accept Office of Internal Oversight Services (OIOS) reports of substandard administration, as was the case with UNMISS, without significant intervention. However, such intervention needs to move beyond tweaking peacekeeping norms and berating the Secretariat to do better. UN peacekeeping requires specific doctrine that relates to expectations of its tactical and administrative performance. That will likely be unpalatable for the troop-contributing countries (TCCs) that feel that it may undermine flexibility for its soldiers and may be objectionable to members of the UNSC that are reluctant to see an independent military identity emerge within the UN. Nonetheless, as the burden increasingly falls on the UN to respond to and diffuse complex crises, that doctrine will be critical to create more certain choice alternatives for SRSGs to accomplish less risk-averse and more optimal outcomes.

Ignorance is bliss?

Opportunities for an SRSG to collect, analyse and act on information in a way that eschews bias and focuses on practical elements of a task should be taken more seriously. However, a non-biased process may lead to the creation of information that compels action that may contradict elements of a persistent bounded rationality. In the current context of UN decision-making, if an SRSG acts outside of the bounded rationality, they risk censure from the UN Secretariat and UNSC and even the loss of their job. However, if they fail to act, it may become public knowledge that they took no action, despite the availability of information that clearly laid out the consequences of that inaction. They could face public condemnation and reputational risk to themselves and the organization. Even if structural reform of peacekeeping processes were possible, incentives will still exist to maintain the subconscious ignorance of relevant information that a bounded rationality provides. It will encourage an SRSG to avoid information that requires action that contradicts the bounded rationality while incentivizing decisions that are *appropriate*, avoiding professional criticism from peers while also lessening culpability for any negative outcomes in the eyes of public judgement.

Acting in a way that is optimal may be not only a rejection of such wilful ignorance but also an uncomfortable act of rebellion. To an employee who has based their professional lives on acting according to systemic appropriateness and have been persistently rewarded for the correctness of their actions by ever-greater promotion and rewards, it will be a difficult psychological proposition to proceed with such a risky course of action. Such decision-making may mean putting peacekeepers' lives in harm's way. It may also mean that an individual never works for the UN again. The difficulty in proving the value of a robust preventive action means that posterity may not even credit their decision. Any lives lost might leave an official with a negative legacy. Within the current decision-making environment, the pursuit of a more optimal peacekeeping decision can constitute an extremely poor professional choice. However, a moral imperative to act to save the lives of civilians, regardless of its professional implications, exists in a frontline role. At some point, an SRSG should be willing to disregard the types of organizational considerations referred to in this book and even question their own values. They must act in the way that is optimal to protect civilians. In exerting that agency, a poor professional choice can also be a profound moral one.

Notes

Preface

1 Steve Bloomfield, 'Why did Nato Cross the Road?' *Monacle*, 2021, No. 100. Available online: https://monocle.com/magazine/issues/100/why-did-nato-cross-the-road/

Chapter 1

1 Some of the most significant tribes considered Equatorian are Azande and Moru in Western Equatoria, Mundari, Bari, Pajulu, Kakwa and Kuku in Central Equatoria as well as Madi, Lango, Lopit, Achioli, Latuka, Lokoya, Didinga and Toposa in Eastern Equatoria.

2 Christopher Tounsel, 'The Equatorial Corps and the Torit Mutiny'. In *Chosen Peoples: Christianity and Political Imagination in South Sudan* (Durham, NC: Duke University Press, 2021), 44–66. https://doi.org/10.2307/j.ctv1qr6sh6.7.

3 Adam Branch and Zachariah Mampilly, 'Winning the War, but Losing the Peace? The Dilemma of SPLM/A Civil Administration and the Tasks Ahead', *The Journal of Modern African Studies*, 43 (2005): 1–20. 10.1017/S0022278X04000588.

4 Jay Johnson, 'South Sudan: Stop Squatters, Land Grabbing, Occupation and Colonization Nonsense', *South Sudan News Agency*, 2013. Available online: https://allafrica.com/stories/201303250041.html

5 'Months after Clashes, Displaced in Lainya Face Humanitarian Crisis', *Radio Tamazuj*, 2016. Available online: https://radiotamazuj.org/en/news/article/months-after-clashes-displaced-in-lainya-face-humanitarian-crisis

6 'Residents: SPLA Killed Five Displaced People in Wonduruba Last Week', *Radio Tamazuj*, 2016. Available online: https://radiotamazuj.org/en/news/article/residents-spla-killed-five-displaced-people-in-wonduruba-last-week

7 Alan Boswell, 'Insecure Power and Violence: The Rise and Fall of Paul Malong and the Mathiang Anyoor', *Small Arms Survey*, 9 (2019): 3.

8 'Nun Shot by SPLA in Yei Passes Away in Hospital', *Radio Tamazuj*, 2016. Available online: https://radiotamazuj.org/en/news/article/nun-shot-by-spla-in-yei-passes-away-in-hospital

9 Bernard Oliya Suwa, 'Postcard of Peace and Forgiveness from "Small London"', *Sudan Tribune*, 2014. Available online: https://sudantribune.com/spip.php?article52956

10 Aryn Baker, 'Why George Clooney is Supporting Coffee Farming in South Sudan', *Time*, 2015. Available online: https://time.com/3918857/george-clooney-south -sudan/

11 Somini Sengupta and Nick Cumming-Bruce, 'Zeid Ra'ad al-Hussein, Top Human Rights Official, Won't Seek a Second Term', *New York Times*, 2017. Available online: https://www.nytimes.com/2017/12/20/world/un-human-rights-al-hussein.html

Chapter 2

1 Kenneth W. Abbott and Duncan Snidal, 'Why States Act Through Formal International Organizations', *Journal of Conflict Resolution*, 42, no. 1 (1998): 3–32. https://doi.org/10.1177/0022002798042001001.

2 For example, see Michael Lipson, 'Peacekeeping: Organized Hypocrisy?' *European Journal of International Relations*, 13, no. 1 (March 2007): 5–34. https://doi.org/10 .1177/1354066107074283.

3 For example, see Hylke Dijkstra, 'Shadow Bureaucracies and the Unilateral Control of International Secretariats: Insights from UN Peacekeeping', *The Review of International Organizations*, 10 (2015): 23–41. https://doi.org/10.10.1007/s11558 -014-9203-7.

4 For example, see Susan Allen and Amy Yuen, 'The Politics of Peacekeeping: UN Security Council Oversight across Peacekeeping Missions', *International Studies Quarterly*, 58 (2013). https://doi.org/10.1111/isqu.12086.

5 John Karlsrud, 'Special Representatives of the Secretary-General as Norm Arbitrators? Understanding Bottom-up Authority in UN Peacekeeping', *Global Governance*, 19, no. 4 (2013): 525–44. Available online: www.jstor.org/stable /24526392; Ingvild Bode, *Individual Agency and Policy Change at the United Nations: The People of the United Nations* (Abingdon: Routledge, 2015).

6 Michael Barnett and Martha Finnemore, *Rules for the World: International Organizations in Global Politics* (Ithaca: Cornell University Press, 2004), 44.

7 Severine Autesserre, *The Trouble with the Congo; Local Violence and the Failure of International Peacebuilding* (Cambridge: Cambridge University Press, 2010).

8 Severine Autesserre, *Peaceland: Conflict Resolution and the Everyday Politics of International Intervention* (Cambridge: Cambridge University Press, 2014).

9 For example, see John W. Meyer and Brian Rowan, 'Institutionalized Organizations: Formal Structure as Myth and Ceremony', *American Journal of Sociology*, 83, no. 2 (Sep 1977): 340–63. https://doi.org/10.1086/226550

10 Terms used in James G. March and Johan P. Olsen, 'The Institutional Dynamics of International Political Orders', *International Organization*, 5, no. 4 (Autumn 1998): 951.

11 For example, see John Karlsrud, 'New Technologies and UN Peacekeeping Operations', in *UN Peacekeeping Doctrine in a New Era*, edited by Cedric de Coning, Chiyuki Aoi and John Karlsrud (Abingdon: Routledge, 2017), 271–87.

12 For example, see Victoria Holt, Max Kelly and Glynn Taylor, *Protecting Civilians in the Context of UN Peacekeeping Operations Successes, Setbacks and Remaining Challenges* (New York: United Nations, 2019).

13 For example, see Peter A. Hall and Rosemary C. R. Taylor, 'Political Science and the Three New Institutionalisms', *Political Studies*, 44, no. 5 (1996): 936–57. https://doi .org/10.1111/j.1467-9248.1996.tb00343.x.

14 Herbert A. Simon, *Administrative Behavior: A Study of Decision-Making Processes in Administrative Organization*, 4th edn. (New York: Free Process, 1947/1997).

15 Ibid., 119.

16 Herbert A. Simon, 'Invariants of Human Behavior', *Annual Review of Psychology*, 41 (1990): 1–20. https://doi.org/10.1146/annurev.ps.41.020190.000245

17 Solomon E. Asch, 'Studies of Independence and Conformity: I. A Minority of One against a Unanimous Majority', *Psychological Monographs: General and Applied*, 70, no. 9 (1956): 1–70. https://doi.org/10.1037/h0093718.

18 Leon Festinger, *A Theory of Cognitive Dissonance* (Stanford: Stanford Press, 1957).

19 Daniel Kahneman and Amos Tversky, 'Prospect Theory: An Analysis of Decision under Risk', *Econometrica*, 47, no. 2 (1979): 263–91. https://doi:10.2307/1914185.

20 Daniel Kahneman, *Thinking Fast and Slow* (London: Penguin, 2011).

21 For example, see Amitai Etzioni, 'Social Psychological Aspects of International Relations', in *Handbook of Social Psychology*, edited by Lindzey Gardner and Elliot Aronson, vol. 5 (Reading: Addison-Weasley, 1969), 538–601.

22 For example, see Margaret G. Hermann, 'Explaining Foreign Policy Behavior Using the Personal Characteristics of Political Leaders', *International Studies Quarterly*, 24, no. 1 (1980): 7–46. https://doi.org/10.2307/2600126.

23 For example, see Philip E. Tetlock, *Expert Political Judgment: How Good Is It? How Can We Know?* (Princeton: Princeton University Press, 2005).

24 Sabine Saurugger, 'Sociological Institutionalism and European Integration', *Oxford Research Encyclopedia of Politics*, 24 May 2017. https://doi.org/10.1093/acrefore /9780190228637.013.179.

25 For example, see Max H. Bazerman, *Judgement in Managerial Decision Making* (New York: Wiley, 2006). And Robert Prentice, 'Enron: A Brief Behavioral Autopsy', *American Business Law Journal*, 40, no. 2 (2008). https://doi-org.chain.kent.ac.uk/10 .1111/j.1744-1714.2002.tb00851.x

26 Herbert, *Administrative Behavior*.

27 Matthew McKay and Patrick Fanning, *Self-esteem: A Proven Program of Cognitive Techniques for Assessing, Improving and Maintaining Your Self-Esteem* (Oakland: New Harbinger, 2016).

28 Walter Mischel and Yuichi Shoda, 'A Cognitive-Affective System Theory of Personality: Reconceptualizing Situations, Dispositions, Dynamics, and Invariance in Personality Structure', *Psychological Review*, 102, no. 2 (1995): 246–68. https://doi .org/10.1037/0033-295X.102.2.246.

29 Thomas Diefenbach and John A. A. Sillince, 'Formal and Informal Hierarchy in Different Types of Organization', *Organization Studies*, 32, no. 11 (2011): 1515–37. https://doi.org/10.1177/0170840611421254.

30 Rahul Chandran and Sebastian von Einsiedel, 'Fixing the UN's Human Resources System', *United Nations University: Centre for Policy Research*, 2 November 2016. Available online: https://cpr.unu.edu/new-ideas-for-a-new-secretary-general-fixing -the-uns-human-resources-system.html

31 Philip Cunliffe, 'The Politics of Global Governance in UN Peacekeeping', *International Peacekeeping*, 16, no. 3 (2009): 323–36. https://doi.org/10.1080/13533310903036384.

32 Karlsrud, 'Special Representatives of the Secretary-General as Norm Arbitrators?'.

33 Ibid., 527.

34 For example, see 'Comprehensive Review of the Whole Question of Peacekeeping Operations in All Their Aspects', UN Doc A/55/305–S/2000/809 (New York: United Nations, 2000).

35 Lipson, 'Peacekeeping: Organized Hypocrisy?'

36 Dijkstra, 'Shadow Bureaucracies'.

37 Harrison M. Trice and Janice M. Beyer, 'Studying Organizational Cultures through Rites and Ceremonials', *The Academy of Management Review*, 9, no. 4 (1984): 653–69. Available online: www.jstor.org/stable/258488.

38 David E. Bowen, Gerald E. Ledford, Jr. and Barry R. Nathan, 'Hiring for the Organization, Not the Job', *The Executive*, 5, no. 4 (1991): 35–51. http://www.jstor .org/stable/4165035.

39 United Nations Security Council, 'Security Council Official Records, Eleventh Year 751st Meeting', UN Doc S/PV.751 (New York: United Nations, 1956).

40 Abraham Zaleznik, 'The Mythological Structure of Organizations and Its Impact', in *The Psychodynamics of Organizations*, edited by Carole Barnett and Larry Hirschorn (Philadelphia: Temple University Press, 1993), 179–89.

41 Ralph R. Frerichs, *Deadly River: Cholera and Cover-Up in Post-Earthquake Haiti* (Ithaca: Cornell University Press, 2016).

42 Jonathan M. Katz, 'U.N. Admits Role in Cholera Epidemic in Haiti', *New York Times*, 17 August 2016.

43 Oliver Holmes, 'Top UN Official to Leave Myanmar Amid Criticism of Rohingya Approach', *The Guardian*, 12 October 2017.

44 Gert Rosenthal, *A Brief and Independent Inquiry into the Involvement of the United Nations in Myanmar from 2010 to 2018* (New York: United Nations, 2019).

45 Mark P. Zanna and J. M. Olson, eds, *The Psychology of Prejudice: The Ontario symposium*, vol. 7 (Mahwah: Lawrence Erlbaum Associates Inc., 1994).

46 For example, see Max H. Bazerman, 'The Relevance of Kahneman and Tversky's Concept of Framing to Organizational Behaviour', *Journal of Management*, 10, no. 3 (1985): 333–43.

47 Raymond S. Nickerson, 'Confirmation Bias: A Ubiquitous Phenomenon in Many Guises', *Review of General Psychology*, 2, no. 2 (1998): 175–220. https://doi.org/10 .1037/1089-2680.2.2.175

48 Asher Koriat, Sarah Lichtenstein, and Baruch Fischhoff, 'Reasons for Confidence', *Journal of Experimental Psychology: Human Learning and Memory*, 6, no. 2 (1980): 107–18. https://doi.org/10.1037/0278-7393.6.2.107.

49 Deanna Kuhn, 'Children and Adults as Intuitive Scientists', *Psychology Review*, 96, no. 4 (1989): 674–89. https://doi.org/10.1037/0033-295x.96.4.674.

50 John H. Lingle and Thomas M. Ostrom, 'Principles of Memory and Cognition in Attitude Formation', in *Cognitive Responses in Persuasive Communications: A Text in Attitude Change*, edited by Richard E. Petty, Thomas M. Ostrom, and Timothy C. Brock (Hillsdale: Erlbaum, 1981), 399–420.

51 Amos Tversky and Daniel Kahneman, 'Availability: A Heuristic for Judging Frequency and Probability', *Cognitive Psychology*, 5 (1973): 207–3. https://doi.org/10 .1016/0010-0285(73)90033-9.

52 John D. Read, 'The Availability Heuristic in Person Identification: The Sometimes Misleading Consequences of Enhanced Contextual Information', *Applied Cognitive Psychology*, 9, no. 2 (1995): 91–121. https://doi.org/10.1002/acp.2350090202.

53 Karyn Riddle, 'Always on My Mind: Exploring How Frequent, Recent, and Vivid Television Portrayals are Used in the Formation of Social Reality Judgments', *Media Psychology*, 13, no. 2 (2010): 155–79. https://doi.org/10.1080/15213261003800140.

54 Daniel Kahneman and Shane Frederick, 'Representativeness Revisited: Attribute Substitution in Intuitive Judgment', in *Heuristics and Biases: The Psychology of Intuitive Judgment*, edited by Thomas Gilovich, Dale Griffin and Daniel Kahneman (Cambridge: Cambridge University Press, 2002), 49–81.

55 Cass Sunstein, 'Moral Heuristics', *Behavioral and Brain Sciences*, 28 (2006): 531. https://doi.org/10.1017/S0140525X05000099.

56 Phil Rosenzweig, *The Halo Effect: … and Eight Other Business Delusions That Deceive Managers* (New York: The Free Press, 2007).

57 Kahneman, *Thinking Fast and Slow*.

58 Irving L. Janis, *Victims of Groupthink: A Psychological Study of Foreign-Policy Decisions and Fiascos* (Boston: Houghton Mifflin, 1972).

59 Victor H. Vroom, *Work and Motivation* (New York: Wiley & Sons, 1964).

60 William G. Ouchi, *Theory Z: How American Business Can Meet the Japanese Challenge* (Boston: Addison-Wesley, 1981).

61 Terrence E. Deal and Allan A. Kennedy, *Corporate Cultures: The Rites and Rituals of Corporate Life* (New York: Perseus, 2000).

62 Barnett and Finnemore, *Rules for the World*, 155.

63　Ibid., 148.

64　Daniel Kahneman and Amos Tversky, 'Choices, Values, and Frames', *American Psychologist*, 39, no. 4 (1984): 341–50. https://doi.org/10.1037/0003-066X.39.4.341.

65　Roch Parayre, 'The Strategic Implications of Sunk Costs: A Behavioral Perspective', *Journal of Economic Behavior and Organization*, 28 (1995): 417–42. https://doi.org/10.1016/0167-2681(95)00045-3

66　Hal Arkes and Catherine Blumer, 'The Psychology of Sunk Cost', *Organizational Behavior and Human Decision Processes*, 35 (1985): 124–40. https://doi.org/10.1016/0749-5978(85)90049-4.

67　Barry M. Staw, 'The Escalation of Commitment: An Update and Appraisal', in *Organizational Decision Making*, edited by Zur Shapira (New York: Cambridge University Press, 1997), 191–215.

68　Theresa F. Kelly and Katherine Milkman, 'Escalation of Commitment', in *Encyclopedia of Management Theory*, edited by Eric Kessler (Thousand Oaks: Sage Publications, Inc., 2013), 256–9.

69　Damian Lilly, 'Protection of Civilians Sites: A New Type of Displacement Settlement?' *Humanitarian Exchange Magazine*, 62 September 2014.

Chapter 3

1　For example, see the considerable evidence compiled by the Enough Project on this subject such as, 'Breaking Report: President's Daughter, Defense Ministry, and Governor Linked to Mining Sector Corruption in South Sudan,' *Enough Project*, 2020. Available online: https://enoughproject.org/press-releases/breaking-report-presidents-daughter-defense-ministry-governor-linked-mining-sector-corruption-south-sudan (accessed 8 December 2021).

2　'PCCA Protests: A Look at Juba, Bor, and Aweil', *Radio Tamazuj*, 2021. Available online: https://radiotamazuj.org/en/news/article/pcca-protests-a-look-at-juba-bor-and-aweil (accessed 9 December 2021).

3　'Juba Mayor Threatens Violent Response Against Planned Protests', *The Sudans Post*, 2021. Available online: https://www.sudanspost.com/juba-mayor-threatens-violent-response-against-planned-protests/ (accessed 8 December 2021).

4　United Nations Office for the Coordination of Humanitarian Affairs, *Humanitarian Needs Overview South Sudan: Humanitarian Programme Cycle 2021* (OCHA, 2021).

5　Sudans Post, 'South Sudan Effects New Salary Structure for Civil Servants, Army Servicemen', *Sudans Post*, 6 October 2021.

6　United Nations Office for the Coordination of Humanitarian Affairs, *Humanitarian Needs Overview South Sudan*.

7   For example, see 'Monyiemiji Give NGOs 72 Hours to Leave Greater Torit, State Gov't Orders Curfew', *Radio Tamzuj*, 2021. Available online: https://radiotamzuj .org/en/news/article/monyiemiji-give-ngos-72-hours-to-leave-otuho-areas-state -gov-t-orders-curfew-in-torit (accessed 5 July 2021).

8   'Funding Crunch Forces WFP to Cut Food Assistance in South Sudan', *World Food Programme*, 2021. Available online: https://www.wfp.org/news/funding-crunch -forces-wfp-cut-food-assistance-south-sudan (accessed 24 November 2021).

9   Daniel Maxwell, Martina Santschi and Rachel Gordon, 'Looking Back to Look Ahead? Reviewing Key Lessons from Operation Lifeline Sudan and Past Humanitarian Operations in South Sudan', *Researching Livelihoods and Services Affected by Conflict*, Working Paper 24 October 2014. Feinstein International Center.

10 Peter Martell, 'South Sudan Celebrate Their Divorce', *BBC*, 9 July 2011. Available online: https://www.bbc.co.uk/news/world-africa-14091903

11 Douglas H. Johnson, 'British Policy in Anglo-Egyptian Sudan Bears Some Responsibility for the Deep-Rooted Divisions Between North and South', *LSE*, 2012. Available online: https://blogs.lse.ac.uk/africaatlse/2012/07/02/british-policy-in -anglo-egyptian-sudan-bears-some-responsibility-for-the-deep-rooted-divisions -between-north-and-south/ (accessed 29 June 2021).

12 Women's Commission for Refugee Women and Children, *From the Ground Up: Education and Livelihoods in Southern Sudan* (New York: WCRWC, 2007).

13 Denis Dumo, 'U.N. Struggling to Deliver Food Aid in South Sudan as Rains Cut Off Vast Areas', *Reuters*, 30 July 2018. Available online: https://uk.reuters.com/article/uk -southsudan-unrest-aid/un-struggling-to-deliver-food-aid-in-south-sudan-as-rains -cut-off-vast-areas-idUKKBN1KK2D6.

14 'South Sudan: Country Overview and Key Facts', *Konrad Adenauer Stiftung*, 2019. Available online: https://www.kas.de/documents/280229/7493755/South+Sudan +Country+Overview.pdf/110c0099-62c6-4be3-e53c-30c6843bc6f4?version=1.0&t =1572941444110 (accessed 29 June 2021).

15 Central Intelligence Agency, 'Country Facts: South Sudan', 29 June 2020. Available online: https://www.cia.gov/library/publications/the-world-factbook/ geos//od.html#:~:text=Population per cent3A,13 per cent2C026 per cent2C129 per cent20(July per cent202017 per cent20est.)&text=Ethnic per cent20groups per cent3A, per cent2C per cent20Fertit per cent20(2011 per cent20est.) (accessed 3 July 2020).

16 Dennis Dumo, 'South Sudan Rebels Say Killed "Many" Government Soldiers', *Reuters*, 18 May 2015. Available online: https://in.reuters.com/article/southsudan -unrest/south-sudan-rebels-say-killed-many-government-soldiers-idINKBN0O31 3120150518.

17 Amnesty International, *Sudan: Who Will Answer for the Crimes?* (London: Amnesty International, 2005), 12. Available online: https://www.amnesty.org/download/ Documents/80000/afr540062005en.pdf.

18 The Autonomous Region of Southern Sudan had existed between the end of the
    First Sudan Civil War in 1972 to 1983, when the second Sudan civil war began and
    was re-established following the CPA. It ended in 2011 with the creation of South
    Sudan.

19 Leslie Goffe, 'Hollywood's Role in South Sudan's Independence', *BBC*, 8 July 2011.
    Available online: https://www.bbc.co.uk/news/world-africa-14050504

20 The United States had suspended aid to Sudan in 1989 following Omar al-Bashir's
    military coup. In the 1990s, Sudan had supported the Iraq regime and hosted
    Osama bin Laden, prompting comprehensive US sanctions and a missile strike on
    installations in Khartoum in 1998.

21 Rebecca Hamilton, 'U.S. Played Key Role in Southern Sudan's Long Journey to
    Independence', *The Atlantic*, 9 July 2011. Available online: https://www.theatlantic
    .com/international/archive/2011/07/us-played-key-role-in-southern-sudans-long
    -journey-to-independence/241660/

22 For example, see John Kerry, 'Chairman Kerry Statement at Hearing on Sudan',
    United States Senate Committee on Foreign Relations, 2012. Available online: https://
    www.foreign.senate.gov/press/chair/release/chairman-kerry-statement-at-hearing
    -on-sudan- (accessed 29 June 2021)

23 'Sudan and South Sudan: Current Issues for Congress and U.S. Policy', *Congressional
    Research Service*, 2012. Available online: https://www.everycrsreport.com/reports/
    R42774.html (accessed 29 June 2012).

24 Colum Lynch, 'Where did Kiir Get His Ten-Gallon Hat?' *Foreign Policy*,
    26 September 2011. Available online: https://foreignpolicy.com/2011/09/26/where
    -did-kiir-get-his-ten-gallon-hat/ (accessed 5 July 2021).

25 William Reno, 'Complex Operations in Weak and Failing States: The Sudan
    Rebel Perspective', *Institute for National Strategic Security*, 1, no. 2 (2010): 111–22.
    Available online: https://www.jstor.org/stable/pdf/26469045.pdf

26 Alexander Dziadosz, 'Exclusive: South Sudan to Split Total Oil Block – Officials',
    2012. Available online: https://www.reuters.com/article/us-southsudan-total-idU
    SBRE88C13V20120913 (accessed 29 June 2021).

27 Samuel Robinson, 'Special Report: In South Sudan, A State of Dependency', *Reuters*.
    Available online: https://www.reuters.com/article/us-south-sudan-aid-idUSBRE
    86909V20120710 (accessed 29 June 2012).

28 'Enormous Challenges Await Southern Sudan After Historic Referendum', *Oxfam*,
    11 January 2011. Available online: https://www.oxfam.org/en/press-releases/
    enormous-challenges-await-southern-sudan-after-historic-referendum (accessed
    6 July 2021).

29 'Sudan: Thousands Die as the OLS Colludes With Khartoum', *Sudan Democratic
    Gazette*, 4 May 1998. Available online: https://allafrica.com/stories/199805040041
    .html (accessed 24 November 2021).

30 "'There is No Protection" Insecurity and Human Rights in Southern Sudan', *Human Rights Watch*, 2009. Available online: https://www.hrw.org/report/2009/02/12/there-no -protection/insecurity-and-human-rights-southern-sudan (accessed 9 December 2021).

31 'The State of Sudan's Comprehensive Peace Agreement, Alert no.1', *IKV PAX Christi*, 2009.

32 Clement Ochan, 'Responding to Violence in Ikotos County, South Sudan: Government and Local Efforts to Restore Order', *Feinstein International Center*, 2007.

33 United Nations Security Council, 'Resolution on Establishing the United Nations Mission in Sudan', S/RES/1590 (New York: United Nations, 2005).

34 Jaïr van der Lijn, *To Paint the Nile Blue: Factors for Success and Failure of UNMIS and UNAMID* (Netherlands Institute of International Relations Clingendael, 2008).

35 Includes military, police and civilian peacekeeper fatalities by malicious acts in UNAMID (thirty-four) and UNMIS (four) out of a global total (seventy-four) between July 2007 and July 2011, and is based on data provided by UNDPO. Available online: https://peacekeeping.un.org/en/peacekeeper-fatalities (accessed 10 September 2019).

36 Dijkstra 'Shadow Bureaucracies'.

37 UNMIL was established with 15,000 soldiers and 1,115 police. Liberia's population in 2003 was approximately 3 million. In 2011, South Sudan was estimated to have a population of 9.8 million.

38 Interview 19 June 2021.

39 This has since changed following the 2018 reforms, which brought the Resident Coordinator role under the administration of the UN Secretariat.

40 The principle of distinction requires a separation of humanitarian and military actors to allow the former to act independently and neutrally.

41 'Financing of the United Nations Mission in South Sudan', UN Doc. A/67/716 (New York: United Nations, 2013).

42 Hilde F. Johnson, *South Sudan: The Untold Story* (London: I. B. Taurus, 2018), 122.

43 'Financing of the United Nations Mission in South Sudan', UN Doc. A/66/532 (New York: United Nations, 2011).

44 Interview 12 May 2020.

45 UN Doc. A/66/532.

46 Tito Justin, 'South Sudan: "UN Doesn't Need Drones, Attack Helicopters"', *Voice of America*, 18 June 2015.

47 Air transportation management (unsatisfactory) AUDIT REPORT 2013/064, medical services (unsatisfactory) AUDIT REPORT 2013/113, local procurement (partially satisfactory) AUDIT REPORT 2013/126, receiving and inspection activities (partially satisfactory) AUDIT REPORT 2013/109, Procurement, administration and management of rations contracts (Partially satisfactory) AUDIT REPORT 2013/56

48 Interview 24 May 2021.

Chapter 4

1 Francesco Checchi, Adrienne Testa, Abdihamid Warsame, Le Quach and Rachel Burns, 'Estimates of Crisis-Attributable Mortality in South Sudan December 2013–April 2018', *London School of Hygiene and Tropical Medicine*, 2018.

2 Matt Brown, 'Violent Attacks on Southern Returnees En Route to Abyei', *Enough Project*, 3 February 2011. Available online: https://enoughproject.org/blog/violent -attacks-abyei-southern-returnees.

3 Armin Rosen, 'From Victim to (Mutual) Aggressor: South Sudan's Disastrous First Year', *The Atlantic*, 8 May 2012.

4 Hannah Wild, Jok Madut Jok and Ronak Patel, 'The Militarization of Cattle Raiding in South Sudan: How a Traditional Practice Became a Tool for Political Violence', *International Journal of Humanitarian Action*, 3, no. 2 (2018). https://doi.org/10 .1186/s41018-018-0030-y

5 Ibid.

6 Boswell, 'Insecure Power and Violence'.

7 Small Arms Survey, 'Fighting for Spoils Armed Insurgencies in Greater Upper Nile', *Small Arms Survey*, November 2011. Available online: http://www.smallar mssurveysudan.org/fileadmin/docs/issue-briefs/HSBA-IB-18-Armed-insurgencies -Greater-Upper-Nile.pdf.

8 Human Rights Watch, 'South Sudan: End Abuses by Disarmament Forces in Jonglei', *Human Rights Watch*, 23 August 2012. Available online: https://www.hrw .org/news/2012/08/23/south-sudan-end-abuses-disarmament-forces-jonglei.

9 'South Sudan: No Justice for Protester Killings', *Human Rights Watch*, 24 May 2013. Available online: https://www.hrw.org/news/2013/05/24/south-sudan-no-justice -protester-killings.

10 Clemence Pinaud, 'South Sudan: Civil War, Predation and the Making of a Military Aristocracy', *African Affairs*, 113, no. 451 (2014): 192–211. https://doi.org/10.1093/ afraf/adu019.

11 Joshua Craze and Jerome Tubiana, 'A State of Disunity: Conflict Dynamics in Unity State, South Sudan 2013–15', *Small Arms Survey*, 2016.

12 However, rampant corruption in the armed forces at this time also meant that an unknown but large number of these soldiers existed only on paper as unscrupulous officers collected their wages.

13 International Institute for Strategic Studies, *The Military Balance 2013* (IISS, 2013).

14 Small Arms Survey, 'Fighting for Spoils Armed Insurgencies in Greater Upper Nile'.

15 David Smith, 'South Sudan President Accuses Officials of Stealing $4bn of Public Money', *The Guardian*, 5 June 2012. Available online: https://www.theguardian.com /world/2012/jun/05/south-sudan-president-accuses-officials-stealing.

16 'Survey of South Sudan Public Opinion April 24 to May 22, 2013', *International Republican Institute*, 2013. Available online: https://www.iri.org/sites/default/files /2013 per cent20July per cent2019 per cent20Survey per cent20of per cent20South per cent20Sudan per cent20Public per cent20Opinion, per cent20April per cent2024-May per cent2022, per cent202013.pdf.

17 Later known as the Fragile State Index.

18 Sophie Brown, 'Report: Political Instability on the Rise', *CNN*, 12 December 2013. Available online: https://edition.cnn.com/2013/12/11/business/maplecroft-political -risk/index.html.

19 Simon Tisdall, 'Riek Machar, the Former Rebel Fighter Ready for a New Battle', *The Guardian*, 4 July 2013. Available online: https://www.theguardian.com/world/2013/ jul/04/riek-machar-south-sudan-ambitions.

20 'Senior SPLM Colleagues Give Kiir Ultimatum Over Party Crisis', *Sudan Tribune*, 6 December 2013. Available online: https://www.sudantribune.com/spip.php ?article49087

21 'Final Report of the African Union Commission of Inquiry on South Sudan', *African Union*, 2014, Addis Ababa, 27.

22 Ibid., 119.

23 'South Sudan: Soldiers Target Ethnic Group in Juba Fighting: Capital's Residents Indiscriminately Fired Upon, Thousands Flee', *Human Rights Watch*, 2013. Available online: https://www.hrw.org/news/2013/12/19/south-sudan-soldiers-target-ethnic -group-juba-fighting

24 These were based at the airport at Tomping in the north-east of the city and the main base at UN House approximately 5 kilometres away on the other side of the city.

25 'South Sudan: A Civil War by Any Other Name', *Brussels; International Crisis Group*, 2014.

26 'South Sudan Crisis Fact Sheet #25', *USAID*, 2014. Available online: https://www .usaid.gov/crisis/south-sudan/fy14/fs25.

27 This is despite the fact that child abduction during raids is a common practice among other communities in South Sudan.

28 Peter Martell, 'The Child Snatchers of South Sudan', *The Telegraph*, 7 December 2009. Available online: https://www.telegraph.co.uk/expat/expatnews/6751222/The -child-snatchers-of-southern-Sudan.html.

29 Hereward Holland, 'Analysis – Jonglei Revolt Gives South Sudan a Security Headache', *Reuters*, 30 September 2012. Available online: https://www.reuters.com/ article/uk-sudan-southsudan-jonglei-idUKBRE88T05A20120930.

30 'South Sudan Horror at Deadly Cattle Vendetta', *BBC*, 16 January 2012. Available online: https://www.bbc.com/news/world-africa-16575153

31 Interview 19 June 2021.

32 Interview 17 June 2021.

33 Johnson, *South Sudan: The Untold Story*, 158.

34 Ibid.

35 Ibid., 159.

36 'South Sudan: Lethal Disarmament', *Amnesty International*, 2012, 17.

37 Wendy Fenton and Sean Loughna, *The Search for Common Ground: Civil–Military Coordination and the Protection of Civilians in South Sudan* (London: Overseas Development Institute, 2012).

38 'Report of the Secretary-General on South Sudan', UN Doc. S/2013/651 (New York: United Nations, 2013).

39 Interview 10 June 2020.

40 Lauren Hutton, *Prolonging the Agony of UNMISS: The Implementation Challenges of a New Mandate During a Civil War* (The Hague: Clingendael Institute, 2014), 12.

41 Interview 8 May 2021.

42 Hilde F. Johnson, *Waging Peace in Sudan: The Inside Story of the Negotiations That Ended Africa's Longest Civil War* (Eastbourne: Sussex Academic Press, 2011), 200–1.

43 Interview 19 June 2021.

44 'From Hope to Horror', *The Economist*, 14 July 2016. Available online: https://www.economist.com/books-and-arts/2016/07/14/from-hope-to-horror.

45 Peter Martell, *First Raise a Flag: How South Sudan Won the Longest War But Lost the Peace* (Oxford: Oxford University Press, 2018), 223.

46 Johnson, *South Sudan: The Untold Story*, 311.

47 'Final Report of the African Union Commission of Inquiry on South Sudan'.

48 Johnson, *South Sudan: The Untold Story*, 243.

49 Ibid., 170.

50 'Special Representative Voices "Cautious Optimism" over Progress in South Sudan, Despite Continuing Violence, Human Rights Violations', (New York: United Nations, 18 November 2013). Available online: https://www.un.org/press/en/2013/sc11178.doc.htm.

51 Hilde F. Johnson, 'Protection of Civilians in the United Nations: A Peacekeeping Illusion?' in *United Nations Peace Operations in a Changing Global Order*, edited by Cedric de Coning and Mateja Peter (Palgrave: MacMillan, 2019), 45–65.

52 'Resolution to Extend the Mandate of UNMISS', UN Doc. S/RES/2109 (New York: United Nations, 2013).

53 'South Sudan: Army Making Ethnic Conflict Worse', *Human Rights Watch*, 19 July 2013. Available online: https://www.hrw.org/news/2013/07/19/south-sudan-army-making-ethnic-conflict-worse.

54 Johnson, *South Sudan: The Untold Story*, 133.

55 Interview 8 May 2021.

56 Johnson, *South Sudan: The Untold Story*, 186.

57 Interview 14 March 2021.

58 Interview 8 May 2021.

59 Interview 24 May 2021.

60 Interview 8 May 2021.
61 Interview 15 June 2021.
62 Interview 8 May 2021.
63 Interview 9 May 2020.
64 Interview 24 May 2021.
65 Interview 7 May 2020.
66 Nicholas Coghlan, *Collapse of a Country: A Diplomat's Memoir of South Sudan* (Montreal: McGill-Queen's University Press, 2017), 108.
67 Interview 2 May 2020.
68 Elizabeth Shackelford, *The Dissent Channel, American Diplomacy in a Dishonest Age* (New York: Public Affairs, 2020), 204.
69 Interview 17 June 2021.

Chapter 5

1 It should be noted that the spelling of Tomping is based on an UNMISS preference for a spelling of the neighbourhood that is likely more correctly known by Thongpiny or Thong Ping. However, as I generally only use the term to refer to the UNMISS base, I have opted to use their organizational spelling. The neighbourhood is also known within the Equatorian community as Juba Na Bari.
2 'South Sudan: War Crimes by Both Sides', *Human Rights Watch*, 26 February 2014. Available online: https://www.hrw.org/news/2014/02/26/south-sudan-war-crimes -both-sides.
3 'Attacks on Civilians in Bentiu & Bor April 2014', 9.
4 Johnson, *South Sudan: The Untold Story*, 210.
5 Interview 17 February 2021.
6 'Attacks on Civilians in Bentiu & Bor April 2014', 9.
7 Ibid., 18.
8 United Nations Mission in South Sudan, 'UNMISS Protection of Civilians Update 16 April 2014', *UNMISS*, 16 April 2014. https://reliefweb.int/sites/reliefweb.int/files/resources/14-04-Update per cent2019.pdf.
9 'Financing of the United Nations Mission in South Sudan', UN Doc. A/67/716 (New York: United Nations, 2013).
10 'Attacks on Civilians in Bentiu & Bor April 2014', 9.
11 Ibid., 18.
12 Ibid., 11.
13 Interview 12 May 2020.
14 Interview 11 June 2020.
15 Ibid.

16 'Attacks on Civilians in Bentiu & Bor April 2014', 20.

17 Interview 11 June 2020.

18 'Attacks on Civilians in Bentiu & Bor April 2014', 19.

19 Ibid., 20.

20 Interview 12 May 2020 *and* Interview 11 June 2020.

21 'Attacks on Civilians in Bentiu & Bor April 2014', 22.

22 Ibid., 21.

23 *Based on readings from audio transcripts from the incident from* interview 11 June (2020).

24 Interview 12 May 2020.

25 'Attacks on Civilians in Bentiu & Bor April 2014', 21.

26 Interview 11 June 2020.

27 'Attacks on Civilians in Bentiu & Bor April 2014', 22.

28 Interview 12 May 2020.

29 According to UNMISS's reporting, peacekeepers only fired outside of the perimeter yet only one body thought to belong to a perpetrator was found outside of the perimeter.

30 'Attacks on Civilians in Bentiu & Bor April 2014', 24.

31 Ibid.

32 Charlton Doki, 'South Sudan Officials Blame UN for Deadly Attack in Bor', *Voice of America*, 18 April 2014. Available online: https://www.voanews.com/africa/south -sudan-officials-blame-un-deadly-attack-bor.

33 'Attacks on Civilians in Bentiu & Bor April 2014', 18.

34 Interview 12 May 2020.

35 Interview 4 May 2020.

36 Shackelford, *The Dissent Channel*, 204.

37 The others being a human rights officer in December 2012 and a civil affairs officer in January 2014.

38 Johnson, *South Sudan: The Untold Story*, 211.

39 Janine Di Giovanni, 'Hilde Johnson is Trying to Stop the Misery in South Sudan', *Newsweek Magazine*, 28 May 2014. Available online: https://www.newsweek.com /2014/06/06/hilde-johnson-trying-stop-misery-south-sudan-252506.html.

40 Michael J. Arensen, *If We Leave, We Are Killed: Lessons Learned from South Sudan Protection of Civilian Sites 2013–2016* (Geneva: IOM, 2016).

41 Ibid., 21.

42 'Guidelines: Civilians Seeking Protection at UNMISS Bases', *UNMISS*, 2013.

43 Lilly, 'Protection of Civilians Sites'.

44 'Report of the Secretary-General on South Sudan', UN Doc. S/2014/158 (New York: United Nations, 2014).

45 'Huge Brawl in PoC Camp Leaves Dozens Injured', *Radio Tamazuj*, 28 October 2014. Available Online: https://radiotamazuj.org/en/news/article/huge-brawl-in -poc-camp-leaves-dozens-injured

46 'Within and Beyond the Gates: The Protection of Civilians by the UN Mission in South Sudan', (Washington, DC: CIVIC, 2015).

47 'South Sudan: Shameful Attitude to Vulnerable Displaced Shown by Leaders of UNMISS', *MSF*, 9 April 2014. Available online: https://www.msf.org.uk/article/south-sudan-shameful-attitude-vulnerable-displaced-shown-leaders-unmiss.

48 Interview 20 June 2021.

49 In the end, it was discovered that an adult had been using an unaccompanied minor to crawl through the small spaces that served as windows. The adult claimed that he had been under the control of the child who he accused of being a witch, an accusation that at least some of the UNPOL were willing to entertain as credible in private conversations. The UNMISS state coordinator wished to expel both individuals from the site; however, they were unsure how to process the minor. The leadership instructed the visibly small child to undergo a medical 'age check' before being airlifted to Akobo, 300 kilometres away in territory held by the SPLA/iO to be with people believed to be relatives.

50 Interview 14 May 2020.

51 Interview 17 February 2021.

52 'Regional Interests at Stake in the South Sudan Crisis', *The New Humanitarian*, 19 March 2014. Available online: https://www.thenewhumanitarian.org/analysis/2014/03/19/regional-interests-stake-south-sudan-crisis

53 Shackelford, *The Dissent Channel*, 215.

54 'Report of the Secretary-General on South Sudan', UN Doc. S/2013/366 (New York: United Nations, 2013).

55 'Report of the Secretary-General on South Sudan', UN Doc. S/2014/821 (New York: United Nations, 2014).

56 'Report of the Independent High-Level Panel on Peace Operations', (New York: United Nations, 2015).

57 'Action for Peacekeeping: Declaration of Shared Commitments on UN Peacekeeping Operations', (New York: United Nations, 2018).

58 A downpour of rain is reported to have stalled earlier attempts to begin the work.

59 Interview 11 June 2020.

60 'Attacks on Civilians in Bentiu & Bor April 2014', 15.

61 Interview 11 June 2020.

62 Between 2012 and 2016, the UN conducted four Boards of Inquiry in South Sudan. These related to two incidents of its helicopters being shot down (2012 and 2014), an attack on its POC site at Malakal in 2016 and the failure of the mission to respond during violence in Juba in 2016.

63 Interview 15 May 2020.

64 Interview 10 June 2020.

65 Johnson, *South Sudan: The Untold Story*, 219.

66 These were the attacks on Malakal in February and Juba in July, and are discussed in greater detail later in the book.

67 Of which thirteen were the result of malicious incidents, according to UNDPO peacekeeping fatalities data.

Chapter 6

1 'Press Conference Statement by Hilde F. Johnson'.

2 'UNMISS POC Site Update 26 June 2014'.

3 Interview 25 June 2021.

4 'South Sudan Food Security Outlook October 2014'.

5 'Report of the Secretary-General on South Sudan Covering the Period from 14 April to 19 August 2015', UN Doc. S/2015/655 (New York: United Nations, 2015).

6 Johnson stepped down as SRSG on 7 July, and Løj was not announced as her replacement until 23 July. She arrived in Juba on 2 September.

7 Interview 8 May 2021.

8 Boutellis and Wyeth, 'Interview with Ellen Margrethe Løj'.

9 Blair, 'In Liberia, the U.N. Mission Helped Restore Confidence in the Rule of Law'.

10 While the Cessation of Hostilities Agreement had effectively collapsed the international community continued to sponsor its mechanisms including its monitoring teams.

11 'Press Conference Transcript Tuesday, 7 October 2014'.

12 Ibid.

13 'Report of the Secretary-General on South Sudan', UN Doc. S/2014/821, 18 November (New York: United Nations, 2014).

14 'SRSG Appeals to IDPs to Respect Protection Sites'.

15 In a coordinated campaign, UNMISS conducted public weapons destructions at Juba POC site (9 December 2014), Malakal POC site (12 December 2014), Bentiu POC site (19 December), Wau POC site (23 December) and Bor POC site (29 December), based on various press releases by UNMISS between 10 December and 30 December 2014; accessed on 4 March 2020 on https://unmiss.unmissions .org/

16 Briggs and Monaghan, 'Protection of Civilians Sites'.

17 'UNMISS Hands over Police Post in Juba'.

18 Interview 13 May 2020.

19 Ibid.

20 'UNMISS Declines IGAD Request to Transport Opposition Leaders to Consultative Conference in Pagak'.

21 Interview 1 May 2020.

22 Interview 14 March 2021.

23 Interview 7 May 2020.

24 Winckler, 'Exceeding Limitations of the United Nations Peacekeeping Bureaucracy'.

25 Interview 1 May 2020.

26 Interview 15 May 2020.

27 Interview 14 May 2020.

28 Interview 7 May 2020.

29 Interview 6 June 2020.

30 Interview 4 May 2020.

31 'UNMISS Restricting Journalists from South Sudan Protection Camps'.

32 Briggs and Monaghan, 'Protection of Civilians Sites', 43.

33 Rubin, 'In South Sudan, Another Human Rights Horror'.

34 Lynch, 'Inside the White House Fight Over the Slaughter in South Sudan'.

35 *Weapons Supplies into South Sudan's Civil War.*

36 For example, see John Kerry's statements. 'John Kerry to South Sudan Leaders: Come to Your Senses, Stop Fighting'.

37 The EU arms embargo was instituted on Sudan in 1994 in response to the civil war. In 2011, it was amended to include the newly created South Sudan, according to the SIPRI database of arms embargoes https://www.sipri.org/databases/embargoes/eu _arms_embargoes/south_sudan; accessed on 9 Jul. 2020.

38 Bodettii, 'How China Came to Dominate South Sudan's Oil'.

39 *Weapons Supplies into South Sudan's Civil War.*

40 'Resolution Renewing the Mandate of UNMISS for an Additional Six Months', UN Doc. S/RES/2187 (New York: United Nations, 2014).

41 'Restart of South Sudan Talks Critical to Avert End-March War Threat'.

42 Interview 17 February 2021.

43 'Final Report of the African Union Commission of Inquiry on South Sudan'.

44 Boswell, 'Insecure Power and Violence'.

45 A dispute between Johnson Olony's Shilluk Aguelek militia and a neighbouring Dinka Padang militia led to the desertion of Olony and his forces when the government appeared to side with his long-time rivals.

46 'Dozens of Children Killed by SPLA Armed Groups: Witnesses'.

47 'Flash Human Rights Report on the Escalation of Fighting in Greater Upper Nile April/May 2015'.

48 'Crisis Impacts on Households in Unity State South Sudan 2014–2015'.

49 'The Conflict in Unity State', (Geneva: Small Arms Survey, 2015).

50 'UNMISS POC Site Update 19 August 2015'.

51 Interview 4 May 2020.

52 Interview 25 June 2021.

53 'Report of the Secretary-General on South Sudan', UN Doc. S/2015/902, 23 November (New York: United Nations, 2015).

54 Interview 14 May 2020.

55 'Special Report of the Secretary-General on the Review of the Mandate of the United Nations Mission in South Sudan', UN Docs. S/2015/899 (New York: United Nations, 2015).

56 Harmer and Czwarno, 'The Effects of Insecurity on Aid Operations in South Sudan'.

57 'Briefing by Special Representative Ellen Margrethe Løj', UN Doc. S/PV.74444 (New York: United Nations, 2015).

58 Interview 14 July 2021.

59 Ibid.

60 'Statement the UN Humanitarian Coordinator in South Sudan, Mr. Toby Lanzer, Up to 100,000 People Displaced in Unity State in May Alone', United Nations, 8 May 2015.

61 Patinkin, 'South Sudan Needs Peace as Much as Food'.

62 'Flash Human Rights Report on the Escalation of Fighting in Greater Upper Nile. April/May'.

63 Interview 6 June 2020.

64 Jones, 'UN Accused of "Shocking" Lack of Action over Murder and Rape in South Sudan'.

65 Løj, 'In Defence of the UN's Role in South Sudan'.

66 Interview 8 May 2021.

67 Briggs and Monaghan, 'Protection of Civilians Sites', 26.

68 Interview 7 May 2020.

69 'Briefing by Special Representative Ellen Margrethe Løj', UN Doc. S/PV.74444 (New York: United Nations, 2015).

70 'UN Peacekeepers Turned Away Yambio Civilians Seeking Shelter from Violence'.

71 This was enshrined in the *Saving Lives Together Framework*, which existed to increase collaboration between NGOs and the UN.

Chapter 7

1 Sarah Vuylsteke, *Identity and Self-determination: The Fertit Opposition in South Sudan* (Small Arms Survey, 2018).

2 'Special Report of the Secretary-General on the Review of the Mandate of the United Nations Mission in South Sudan', UN Docs. S/2015/899 (New York: United Nations, 2015).

3 'UNMISS POC Site Update 28 January 2016', *UNMISS*, 2016. Available online: https://unmiss.unmissions.org/sites/default/files/18-01-_update_no._109.pdf

4 Briggs and Monaghan, 'Protection of Civilians Sites', 59.

5 'UN Delays Leave "Protection" Area Unfenced Amid Horrific Violence in S Sudan's Unity State', *Radio Tamazuj*, 22 May 2015. Available online: https://radiotamazuj .org/en/news/article/un-delays-leave-protection-area-unfenced-amid-horrific -violence-in-s-sudan-s-unity-state

6 Arensen. *If We Leave, We Are Killed.*

7 Based on 142,170 troop days reported to have been carried out to provide static protection of the POC sites out of a total number of 1,282,912 available troop duty days as part of 2014–15 planning based on financing documents presented to the UNGA in 2014 and 2015.

8 Based on 105,408 troop days planned to provide static protection of the POC sites out of a total number of 1,202,528 available troop duty days based on financing documents presented to the UNGA in 2015.

9 Interview 20 June 2021.

10 *A Refuge in Flames; The February 17–18 Violence in Malakal* (Washington, DC: CIVIC, 2016).

11 *UNSG, Note to Correspondents – Board of Inquiry Report on Malakal* (New York: United Nations, 5 August 2016).

12 'UN Delays Leave "Protection" Area Unfenced Amid Horrific Violence in S Sudan's Unity State'.

13 *A Refuge in Flames.*

14 Interview 25 June 2021.

15 Zach Vertin, *A Rope From the Sky; The Making and Unmaking of the World's Newest State* (New York: Pegasus, 2019), 408.

16 D. Akol Ruay Deng, *The Politics of Two Sudans: The South and the North 1821–1969* (Uppsala: Nordiska Afrikainstitutet, 1994).

17 'Minutes of Permanent Ceasefire and Transitional Security Arrangements (PCTSA) Workshop', *IGAD*, 2015. Available online: https://www.usip.org/south-sudan-peace -process-digital-library/permanent-ceasefire-and-transitional-security

18 'South Sudan's Rival Forces Clash in Upper Nile State', *South Sudan News Agency*, 25 December 2015.

19 Ayen Bior, 'UN Report: Rights Violations, Fighting Spike in South Sudan', *Voice of America*, 15 March 2017. Available online: https://www.voanews.com/archive/un -report-rights-violations-fighting-spike-south-sudan

20 In February 2015, there were 21,368 people seeking protection at Malakal POC site (UNMISS, 2015e). This peaked at 48,840 in August (UNMISS, 2015f). By December, the recorded number remained at 47,791 (UNMISS, 2015g).

21 'MSF Demands UN Give More Space to Displaced in Malakal Amid "Deplorable" Conditions', *Radio Tamazuj*, 19 November 2015. Available online: https:// radiotamazuj.org/en/news/article/msf-demands-un-give-more-space-to-displaced -in-malakal-amid-deplorable-conditions.

22 'Five Protesters Injured in Malakal PoC', *Radio Tamazuj*, 24 June 2015. Available online: https://radiotamazuj.org/en/news/article/five-protesters-injured-in-malakal-poc.
23 Interview 17 February 2021.
24 'MSF Internal Review of the February 2016 Attack on the Malakal Protection of Civilians Site and the Post-Event Situation', *MSF*, June 2016.
25 *A Refuge in Flames*, 24.
26 *UNSG, Note to Correspondents – Board of Inquiry Report on Malakal*.
27 Ibid.
28 'MSF Internal Review of the February 2016 Attack on the Malakal'.
29 *UNSG, Note to Correspondents – Board of Inquiry Report on Malakal*.
30 Ibid.
31 'MSF Internal Review of the February 2016 Attack on the Malakal'.
32 Ibid.
33 *A Refuge in Flames*, 33.
34 *UNSG, Note to Correspondents – Board of Inquiry Report on Malakal*.
35 Interview 26 June 2021.
36 'Budget for the United Nations Mission in South Sudan for the period from 1 July 2016 to 30 June 2017', UN Docs. A/70/791 (New York: United Nations, 2016).
37 *UNSG, Note to Correspondents – Board of Inquiry Report on Malakal*.
38 Michelle Nichols, 'U.N. Reaction to Malakal Violence in South Sudan Marred by Confusion', *Reuters*, 2016. Available online: https://www.reuters.com/article/us-southsudan-unrest-un-idUSKCN0Z731G.

Chapter 8

1 IOM was founded as an independent technical agency and inter-governmental organization. In September 2016, it became a related organization of the United Nations.
2 Martell, *First Raise a Flag*.
3 *For example, see* Vertin, *A Rope From the Sky*, 376.
4 *For example, see* Sharath Srinivasan, *When Peace Kills Politics: International Intervention and Unending Wars in the Sudans* (London: Hurst, 2021), 288–71.
5 Vertin, *A Rope From the Sky*, 399.
6 Interview 15 June 2021.
7 'Outcome of the Meeting of the Principal Signatory Parties to the Agreement on Planning Implementation of the Provisions in Chapter II the Agreement 21 October–3 November 2015', *IGAD*, 2015. Available online: https://www.usip.org/south-sudan-peace-process-digital-library/outcome-meeting-principal-signatory-parties-agreement

8 'October Monthly Security Report', *South Sudan NGO Forum*, 2016 (Personal archives).

9 'Embassy Cable: Juba "More Dangerous Than Ever"'. *Radio Tamazuj*, 3 May 2016. Available online: https://radiotamazuj.org/en/news/article/embassy-cable-juba-more-dangerous-than-ever

10 'South Sudan Govt Accused of Expelling Ceasefire Monitors from W Equatoria, Again', *Radio Tamazuj*, 14 April 2016. Available online: https://radiotamazuj.org/en/news/article/south-sudan-govt-accused-of-expelling-ceasefire-monitors-from-w-equatoria-again; Emmanuel Akile, 'Ceasefire Monitors Seek Refuge at UN Torit Base', *Eye Radio*, 1 July 2016. https://eyeradio.org/ceasefire-monitors-seek-refuge-torit-base/

11 'Makuei Behind Expulsion of Peace Monitor from South Sudan: Document', *Radio Tamazuj*, 2016.

12 Daniel Finnan, 'South Sudan: Ceasefire Violations Continue, Conflict Spreading, Say Monitors', *Radio France Internationale*, 28 March 2016. Available online: https://www.rfi.fr/en/africa/20160328-south-sudan-ceasefire-violations-continue-conflict-spreading-say-monitors

13 'South Sudan Expels Ceasefire Monitors from Yambio', *Radio Tamazuj*, 24 March 2016. Available online: https://radiotamazuj.org/en/news/article/south-sudan-expels-ceasefire-monitors-from-yambio

14 Ayuen Panchol, 'Government Rejects PLO Lumumba', *Eye Radio*, 6 November 2015. https://eyeradio.org/govt-rejects-plo-lumumba/

15 Karin Zeitvogel and Waakhe Simon Wudu, 'IGAD: Creating New States in South Sudan Violates Peace Deal', *Voice of America*, 13 October 2015. Available online: https://www.voanews.com/archive/igad-creating-new-states-south-sudan-violates-peace-deal.

16 'Report of the Secretary-General on South Sudan', UN Docs. S/2016/138 (New York: United Nations, 2016).

17 'Final Report of the South Sudan Sanctions Committee Panel of Experts', UN Doc. S/2016/70 (New York: United Nations, 2016).

18 Interview 14 May 2020.

19 John Young, 'South Sudan's Civil War; Violence, Insurgency and Failed Peacemaking', *Zed Books*, 2019, 152.

20 Coghlan, *Collapse of a Country.*

21 Ibid.

22 Ibid.

23 'Mogae has "Heavy Heart" over Struggling Peace Deal', *Radio Tamazuj*, 24 June 2016. Available on: https://radiotamazuj.org/en/news/article/mogae-has-heavy-heart-over-struggling-peace-deal

24 Interview 7 May 2020.

25 Interview 17 February 2021.

26 Interview 14 May 2020.

27 Simona Foltyn, 'Violence Erupts Again in South Sudan as Faith in Peace Deal Flounders', *The Guardian*, 2016. Available online: https://www.theguardian.com /global-development/2016/jul/05/violence-erupts-again-in-south-sudan-wau-as -faith-in-peace-deal-flounders

28 *Under Fire: The July 2016 Violence in Juba and UN Response* (Washington DC: CIVIC, 2016).

29 When asked, UNMISS were unable to confirm that such a request was ever made.

30 'Budget for the United Nations Mission in South Sudan for the period from 1 July 2016 to 30 June 2017'.

31   *Under Fire: The July 2016 Violence in Juba and UN Response.*

32 'Report of the Panel of Experts on South Sudan', UN Docs. S/2016/793 (New York: United Nations, 2016).

33 'Executive Summary of the Independent Special Investigation into the Violence in Juba in 2016 and the Response by the United Nations Mission in South Sudan', UN Docs. S/2016/924 (New York: United Nations, 2016).

34 Ibid.

35 Matt Wells, 'The UN has Failed Its Peacekeepers in S Sudan', *Al Jazeera*, 10 September 2016. Available online: https://www.aljazeera.com/indepth/opinion /2016/09/failed-peacekeepers-sudan-160908091206526.html

36 *SPLA Committed Widespread Violations During and After July Fighting in South Sudan* (Geneva: United Nations, 2016).

37 Sadie Levy Gale, 'UN Peacekeepers Looked on as Women Were Raped in Camps by South Sudanese Soldiers, Witnesses Say', *The Independent*, 2016. Available online: https://www.independent.co.uk/news/world/africa/south-sudan-rape-soldiers -united-nations-peacekeepers-juba-dinka-nuer-a7160311.html

38 'At Least 300 Killed in Latest South Sudan Violence: UN', *AFP*, July 2016. Available online: https://www.bbc.com/news/world-africa-52745377#:~:text=At per cent20least per cent20300 per cent20people per cent20have,workers per cent20were per cent20among per cent20those per cent20killed.

39 *SPLA Committed Widespread Violations During and After July fighting in South Sudan.*

40 Faith Karimi, 'South Sudan: Did Clashes Start over Facebook Post?' *CNN*, 15 July. https://edition.cnn.com/2016/07/13/africa/south-sudan-violence-questions/index .html

41 'JMEC Criticizes Nomination of Taban Deng Gai as "Illegitimate"', *Sudan Tribune*, 23 July 2016. Available online: https://sudantribune.com/spip.php?article59705

42 Interview 14 May 2020.

43 Following the inauguration of the newly assembled Transitional National Legislative Assembly on 18 August, UNMISS met with its leadership. On 23 August, UNMISS met with the minister of justice to discuss their support to transitional justice. On 25 August, Løj discussed with the TGoNU how it and UNMISS might *'harmonize its understanding of the mandated tasks under resolution'*.

44 Daniel Danis, 'Replacement of Riek in Line with Peace Deal – Kerry', *Eye Radio*, 23 August 2016. Available online: https://eyeradio.org/replacement-riek-line-peace -deal-kerry/

45 Young, 'South Sudan's Civil War'.

46 'Rebels Warn of Clamp Down on Riek Machar', *Radio Tamazuj*, 23 November 2016. Available online: https://radiotamazuj.org/en/news/article/rebels-warn-of-clamp -down-on-riek-machar#:~:text=In per cent20last per cent20September per cent2C per cent20Booth per cent20said,continuing per cent20instability per cent20in per cent20the per cent20country

47 'High-level Detainee Accuses Kenya, South Sudan of Kidnapping', *Voice of America*, 6 February 2016. Available online: https://www.voanews.com/africa/high-level -detainee-accuses-kenya-south-sudan-kidnapping

48 Jonathan Pedneault, *Safe Haven No More in South Sudan* (Human Rights Watch, 2016).

49 'Media Briefing by Adama Dieng, United Nations Special Adviser on the Prevention of Genocide on his visit to South Sudan', (New York: United Nations, 2016).

50 'UN Human Rights Experts Says International Community has an Obligation to Prevent Ethnic Cleansing in South Sudan', (Geneva: United Nations, 2016).

51 Checchi et. al. 'Estimates of Crisis-Attributable Mortality in South Sudan'.

52 Rocco Nuri, '100,000 Fearful Civilians Trapped in South Sudan Town', *UNHCR*, 2016.

53 'Report of the Secretary-General on South Sudan', UN Docs. S/2016/950 (New York: United Nations, 2016).

54 Briggs and Monaghan, 'Protection of Civilians Sites', 89.

55 'Executive Summary of the Independent Special Investigation into the Violence in Juba in 2016 and the Response by the United Nations Mission in South Sudan', UN Docs. S/2016/924 (New York: United Nations, 2016).

56 Margaret Besheer, 'Kenya in Uproar after UN Blames General for S. Sudan Violence', *Voice of America*, 3 November 2016. Available online: https://www .voanews.com/africa/kenya-uproar-after-un-blames-general-s-sudan-violence

57 Interview 24 May 2021.

58 'Executive Summary of the Independent Special Investigation into the Violence in Juba in 2016 and the Response by the United Nations Mission in South Sudan', UN Docs. S/2016/924 (New York: United Nations, 2016).

Chapter 9

1 Lynch, 'Inside the White House Fight Over the Slaughter in South Sudan'.

2 'Ellen Løj briefing the UNSC', S/PV.7814. New York: United Nations, 2016.

3 Ibid.

4 Shearer spent more than thirteen years in operational roles in emergency contexts that included Iraq, Lebanon, Rwanda, Somalia and Sri Lanka.

5 Interview 8 May 2021.

6 'Update on Implementation of Special Investigation Recommendations', UN Docs. S/2017/328 (New York: United Nations, 2017).

7 Interview 14 March 2021.

8 Interview 1 May 2020.

9 Interview 14 July 2021.

10 Interview 8 May 2021.

11 Waakhe Simon Wudu and Ayen Bior, 'South Sudan Accused of Blocking Aid, Despite Famine', *Voice of America*, 22 Febuary 2017. Available online: https://www.voanews.com/africa/south-sudan-accused-blocking-aid-despite-famine#:~:text=aid percent20agenciespercent20declaredpercent20faminepercent20exists, checkpoints percent20approachingpercent20faminepercent2Dstrickenpercent20areas.

12 David Shearer, 'Why South Sudan's Leaders are to Blame for the Country's Famine', *Newsweek*, 3 March 2017.

13 Two examples of this include UNMISS press releases about an intervention by Chinese peacekeepers in Yei to rescue UN staff and an intervention in Bentiu by Mongolian peacekeepers to rescue fifty civilians, both in 2017.

14 'The Mass Displacement of the Shilluk Population from the West Bank of the White Nile, South Sudan', *Amnesty International*, June 2017.

15 'South Sudan Flash Update on Upper Nile', *OCHA*, 27 April 2017.

16 'Protection Trends South Sudan January - April 2017', *Protection Cluster*, May 2017.

17 'South Sudan: UN Deplores Lack of Information on 20,000 People Displaced in Upper Nile', *UNMISS*, 16 Febuary 2017.

18 'South Sudan / Aburoc Peacekeeping [Video]', *UN Audiovisual Library*, 22 June 2017. Available online: https://www.unmultimedia.org/avlibrary/asset/1916/1916033/

19 That only includes those major attacks which involved significant loss of life in 2013, 2014 and 2016 (2).

20 In June 2015, there were 11,350 UNMISS peacekeeping soldiers in country compared to 11,512 in April 2017.

21 China, Russia, Angola, Egypt, Senegal, Malaysia, Venezuela and Japan abstained.

22 'Report of the Secretary-General on South Sudan', UN Docs. S/2017/505 (New York: United Nations, 2017).

23 'Moving Toward Mobility; Providing Protection to Civilians Through Static Presence and Mobile Peacekeeping in South Sudan', (Washington, DC: CIVIC, 2019).

24 Interview 8 May 2021.

25 Interview 14 July 2021.

26 Sam Mednick, 'UN Pullout Triggers Safety Concerns in South Sudan Displacement Camps', *The New Humanitarian*, 2021. Available online: https://www .thenewhumanitarian.org/news-feature/2021/18/5/un-pullout-triggers-security -concerns-in-south-south-displacement-camps

27 Interview 21 October 2021.

28 Interview 8 May 2021.

29 Interview 17 February 2021.

30 'Annual Brief on Violence Affecting Civilians', *UNMISS*, 2021. Available online: https://reliefweb.int/sites/reliefweb.int/files/resources/UNMISS%20annual%20brief _violence%20against%20civilians_2020.pdf

31 'South Sudan: UN Urges Accountability for Key Figures Supporting Militias in Greater Jonglei', *United Nations*, 2021. Available online: https://www.ohchr.org/EN/ NewsEvents/Pages/DisplayNews.aspx?NewsID=26894&LangID=E

32 'Statement by Yasmin Sooka Chair of the UN Commission on Human Rights in South Sudan to the Human Rights Council', *United Nations*, 2021. Available online: https://www.ohchr.org/EN/HRBodies/HRC/Pages/NewsDetail.aspx?NewsID =27523&LangID=E

33 Sam Mednick, 'Old Grudges and Empty Coffers: South Sudan's Precarious Peace Process', *The New Humanitarian*, 2021. Available online: https://www .thenewhumanitarian.org/news-feature/2021/01/21/south-sudan-peace-deal -violence-famine

34 Ibid.

35 'RJMEC Expresses Concern at Reports of Defections or Accepting Defections', *RJMEC*, 2020. Available online: https://jmecsouthsudan.org/index.php/press -release/item/530-rjmec-expresses-concern-at-reports-of-defections-or-accepting -defections

36 Interview 12 June 2021.

References

'A Refuge in Flames; The February 17–18 Violence in Malakal'. Washington: CIVIC, 2016.

'Action for Peacekeeping: Declaration of Shared Commitments on UN Peacekeeping Operations'. New York: United Nations, 2018.

'Annual Brief on Violence Affecting Civilians'. *UNMISS*, 2021.

'At Least 300 Killed in Latest South Sudan Violence: UN'. *AFP*, July 2016.

'Breaking Report: President's Daughter, Defense Ministry, and Governor Linked to Mining Sector Corruption in South Sudan'. *Enough Project*, 2020.

'Briefing by Special Representative Ellen Margrethe Løj'. UN Doc. S/PV.74444. New York: United Nations, 2015.

'Budget for the United Nations Mission in South Sudan for the Period from 1 July 2016 to 30 June 2017'. UN Docs. A/70/791. New York: United Nations, 2017.

'Comprehensive Review of the Whole Question of Peacekeeping Operations in All Their Aspects'. UN Doc A/55/305–S/2000/809. New York: United Nations, 2000.

'Crisis Impacts on Households in Unity State South Sudan 2014–2015'. *Office of the Deputy Humanitarian Coordinator for South Sudan*, 2016.

'Dozens of Children Killed by SPLA Armed Groups: Witnesses'. *Radio Tamazuj*, 18 May 2015.

'Ellen Løj Briefing the UNSC'. UN Doc S/PV.7814. New York: United Nations, 2016.

'Embassy Cable: Juba "More Dangerous Than Ever"'. *Radio Tamazuj*, 3 May 2016.

'Enormous Challenges Await Southern Sudan After Historic Referendum'. *Oxfam*, 11 January 2011.

'Executive Summary of the Independent Special Investigation into the Violence in Juba in 2016 and the Response by the United Nations Mission in South Sudan'. UN Docs. S/2016/924. New York: United Nations, 2016.

'Fighting for Spoils Armed Insurgencies in Greater Upper Nile'. *HSBA Small Arms Survey*, November 2011.

'Final Report of the African Union Commission of Inquiry on South Sudan'. *African Union*. Addis Ababa, 2014.

'Final Report of the South Sudan Sanctions Committee Panel of Experts'. UN Doc. S/2016/70. New York: United Nations, 2016.

'Financing of the United Nations Mission in South Sudan'. UN Doc. A/67/716. New York: United Nations, 2013.

'Financing of the United Nations Mission in South Sudan'. UN Doc. A/66/532. New York: United Nations, 2011.

'Financing of the United Nations Mission in South Sudan'. UN Doc. A/67/716. New York: United Nations, 2013.

'Five Protesters Injured in Malakal PoC'. *Radio Tamazuj*, 24 June 2015.

'Flash Human Rights Report on the Escalation of Fighting in Greater Upper Nile April/May 2015'. *UNMISS*, 29 June 2015.

'From Hope to Horror'. *The Economist*, 14 July 2016.

'From the Ground Up: Education and Livelihoods in Southern Sudan'. New York: WCRWC, 2007.

'Funding Crunch Forces WFP to Cut Food Assistance in South Sudan'. *World Food Programme*, 2021.

'Guidelines: Civilians Seeking Protection at UNMISS Bases'. *UNMISS*, 2013.

'High-level Detainee Accuses Kenya, South Sudan of Kidnapping'. *Voice of America*, 6 February 2016.

'Huge Brawl in PoC Camp Leaves Dozens Injured'. *Radio Tamazuj*, 28 October 2014.

'Humanitarian Needs Overview South Sudan: Humanitarian Programme Cycle 2021'. *OCHA*, 2021.

'JMEC Criticizes Nomination of Taban Deng Gai as "Illegitimate" '. *Sudan Tribune*, 23 July 2016.

'John Kerry to South Sudan Leaders: Come to Your Senses, Stop Fighting'. (2015). *Voice of America*, 5 May. Available online: https://www.voanews.com/africa/john-kerry-south-sudan-leaders-come-your-senses-stop-fighting

'Juba Mayor Threatens Violent Response Against Planned Protests'. *The Sudans Post*, 2021.

'Makuei Behind Expulsion of Peace Monitor from South Sudan: Document'. *Radio Tamazuj*, 2016.

'Media Briefing by Adama Dieng, United Nations Special Adviser on the Prevention of Genocide on his visit to South Sudan'. New York: United Nations, 2016.

'Minutes of Permanent Ceasefire and Transitional Security Arrangements (PCTSA) Workshop'. *IGAD*, 2015.

'Mogae has "Heavy Heart" over Struggling Peace Deal'. *Radio Tamazuj*, 24 June 2016.

'Months after Clashes, Displaced in Lainya Face Humanitarian Crisis'. *Radio Tamazuj*, 2016.

'Monyiemiji Give NGOs 72 Hours to Leave Greater Torit, State Gov't Orders Curfew'. *Radio Tamazuj*, 2021.

'Moving Toward Mobility; Providing Protection to Civilians Through Static Presence and Mobile Peacekeeping in South Sudan'. Washington: CIVIC, 2019.

'MSF Demands UN Give More Space to Displaced in Malakal Amid "Deplorable" Conditions'. *Radio Tamazuj*, 19 November 2015.

'MSF Internal Review of the February 2016 Attack on the Malakal Protection of Civilians Site and the Post-Event Situation'. *MSF*, June 2016.

'Nun Shot by SPLA in Yei Passes Away in Hospital'. *Radio Tamazuj*, 2016. Available online: https://radiotamazuj.org/en/news/article/nun-shot-by-spla-in-yei-passes-away-in-hospital

'October Monthly Security Report'. *South Sudan NGO Forum*. Personal archives, 2016.

'Outcome of the Meeting of the Principal Signatory Parties to the Agreement on Planning Implementation of the Provisions in Chapter II the Agreement 21 October – 3 November 2015'. *IGAD*, 2015.

'PCCA Protests: A Look at Juba, Bor, and Aweil'. *Radio Tamazuj*, 2021.

'Press Conference Statement by Hilde F. Johnson'. *United Nations*, 8 July 2014.

'Press Conference Transcript Tuesday, 7 October 2014'. *UNMISS*, 2014.

'Protection Trends South Sudan January–April 2017'. *Protection Cluster*, May 2017.

'Rebels Warn of Clamp Down on Riek Machar'. *Radio Tamazuj*, 23 November 2016.

'Regional Interests at Stake in the South Sudan Crisis'. *The New Humanitarian*, 19 March 2014.

'Report of the Independent High-Level Panel on Peace Operations'. New York: United Nations, 2015.

'Report of the Panel of Experts on South Sudan'. UN Docs. S/2016/793. New York: United Nations, 2016.

'Report of the Secretary-General on South Sudan Covering the Period from 14 April to 19 August 2015'. UN Doc. S/2015/655. New York: United Nations, 2015.

'Report of the Secretary-General on South Sudan'. UN Doc. S/2013/651. New York: United Nations, 2013.

'Report of the Secretary-General on South Sudan'. UN Doc. S/2013/366. New York: United Nations, 2013.

'Report of the Secretary-General on South Sudan'. UN Doc. S/2014/158. New York: United Nations, 2014.

'Report of the Secretary-General on South Sudan'. UN Doc. S/2014/821. New York: United Nations, 2014.

'Report of the Secretary-General on South Sudan'. UN Doc. S/2014/821. New York: United Nations, 2014.

'Report of the Secretary-General on South Sudan'. UN Doc. S/2015/902. New York: United Nations, 2015.

'Report of the Secretary-General on South Sudan'. UN Docs. S/2016/138. New York: United Nations, 2016.

'Report of the Secretary-General on South Sudan'. UN Docs. S/2016/950. New York: United Nations, 2016.

'Report of the Secretary-General on South Sudan'. UN Docs. S/2017/505. New York: United Nations, 2017.

'Residents: SPLA Killed Five Displaced People in Wonduruba Last Week'. *Radio Tamazuj*, 2016.

'Resolution on Establishing the United Nations Mission in Sudan'. UN Doc S/RES/1590. New York: United Nations, 2005.

'Resolution Renewing the Mandate of UNMISS for an Additional Six Months'. UN Doc. S/RES/2187. New York: United Nations, 2014.

'Resolution to Extend the Mandate of UNMISS'. UN Doc. S/RES/2109. New York: United Nations, 2013.

'Restart of South Sudan Talks Critical to Avert End-March War Threat'. Brussels: ICG, 2015.

'RJMEC Expresses Concern at Reports of Defections or Accepting Defections'. *RJMEC*, 2020.

'Security Council Official Records, Eleventh Year 751st Meeting'. UN Doc S/PV.751. New York: United Nations, 1956.

'Senior SPLM Colleagues Give Kiir Ultimatum Over Party Crisis'. *Sudan Tribune*, 6 December 2013.

'South Sudan / Aburoc Peacekeeping [Video]'. *UN Audiovisual Library*, 22 June 2017.

'South Sudan Crisis Fact Sheet #25'. *USAID*, 2014.

'South Sudan Effects New Salary Structure for Civil Servants, Army Servicemen'. *Sudans Post*, 6 October 2021.

'South Sudan Expels Ceasefire Monitors from Yambio'. *Radio Tamazuj*, 24 March 2016.

'South Sudan Flash Update on Upper Nile'. *OCHA*, 27 April 2017.

'South Sudan Food Security Outlook October 2014'. *FEWS NET*, 2014.

'South Sudan Govt Accused of Expelling Ceasefire Monitors from W Equatoria, Again'. *Radio Tamazuj*, 14 April 2016.

'South Sudan Horror at Deadly Cattle Vendetta'. *BBC*, 16 January 2012.

'South Sudan: A Civil War by Any Other Name'. Brussels: International Crisis Group, 2014.

'South Sudan: Army Making Ethnic Conflict Worse'. *Human Rights Watch*, July 2013.

'South Sudan: Country Overview and Key Facts'. *Konrad Adenauer Stiftung*, 2019.

'South Sudan: End Abuses by Disarmament Forces in Jonglei'. *Human Rights Watch*, 23 August 2012.

'South Sudan: Lethal Disarmament'. *Amnesty International*, 2012.

'South Sudan: No Justice for Protester Killings'. *Human Rights Watch*, 24 May 2013.

'South Sudan: Shameful Attitude to Vulnerable Displaced Shown by Leaders of UNMISS'. *MSF*, 9 April 2014.

'South Sudan: Soldiers Target Ethnic Group in Juba Fighting: Capital's Residents Indiscriminately Fired Upon, Thousands Flee'. *Human Rights Watch*, 2013.

'South Sudan: UN Deplores Lack of Information on 20,000 People Displaced in Upper Nile'. *UNMISS*, 16 February 2017.

'South Sudan: UN Urges Accountability for Key Figures Supporting Militias in Greater Jonglei'. United Nations, 2021.

'South Sudan: War Crimes by Both Sides'. *Human Rights Watch*, 26 February 2014.

'South Sudan's Rival Forces Clash in Upper Nile State'. *South Sudan News Agency*, 25 December 2015.

'Special Report of the Secretary-General on the Review of the Mandate of the United Nations Mission in South Sudan', UN Docs. S/2015/899. New York: United Nations, 2015.

'Special Representative Voices "Cautious Optimism" over Progress in South Sudan, Despite Continuing Violence, Human Rights Violations'. New York: United Nations, 18 November 2013.

'SPLA Committed Widespread Violations During and After July Fighting in South Sudan'. Geneva: United Nations, 2016.

'SRSG Appeals to IDPs to Respect Protection Sites'. *UNMISS*, 20 November 2014.

'Statement by the UN Humanitarian Coordinator in South Sudan, Mr. Toby Lanzer, Up to 100,000 People Displaced in Unity State in May Alone'. *United Nations*, 8 May 2015.

'Statement by Yasmin Sooka Chair of the UN Commission on Human Rights in South Sudan to the Human Rights Council'. *United Nations*, 2021.

'Sudan and South Sudan: Current Issues for Congress and U.S. Policy'. *Congressional Research Service*, 2012.

'Sudan: Thousands Die as the OLS Colludes With Khartoum'. *Sudan Democratic Gazette*, 4 May 1998.

'The Conflict in Unity State'. Geneva: Small Arms Survey, 2015.

'The Mass Displacement of the Shilluk Population from the West Bank of the White Nile, South Sudan'. *Amnesty International*, June 2017.

'The State of Sudan's Comprehensive Peace Agreement, Alert no.1'. *IKV PAX Christi*, 2009.

'"There is No Protection" Insecurity and Human Rights in Southern Sudan'. *Human Rights Watch*, 2009.

'UN Delays Leave "Protection" Area Unfenced Amid Horrific Violence in S Sudan's Unity State'. *Radio Tamazuj*, 22 May 2015.

'UN Human Rights Experts Says International Community has an Obligation to Prevent Ethnic Cleansing in South Sudan'. Geneva: United Nations, 2016.

'UN Peacekeepers Turned Away Yambio Civilians Seeking Shelter from Violence'. *Radio Tamazuj*, 3 August 2015.

'Under Fire: The July 2016 Violence in Juba and UN Response'. Washington: CIVIC, 2016.

'UNMISS Declines IGAD Request to Transport Opposition Leaders to Consultative Conference in Pagak'. *UNMISS*, 27 November 2014.

'UNMISS Hands Over Police Post in Juba'. *UNMISS*, 25 November 2014.

'UNMISS POC Site Update 16 April 2014'. *UNMISS*, 2014.

'UNMISS POC Site Update 19 August 2015'. *UNMISS*, 19 August 2015.

'UNMISS POC Site Update 26 June 2014'. *UNMISS*, 26 June 2014.

'UNMISS POC Site Update 28 January 2016'. *UNMISS*, 28 January 2016.

'UNMISS Restricting Journalists from South Sudan Protection Camps'. *Radio Tamazuj*, 3 April 2016.

'UNSG, Note to Correspondents – Board of Inquiry Report on Malakal'. New York: United Nations, 2016.

'Update on Implementation of Special Investigation Recommendations'. UN Docs. S/2017/328. New York: United Nations, 2017.

'Weapons Supplies into South Sudan's Civil War'. London: Conflict Armament Research, 2018.

'Within and Beyond the Gates: The Protection of Civilians by the UN Mission in South Sudan'. Washington: CIVIC, 2015.

Abbott, Kenneth W. and Duncan Snidal. 'Why States Act Through Formal International Organizations'. *Journal of Conflict Resolution*, 42, no. 1 (1998): 3–32.

Allen, Susan and Amy Yuen. 'The Politics of Peacekeeping: UN Security Council Oversight Across Peacekeeping Missions'. *International Studies Quarterly*, 58 (2013): 621–32.

Amnesty International, *Sudan: Who Will Answer for the Crimes?* London: Amnesty International, 2005. Available online: https://www.amnesty.org/download/Documents/80000/afr540062005en.pdf.

Arensen, Michael J. *If We Leave, We Are Killed: Lessons Learned from South Sudan Protection of Civilian Sites 2013–2016*. Geneva: IOM, 2016.

Arkes, Hal and Catherine Blumer. 'The Psychology of Sunk Cost'. *Organizational Behavior and Human Decision Processes*, 35 (1985): 124–40. https://doi.org/10.1016/0749-5978(85)90049-4.

Asch, Solomon E. 'Studies of Independence and Conformity: I. A Minority of One Against a Unanimous Majority'. *Psychological Monographs: General and Applied*, 70, no. 9 (1956): 1–70.

Autesserre, Severine. *Peaceland: Conflict Resolution and the Everyday Politics of International Intervention*. Cambridge: Cambridge University Press, 2014.

Autesserre, Severine. *The Trouble with the Congo; Local Violence and the Failure of International Peacebuilding*. Cambridge: Cambridge University Press, 2010.

Baker, Aryn. 'Why George Clooney is Supporting Coffee Farming in South Sudan'. *Time Magazine*, 2015.

Barnett, Michael and Martha Finnemore. *Rules for the World: International Organizations in Global Politics*. Ithaca: Cornell University Press, 2004.

Bazerman, Max H. *Judgement in Managerial Decision Making*. New York: Wiley, 2006.

Bazerman, Max H. 'The Relevance of Kahneman and Tversky's Concept of Framing to Organizational Behaviour'. *Journal of Management*, 10, no. 3 (1985): 333–43.

Besheer, Margaret. 'Kenya in Uproar After UN Blames General for S. Sudan Violence'. *Voice of America*, 3 November 2016.

Bior, Ayen. 'UN Report: Rights Violations, Fighting Spike in South Sudan'. *Voice of America*, 15 March 2017.

Blair, Robert. 'In Liberia, the U.N. Mission Helped Restore Confidence in the Rule of Law'. *The Washington Post*, 30 April 2019.

Bloomfield, Steve. 'Why did Nato Cross the Road?' *Monacle*, No. 100. 2021.

Bode, Ingvild. *Individual Agency and Policy Change at the United Nations: The People of the United Nations*. Abingdon: Routledge, 2015.

Bodettii, Austin. 'How China Came to Dominate South Sudan's Oil'. *The Diplomat*, 11 February 2019.

Boswell, Alan. 'Insecure Power and Violence: The Rise and Fall of Paul Malong and the Mathiang Anyoor'. Geneva: Small Arms Survey, 2019. https://www.smallarmssurvey .org/sites/default/files/resources/HSBA-BP-Mathiang-Anyoor.pdf.

Boutellis, A. and V. Wyeth, 'Interview with Ellen Margrethe Løj, Former SRSG for Liberia and Head of UNMIL'. *IPI Global Observatory*, 13 March 2012.

Bowen, David E., Gerald E. Ledford, Jr. and Barry R. Nathan. 'Hiring for the Organization, Not the Job'. *The Executive*, 5, no. 4 (1991): 35–51.

Branch, Adam and Zachariah Mampilly. 'Winning the War, but Losing the Peace? The Dilemma of SPLM/A Civil Administration and the Tasks Ahead'. *The Journal of Modern African Studies*, 43(2005): 1–20.

Briggs, Caelin and Lisa Monaghan. 'Protection of Civilians Sites: Lessons from South Sudan for Future Operations'. *Norwegian Refugee Council*, 2017.

Brown, Matt. 'Violent Attacks on Southern Returnees En Route to Abyei'. *Enough Project*, 3 February 2011.

Brown, Sophie. 'Report: Political Instability on the Rise'. *CNN*, 12 December 2013.

Chandran, Rahul and Sebastian von Einsiedel. 'Fixing the UN's Human Resources System'. *United Nations University: Centre for Policy Research*, 2 November 2016.

Checchi, Francesco, Adrienne Testa and Abdihamid Warsame and Rachel Burns Le Quach. 'Estimates of Crisis-Attributable Mortality in South Sudan December 2013– April 2018'. *London School of Hygiene and Tropical Medicine*, 2018.

Coghlan, Nicholas. *Collapse of a Country: A Diplomat's Memoir of South Sudan*. Montreal: McGill-Queen's University Press, 2017.

Craze, Joshua and Jerome Tubiana. 'A State of Disunity: Conflict Dynamics in Unity State, South Sudan 2013–15'. *Small Arms Survey*, 2016.

Cunliffe, Philip. 'The Politics of Global Governance in UN Peacekeeping'. *International Peacekeeping*, 16, no. 3 (2009): 323–36.

Danis, Daniel. 'Replacement of Riek in Line with Peace Deal – Kerry'. *Eye Radio*, 23 August 2016.

Deal, Terrence E. and Allan A. Kennedy. *Corporate Cultures: The Rites and Rituals of Corporate Life*. New York: Perseus, 2000.

Deng, D. Akol Ruay. *The Politics of Two Sudans: The South and the North 1821–1969*. Uppsala: Nordiska Afrikainstitutet, 1994.

Di Giovanni, Janine. 'Hilde Johnson is Trying to Stop the Misery in South Sudan'. *Newsweek Magazine*, 28 May 2014.

Diefenbach, Thomas and John A. A. Sillince. 'Formal and Informal Hierarchy in Different Types of Organization'. *Organization Studies*, 32, no. 11 (2011): 1515–37. https://doi.org/10.1177/0170840611421254.

Dijkstra, Hylke. 'Shadow Bureaucracies and the Unilateral Control of International Secretariats: Insights from UN Peacekeeping'. *The Review of International Organizations*, 10 (2015): 23–41.

Doki, Charlton. 'South Sudan Officials Blame UN for Deadly Attack in Bor'. *Voice of America*, April 18 2014.

Dumo, Denis. 'South Sudan Rebels Say Killed "Many" Government Soldiers'. *Reuters*, 18 May 2015.

Dumo, Denis. 'U.N. Struggling to Deliver Food Aid in South Sudan as Rains Cut Off Vast Areas'. *Reuters*, 30 July 2018.

Dziadosz, Alexander. 'Exclusive: South Sudan to Split Total Oil Block – Officials'. *Reuters*, 2012.

Etzioni, Amitai. 'Social Psychological Aspects of International Relations'. In *Handbook of Social Psychology*, edited by Lindzey Gardner and Elliot Aronson, vol. 5, 538–601. Reading: Addison-Weasley, 1969.

Fenton, Wendy and Sean Loughna. *The Search for Common Ground: Civil–Military Coordination and the Protection of Civilians in South Sudan*. London: Overseas Development Institute, 2012.

Festinger, Leon. *A Theory of Cognitive Dissonance*. California: Stanford Press, 1957.

Finnan, Daniel. 'South Sudan: Ceasefire Violations Continue, Conflict Spreading, Say Monitors'. *Radio France Internationale*, 28 March 2016.

Foltyn, Simona. 'Violence Erupts Again in South Sudan as Faith in Peace Deal Flounders'. *The Guardian*, 2016.

Frerichs, Ralph R. *Deadly River: Cholera and Cover-Up in Post-Earthquake Haiti*. Ithaca: Cornell University Press, 2016.

Gale, Sadie Levy. 'UN Peacekeepers Looked on as Women Were Raped in Camps by South Sudanese Soldiers, Witnesses Say'. *The Independent*, 2016.

Goffe, Leslie. 'Hollywood's Role in South Sudan's Independence'. *BBC*, 8 July 2011.

Hall, Peter A. and Rosemary C. R. Taylor. 'Political Science and the Three New Institutionalisms'. *Political Studies*, 44, no. 5 (1996): 936–57.

Hamilton, Rebecca. 'U.S. Played Key Role in Southern Sudan's Long Journey to Independence'. *The Atlantic*, 9 July 2011.

Harmer, Adele and Monica Czwarno. 'The Effects of Insecurity on Aid Operations in South Sudan'. *Humanitarian Practice Network*, 2017.

Hermann, Margaret G. 'Explaining Foreign Policy Behavior Using the Personal Characteristics of Political Leaders'. *International Studies Quarterly*, 24, no. 1 (1980): 7–46.

Holland, Hereward. 'Analysis – Jonglei Revolt Gives South Sudan a Security Headache'. *Reuters*, 30 September 2012.

Holmes, Oliver. 'Top UN Official to Leave Myanmar Amid Criticism of Rohingya Approach'. *The Guardian*, 12 October 2017.

Holt, Victoria, Max Kelly and Glynn Taylor. *Protecting Civilians in the Context of UN Peacekeeping Operations Successes, Setbacks and Remaining Challenges*. New York: United Nations, 2009.

Hutton, Lauren. *Prolonging the Agony of UNMISS: The Implementation Challenges of a New Mandate During a Civil War*. The Hague: Clingendael Institute, 2014.

James, G. and Johan P. Olsen. 'The Institutional Dynamics of International Political Orders'. *International Organization*, 5 (1998): 4.

Janis, Irving L. *Victims of Groupthink: A Psychological Study of Foreign-Policy Decisions and Fiascos*. Boston: Houghton Mifflin, 1972.

Johnson, Douglas H. 'British Policy in Anglo-Egyptian Sudan Bears Some Responsibility for the Deep-Rooted Divisions Between North and South'. *LSE*, 2012.

Johnson, Hilde F. 'Protection of Civilians in the United Nations: A Peacekeeping Illusion?' In *United Nations Peace Operations in a Changing Global Order*, edited by Cedric de Coning and Mateja Peter, 45–65. Palgrave: MacMillan, 2019.

Johnson, Hilde F. *South Sudan: The Untold Story*. London: I. B. Taurus, 2018.

Johnson, Hilde F. *Waging Peace in Sudan: The Inside Story of the Negotiations That Ended Africa's Longest Civil War*. Eastbourne: Sussex Academic Press, 2011.

Johnson, Jay. 'South Sudan: Stop Squatters, Land Grabbing, Occupation and Colonization Nonsense'. *South Sudan News Agency*, 2013.

Jones, Sam. 'UN Accused of "Shocking" Lack of Action over Murder and Rape in South Sudan'. *The Guardian*, 2015.

Justin, Tito. 'South Sudan: "UN Doesn't Need Drones, Attack Helicopters"'. *Voice of America*, 18 June 2015.

Kahneman, Daniel. *Thinking Fast and Slow*. London: Penguin, 2011.

Kahneman, Daniel and Shane Frederick. 'Representativeness Revisited: Attribute Substitution in Intuitive Judgment'. In *Heuristics and Biases: The Psychology of Intuitive Judgment*, edited by Thomas Gilovich, Dale Griffin and Daniel Kahneman, 49–81. Cambridge: Cambridge University Press, 2002.

Kahneman, Daniel and Amos Tversky. 'Choices, Values, and Frames'. *American Psychologist*, 39, no. 4 (1984): 341–50. https://doi.org/10.1037/0003-066X.39.4.341.

Kahneman, Daniel and Amos Tversky. 'Prospect Theory: An Analysis of Decision under Risk'. *Econometrica*, 47, no. 2 (1979): 263–91.

Karimi, Faith. 'South Sudan: Did Clashes Start over Facebook Post?' *CNN*, 15 July 2016.

Karlsrud, John. 'New Technologies and UN Peacekeeping Operations'. In *UN Peacekeeping Doctrine in a New Era*, edited by Cedric de Coning, Chiyuki Aoi and John Karlsrud, 271–87. Abingdon: Routledge, 2017.

Karlsrud, John. 'Special Representatives of the Secretary-General as Norm Arbitrators? Understanding Bottom-up Authority in UN Peacekeeping'. *Global Governance*, 19, no. 4 (2013): 525–44.

Katz, Jonathan M. 'U.N. Admits Role in Cholera Epidemic in Haiti'. *New York Times*, 17 August 2016.

Kelly, Theresa F and Katherine Milkman. 'Escalation of Commitment'. In *Encyclopaedia of Management Theory*, edited by Eric Kessler, 256–9. Thousand Oaks: Sage Publications, 2013.

Kerry, John. 'Chairman Kerry Statement at Hearing on Sudan'. *United States Senate Committee on Foreign Relations*, 2012.

Koriat, Asher, Sarah Lichtenstein and Baruch Fischhoff. 'Reasons for Confidence'. *Journal of Experimental Psychology: Human Learning and Memory*, 6, no. 2 (1980): 107–18.

Kuhn, Deanna. 'Children and Adults as Intuitive Scientists'. *Psychology Review*, 96, no. 4 (1989): 674–89.

Lilly, Damian. 'Protection of Civilians Sites: A New Type of Displacement Settlement?'. *Humanitarian Exchange Magazine*, 62. September, 2014.

Lingle, John H. and Thomas M. Ostrom. 'Principles of Memory and Cognition in Attitude Formation'. In *Cognitive Responses in Persuasive Communications: A Text in Attitude Change*, edited by Richard E. Petty, Thomas M. Ostrom and Timothy C. Brock, 399–420. Hillsdale: Erlbaum, 1981.

Lipson, Michael. 'Peacekeeping: Organized Hypocrisy?' *European Journal of International Relations*, 13, no. 1 (2007): 5–34.

Løj, Ellen M. 'In Defence of the UN's Role in South Sudan'. *The Guardian*, 17 December 2015.

Lynch, Colum. 'Inside the White House Fight Over the Slaughter in South Sudan'. *Foreign Policy*, 26 January 2015.

Lynch, Colum. 'Where did Kiir Get His Ten-Gallon Hat?' *Foreign Policy*, 26 September 2011.

Martell, Peter. *First Raise a Flag: How South Sudan Won the Longest War But Lost the Peace*. Oxford University Press, 2018.

Martell, Peter. 'South Sudan Celebrate Their Divorce'. *BBC*, 9 July 2011.

Martell, Peter. 'The Child Snatchers of South Sudan'. *The Telegraph*, 7 December 2009.

Maxwell, Daniel, Martina Santschi and Rachel Gordon. 'Looking Back to Look Ahead? Reviewing Key Lessons from Operation Lifeline Sudan and Past Humanitarian Operations in South Sudan'. Researching livelihoods and services affected by conflict. Working Paper 24 October. Feinstein International Center, 2014.

McKay, Matthew and Patrick Fanning. *Self-esteem: A Proven Program of Cognitive Techniques for Assessing, Improving, and Maintaining Your Self-Esteem*. Oakland: New Harbinger, 2016.

Mednick, Sam. 'Old Grudges and Empty Coffers: South Sudan's Precarious Peace Process'. *The New Humanitarian*, 2021.

Mednick, Sam. 'UN Pullout Triggers Safety Concerns in South Sudan Displacement Camps'. *The New Humanitarian*, 2021.

Meyer, John W. and Brian Rowan. 'Institutionalized Organizations: Formal Structure as Myth and Ceremony'. *American Journal of Sociology*, 83, no. 2 (1977): 340–63.

Mischel, Walter and Yuichi Shoda. 'A Cognitive-Affective System Theory of Personality: Reconceptualizing Situations, Dispositions, Dynamics, and Invariance in Personality Structure'. *Psychological Review*, 102, no. 2 (1995): 246–68.

Nichols, Michelle. 'U.N. Reaction to Malakal Violence in South Sudan Marred by Confusion'. *Reuters*, 2016.

Nickerson, Raymond S. 'Confirmation Bias: A Ubiquitous Phenomenon in Many Guises'. *Review of General Psychology*, 2, no. 2 (1998): 175–220.

Nuri, Rocco. '100,000 Fearful Civilians Trapped in South Sudan Town'. *UNHCR*, 2016.

Ochan, Clement. *Responding to Violence in Ikotos County, South Sudan: Government and Local Efforts to Restore Order*. Feinstein International Center, 2007.

Oliya Suwa, Bernard. 'Postcard of Peace and Forgiveness from "Small London"'. *Sudan Tribune*, 2014.

Ouchi, William G. *Theory Z: How American Business Can Meet the Japanese Challenge*. Boston: Addison-Wesley, 1981.

Panchol, Ayuen. 'Government Rejects PLO Lumumba'. *Eye Radio*, 6 November 2015.

Parayre, Roch. 'The Strategic Implications of Sunk Costs: A Behavioral Perspective'. *Journal of Economic Behavior and Organization*, 28 (1995): 417–42.

Patinkin, Jason. 'South Sudan Needs Peace as Much as Food'. *The New Humanitarian*, 20 March 2017.

Pedneault, Jonathan. 'Safe Haven No More in South Sudan'. *Human Rights Watch*, 2016.

Pinaud, Clemence. 'South Sudan: Civil War, Predation and the Making of a Military Aristocracy'. *African Affairs*, 113/451 (2014): 192–211.

Prentice, Robert. 'Enron: A Brief Behavioral Autopsy'. *American Business Law Journal*, 40, no. 2 (2008): 417–44.

Read, John D. 'The Availability Heuristic in Person Identification: The Sometimes Misleading Consequences of Enhanced Contextual Information'. *Applied Cognitive Psychology*, 9, no. 2 (1995): 91–121.

Reno, William. 'Complex Operations in Weak and Failing States: The Sudan Rebel Perspective'. *Institute for National Strategic Security*, 1, no. 2 (2010): 111–22.

Riddle, Karyn. 'Always on My Mind: Exploring How Frequent, Recent, and Vivid Television Portrayals Are Used in the Formation of Social Reality Judgments'. *Media Psychology*, 13, no. 2 (2010): 155–79.

Robinson, Samuel. 'Special Report: In South Sudan, a State of Dependency'. *Reuters*, 2012.

Rosen, Armin. 'From Victim to (Mutual) Aggressor: South Sudan's Disastrous First Year'. *The Atlantic*, 8 May 2012.

Rosenthal, Gert. *A Brief and Independent Inquiry into the Involvement of the United Nations in Myanmar from 2010 to 2018*. New York: United Nations, 2019.

Rosenzweig, Phil. *The Halo Effect:…and Eight Other Business Delusions that Deceive Managers*. New York: The Free Press, 2007.

Rubin, Jennifer. 'In South Sudan, Another Human Rights Horror'. *The Washington Post*, 2 July 2014.

Saurugger, Sabine. 'Sociological Institutionalism and European Integration'. *Oxford Research Encyclopaedia of Politics*, 2017.

Sengupta, Somini and Nick Cumming-Bruce. 'Zeid Ra'ad al-Hussein, Top Human Rights Official, Won't Seek a Second Term'. *New York Times*, 2017.

Shackelford, Elizabeth. *The Dissent Channel, American Diplomacy in a Dishonest Age*. New York: Public Affairs, 2020.

Shearer, David. 'Why South Sudan's Leaders are to Blame for the Country's Famine'. *Newsweek*, 3 March 2017.

Simon, Herbert A. *Administrative Behavior: A Study of Decision-Making Processes in Administrative Organization*, 4th edn. New York: Free Press, 1947/1997.

Simon, Herbert A. 'Invariants of Human Behavior'. *Annual Review of Psychology*, 41(1990): 1–20.

Small Arms Survey. 'Fighting for Spoils Armed Insurgencies in Greater Upper Nile'. *Small Arms Survey*, November 2011.

Smith, David. 'South Sudan President Accuses Officials of Stealing $4bn of Public Money'. *The Guardian*, 5 June 2012.

Srinivasan, Sharath. *When Peace Kills Politics: International intervention and unending wars in the Sudans*. London: Hurst, 2021.

Staw, Barry M. 'The Escalation of Commitment: An Update and Appraisal'. In *Organizational Decision Making*, edited by Zur Shapira, 191–215. New York: Cambridge University Press, 1997.

Sunstein, Cass. 'Moral Heuristics'. *Behavioral and Brain Sciences*, 28 (2006): 531.

Survey of South Sudan Public Opinion April 24 to May 22, 2013. (2013). International Republican Institute. Available online: https://www.iri.org/sites/default/files/2013 per cent20July per cent2019 per cent20Survey per cent20of per cent20South per cent20Sudan per cent20Public per cent20Opinion, per cent20April per cent2024-May per cent2022, per cent202013.pdf.

Tetlock, Philip E. *Expert Political Judgment: How Good is It? How Can We Know?* Princeton University Press, 2005.

Tisdall, Simon. 'Riek Machar, the Former Rebel Fighter Ready for a New Battle'. *The Guardian*, 4 July 2013.

Tounsel, Christopher. 'The Equatorial Corps and the Torit Mutiny'. In *Chosen Peoples: Christianity and Political Imagination in South Sudan*. Durham: Duke University Press, 2021.

Trice, Harrison M. and Janice M. Beyer. 'Studying Organizational Cultures through Rites and Ceremonials'. *The Academy of Management Review*, 9, no. 4 (1984): 653–69.

Tversky, Amos and Daniel Kahneman. 'Availability: A Heuristic for Judging Frequency and Probability'. *Cognitive Psychology*, 5 (1973): 207–3.

van der Lijn, Jaïr. *To Paint the Nile Blue: Factors for success and failure of UNMIS and UNAMID*. Netherlands Institute of International Relations Clingendael, 2008.

Vertin, Zach. *A Rope From the Sky; The Making and Unmaking of the World's Newest State*. New York: Pegasus, 2019.

Vroom, Victor H. *Work and Motivation*. New York: Wiley & Sons, 1964.

Vuylsteke, Sarah. Identity and Self-determination: The Fertit Opposition in South Sudan. Small Arms Survey, 2018.

Wells, Matt. 'The UN has Failed Its Peacekeepers in S Sudan'. *Al Jazeera*, 10 September 2016.

Wild, Hannah, Jok, Jok Madut and Patel, Ronak. 'The Militarization of Cattle Raiding in South Sudan: How a Traditional Practice Became a Tool for Political Violence', *International Journal of Humanitarian Action*, 3, no. 2 (2018): 1–11.

Winckler, Joel Gwyn. 'Exceeding Limitations of the United Nations Peacekeeping
    Bureaucracy: Strategies of Officials to Influence Peacekeeping Activities within the
    United Nations Mission in Liberia and the Department of Peacekeeping Operations'.
    International Peacekeeping, 22, no. 1 (2015): 43–64.
Wudu, Waakhe Simon and Ayen Bior. 'South Sudan Accused of Blocking Aid, Despite
    Famine'. *Voice of America*, 22 February 2017.
Young, John. 'South Sudan's Civil War; Violence, Insurgency and Failed Peacemaking'.
    Zed Books, 2019.
Zaleznik, Abraham. 'The Mythological Structure of Organization s and Its Impact'. In
    The Psychodynamics of Organizations, edited by Carole Barnett and Larry Hirschorn,
    179–89. Philadelphia: Temple University Press, 1993.
Zanna, Mark. *The Psychology of Prejudice*. Mahwah: Lawrence Erlbaum Associates Inc.,
    1994.
Zeitvogel, Karin and Waakhe Simon Wudu. 'IGAD: Creating New States in South
    Sudan Violates Peace Deal'. *Voice of America*, 13 October 2015

Index

www.ingramcontent.com/pod-product-compliance
Lightning Source LLC
Chambersburg PA
CBHW050437280326
41932CB00013BA/2149